Dark Signals

*A Navy Radio Operator in the Tonkin Gulf
and
South China Sea, 1964-1965*

Si Dunn

Sagecreek Productions LLC   Austin, Texas

DARK SIGNALS
A Navy Radio Operator in the Tonkin Gulf and South China Sea,
1964-1965

Cover photograph by Si Dunn

Sagecreek Productions, LLC
3800 N. Lamar Blvd., Suite 730-131
Austin, TX 78756-4011
contact_scp@sagecreekproductions.com

ISBN 978-0-985-17350-0

*Dedicated to all who served aboard the **USS Lenah S. Higbee** (DD-806), a gallant destroyer that fought in three wars and was the U.S. Navy's first combat ship named for a woman.*

Chief Nurse Lenah H. Sutcliffe Higbee, Superintendent of the Navy Nurse Corps, 1911-1922. Recipient of the Navy Cross during World War I. Namesake of the destroyer *USS Higbee*.

(U.S. Navy Photograph. Photographer unknown.)

PREFACE

A military memoir presents many challenges to a writer, whether the recollections are prepared five hours or five decades after the depicted events.

Send 250 people – a ship's crew, for example – into the midst of tense historical events, and each person will emerge with different memories, perceptions and opinions of what happened and what did *not* happen.

I left the South China Sea and lower reaches of the Tonkin Gulf in early May, 1965. Even then, the Vietnam War already had become, in the words of Phillip Knightley in *The First Casualty*, "a war like no other, a war with no front line, no easily identifiable enemy, no simply explained cause, no clearly designated villain on whom to focus the nation's hate, no menace to the homeland, no need for general sacrifice, and therefore, no nationwide fervor of patriotism. It was a vicious war, in a tiny, distant, devastated, and backward nation…."

Today, the Vietnam conflict is remembered primarily as a ground war and air war. Yet naval operations generated some of the conflict's key trigger points, as well as incidents of lasting controversy.

Some aspects of American naval actions in the Tonkin Gulf and South China Sea in 1964 and 1965 remained classified until the early years of the 21st century. And some information from that time period perhaps is still classified.

Numerous other crises and conflicts have erupted since the end of the Vietnam War, creating countless new documents and controversies to compete for attention and memory. As a result, many details of the conflict now are encased in aging books, magazines and newspaper articles that few people, except historians, students and aging veterans, likely will read again.

Still, many people ask me "What was it like? What did you do there?"

Over the years, I have become reasonably adept at giving brief, hand-waving answers that elicit winces or laughs. But what was it *really* like for me? To attempt to find out – and hopefully provide deeper answers for family, friends and others who are curious – I decided to write this book.

Researching and writing *Dark Signals*, however, has proven a much tougher task than I imagined. This memoir could not have been completed without help from many individuals, agencies and organizations.

First and foremost, my wife, Carmen Mitchell, a writer, journalist and editor in her own right, encouraged and challenged me to complete the book proposal and early chapters and enter them into competition at the 2008 Mayborn Literary Nonfiction Conference.

To my surprise and delight, *Dark Signals* won a noteworthy award: 1st runner-up. Since then, Carmen has read each new draft and maintained a drumbeat of reminders to keep pushing ahead with the research and completing the manuscript.

I am grateful to the Mayborn Institute at the University of North Texas for its early support of this project and to Ron Chrisman of UNT Press and Thomas J. Cutler of the Naval Institute Press for their astute feedback.

I owe special thanks, as well, to some of my former shipmates, including radioman Richard Rodriguez, radioman James L. Davis, electronics technician Frank Schley and retired Rear Admiral Tim Jenkins, who, as a young lieutenant junior grade, was the *USS Higbee*'s operations officer when I served in his department in 1964-1965.

They, along with Raymond Heflin, the Radioman First Class petty officer who was my immediate supervisor, helped me dig beneath a number of time-enhanced "sea stories" and get closer to the realities of my experiences in the South China Sea and Tonkin Gulf.

Regrettably, Ray Heflin did not live to see this book published.

I also wish to thank several former enlisted sailors and officers who served aboard other ships or in other commands associated with the events and actions that I experienced. They helped provide greater depth, clarity and accuracy to my recollections. Their contributions are noted in this book.

I lost contact long ago with some of my other *Higbee* shipmates. And, despite the increasingly deep and long reach of the Internet and other electronic means, I have not been able to locate them again, to seek their memories and permission to use their names. They have, for me, disappeared into the great fabric of America.

Therefore, reluctantly, I have adopted a technique that many other military memoir writers have to employ. I have created new characters to stand in for some of the long-lost crewmen. These new characters speak lines and perform actions as I recall them.

They are, however, I readily admit, flimsy substitutes for the real people who were there with me.

Ultimately, this book represents events, conversations and actions as I recall them, with help, where possible, from published and unpublished documents, photographs, and interviews. The interpretations, opinions and assertions I offer with these materials are mine alone.

Above: The Gearing Class destroyer *USS Higbee* (DD-806).
(U.S. Navy photograph by PH2 L.D. Crouse)

Below: One of the fortresses guarding the moat and stone wall
surrounding the Japanese Imperial Palace, Tokyo, 1964.
(Photo by Si Dunn)

CHAPTER 1

"War!"

"The secret of war lies in the communications."

- Napoleon Bonaparte

Yokosuka, Japan
August 2, 1964

I was in sitting in Club Kobe, slumped in a garish red vinyl-covered booth. "The Kobe," as it was known, was one of dozens of sailor bars lining, or branching off from, Yokosuka's narrow and seedy Honcho Street. As I sipped from a dark, sweaty bottle of Asahi beer, the main thought on my mind was a vague sense of irony and disconnection. In the ancient Land of the Rising Sun, I was listening to a jukebox loudly booming a new hit song, "House of the Rising Sun," by Eric Burdon and the Animals.[1]

It was early evening, and I was drinking a beer for just the second time in my life. I didn't like the bitter brew nearly as much as I liked the sweet drinks of my recent youth: Coca-Cola, RC, Pepsi, Grapette, and Nehi. Yet, to be a sailor in a Seventh Fleet sailor bar, I had to at least *appear* to be drinking.

I was sharing the big, tacky booth with two sailors I barely knew. They had arrived after getting hot baths and massages at a bath house in another part of Yokosuka. Now the three of us were bitching about nothing that mattered – minor incidents on our ship – as we eyed the bar girls who soon would move over to sit with us and try to con us into buying them drinks at inflated prices. Hustling drinks was one of two main ways they could make money in The Kobe or other bars. Each bar paid a *jo-san* a small commission for every watered-down drink a sailor or Marine bought for her.

Later, within a couple of hours of closing time, if her booth boyfriend still had any money, he could pay another 10,000 yen—about $30 at that time—to buy her out of the bar and spend the rest of the night at her tiny apartment or in one of Yokosuka's small "honeymoon" hotels that catered to American servicemen's trysts.

My booth-mates, Smoak and Markham, were "regular Navy"—four-year enlistees. Smoak was a muscular, stocky Machinists Mate Seaman (MMSN). Markham was a tall, wiry Boatswains Mate Seaman (BMSN). We had absolutely nothing in common except being crewmen on the same World War II-era Gearing Class destroyer, the *USS Lenah S. Higbee* (DD-806).[2] We also knew each other only by our last names. Enlisted sailors always addressed each other – or were spoken to or yelled at – by surname or simplified versions of difficult last names, such as "Ski" instead of Mazinowski. I had no idea what Smoak's and Markham's first names were, and I secretly hoped they *never* discover mine: *Silas*.

Likewise, they did not realize I was a Navy Reservist. My boot camp had lasted just two intense weeks instead of the usual two months for Navy regulars. And my required tour of active duty was only 24 months, half as long as theirs. Smoak lit a cigarette and complained about something Chief So-and-So told him to fix just before liberty call, and Markham nodded knowingly.

The two sailors and the hulking booth all dwarfed me. I was a skinny 20-year-old Radioman 3rd Class (RM3) of barely average height. As a petty officer third class, I was the approximate equivalent of an Army corporal. I outranked Smoak and Markham, and, technically, I could give them orders. But, as I took another tentative sip of beer, I had no idea what those orders might be.

I had now made it through almost 13 months of my required 24-month duty tour. And I was, at last, beginning to feel something like a sailor. In the first few months, I had been stationed at Hunter's Point Naval Shipyard near San Francisco, working in a small communications office while the *Higbee* was in dry dock for repairs and extensive upgrades. Then, from port facilities in Long Beach, Calif., I had briefly gone to sea on temporary duty aboard a Guardian-class radar picket ship, the aging *USS Locator* (AGR-6), and discovered how truly susceptible I was to seasickness.

When the newly modernized *Higbee* started underway training and high-speed shakedown maneuvers along the West Coast in spring, 1964, I had begun begging almost daily for a transfer to shore duty. But nothing happened, even after officers and chiefs sometimes found me lying in a passageway or on a deck, semi-conscious, gagging, groaning in pain and spattered with vomit. The Navy, I was told repeatedly, needed every shipboard radio operator it could find. I would just have to cope and tough it out.

Now in early August, I was just one more sailor among tens of thousands in the Navy's massive Seventh Fleet. Its hundreds of ships patrolled 48 million square miles of the Western Pacific (WestPac) and Indian Ocean and used Yokosuka as home port.[3] Aboard the *Higbee*, however, I was a bit less of a cipher. I was one of ten radio operators assigned to keep the destroyer's radio room manned in shifts, or "watches," and operating around the clock.

Nearly 400 feet long and displacing 3,400 tons, the *Higbee* was one of the dozens of Gearing Class "tin cans" built and commissioned just in time to see combat in the Pacific during World War II's final months. In one battle in 1945, the *Higbee* shot down six Japanese planes – four in just 22 minutes.[4]

The ship also had completed three combat tours during the Korean War and was involved in actions that included shelling North Korean forces and supporting Gen. Douglas MacArthur's surprise amphibious landing at Inchon, South Korea, in mid-September, 1950.[5] Now, gently bobbing at a Yokosuka Naval Station pier about a mile from Club Kobe, the aging but refurbished destroyer was a 33-knot platform for some of the Navy's latest antisubmarine warfare (ASW) weapons, as well as new sonar, radar and communications gear.

American destroyers traditionally had been named for naval heroes and political leaders, predominantly men. In 1964, the *Higbee* still was the Navy's first and only combat ship named for a woman.[6] Lenah Sutcliffe Higbee had served as commandant of the Navy nurse corps from 1911 to 1921 and was the first woman to receive the Navy Cross while living.[7] Not surprisingly, DD-806 had picked up several nicknames in the two decades before I reported aboard. The kindest included: "the Leaping Lenah"; "the Leaking Lenah"; the "Hick-Bee"; and "DD Eight Oh Sucks."

In heavy seas, the *Higbee*, like destroyers, shuddered and leaped upward when it slammed into a large wave. Then it wallowed over the crest and dropped hard into the wave's trough. Roller coasters were tame compared to the dangerous ride of a Gearing Class tin can in rough water. Walking inside the ship when its bow suddenly rose was like struggling to move up a steep mountain path while weighted down with extra gravity. When the bow plunged into the trough, the sensation was like being almost weightless inside a rapidly falling elevator. Complicating every sailor's struggle to walk, the ship also made quick, side-to-side motions as it rose and fell. The smart destroyer crewman learned to move about with knees loose and hands and arms out, ready to grab or brace against anything that could stop him from smashing into bulkheads, pipes and fittings.

The *Higbee*'s aging hull often took in large quantities of water from stormy seas. And, when the bilge pumps seemed hard-pressed to keep up with the inflow, grim rumors sometimes spread, warning that the Leakin' Lenah was about to go down. I took these rumors seriously; I was a natural worrier. Indeed, during the three-week crossing from California to Japan, I had carefully rehearsed all procedures for sending out an SOS distress call, destroying equipment and sensitive files, and abandoning ship.

I had learned where the life rafts were stored. And I had studied up on how to work the bright-yellow, World War II-era, AN/CRT-3 "Gibson Girl" lifeboat transmitter that allegedly would broadcast automatic distress signals as long as I could keep turning its hand crank. As an added precaution, I also kept a spare, inflatable life vest hidden behind some of the *Higbee*'s radio gear – just in case there was no time to do anything else except grab it and leap, screaming, into the sea.

Some sailors in another Club Kobe booth decided to play "House of the Rising Sun" again. Smoak and Carver now were talking to each other about a recent scuffle involving two other *Higbee* crewmen. A pair of deck apes had gone at each other with fists and "swabs" – their mops. My mind, meanwhile, was split: half listening to them and the song and half drifting through parts of the universe far from Honcho Street.

The *Higbee* now had been moored at the U.S. Naval Station in Yokosuka, near the southern edge of Tokyo Bay, for almost three weeks. And, during some of this time, I had not been allowed to go on liberty.

Chief Radioman Randall Linn, a short, intense man in his late forties, periodically had restricted me to the ship and made me stand extra in-port radio watches. I kept doing things that made him mad – and not by choice. "Regular" Navy since World War II, Chief Linn, openly detested enlisted Reservists. So he stayed alert to chances to catch me doing something he disliked. Anger seemed to be his main happiness.

Recently, I had failed to follow his exact instructions on a pair of small tasks, and he had roared at me for what seemed an hour when I tried to make excuses.

First, I had carelessly smeared a bit of paint on a small rubber seal while painting an escape hatch in one of the radio spaces. Second, I had not quite swept up every speck of dust from the nonslip flooring in Radio Central, the ship's main radio room. The Chief had spotted a small smear of dust near an air intake grille for one of the high-frequency radio transmitters' cooling fans.

Chief Linn's face often turned purple when he hit full boil, and I never divined the exact root of his anti-Reservist rage. But I was the lone 24-month enlistee in the *Higbee*'s ten-man radio gang and almost the only "two-year wonder" in the ship's crew of 240 enlisted men and officers.

Whenever possible, I tried to avoid contact with Chief Linn. But this was tough to do on a small ship where there was almost no place to hide.

Fortunately, the Chief's lead radioman, a soft-spoken 1st Class petty officer named Raymond Heflin, had quiet sympathy for my plight, particularly my too-easy tendency to get seasick. ("I have never seen anyone get as sick and look as bad as you did," he would tell me more than 30 years later.)[8] RM1 Heflin's job was to directly supervise the eight other lower-ranking radiomen. "Hef," as we called him, frequently did what he could to keep Chief Linn satisfied, distracted and free to leave Radio Central as soon as possible.

We wanted the Chief to just leave us the hell alone – a feeling many enlisted sailors traditionally have held toward the chiefs in charge of them. To those of us in the lower ranks, a chief petty officer's job mostly seemed to involve standing around with a coffee cup and criticizing anything anyone tried to do. A CPO was supposed to be both a leader and a technical expert, by virtue of training and long experience. Chief Linn, I had observed, didn't seem to know much about the *Higbee*'s new radio equipment. So I suspected he was using anger over small tasks to try to hide that shortcoming.

Aboard destroyers such as the *Higbee*, the Chief Radioman reported to the ship's communications officer, typically a young ensign or a new lieutenant junior grade. The communications officer reported to the operations officer, a more experienced lieutenant junior grade (jg) or lieutenant. And the operations officer reported to the ship's executive officer and captain.

When someone in that chain of command became unhappy with something involving communications or one of the radiomen, it was the Chief Radioman's job to fix the problem. When Chief Linn heard something negative from an officer, he immediately became "shaky"— that was our term for it. He grew visibly nervous, quick to tongue-lash and ready to pounce on any slight misstep.

I drew much of his wrath, whether I deserved it or not. And sometimes I *did* deserve it. I never could seem to get myself completely squared away as a sailor. Something usually was slightly askew with my uniform, my haircut, my shoeshine, my movements across the radio room, or in how I responded to the Chief's orders.

Even when I did something exactly right, Chief Randall Linn knew exactly how to spot something "wrong." He just made up something and tore into me.

Hef, however, considered me perhaps his best overall radio operator, even if I was an imperfect sailor. I could copy Morse code transmissions (commonly known as CW) faster and more accurately than the *Higbee*'s other radiomen, including the Chief. I could tune encrypted radio-teletype signals into accurate reception by ear rather than by relying on bouncing, confusing oscilloscope displays.

Civilian experience and training as a ham radio operator had given me the skills and experience necessary to adjust and operate the ship's new transmitters, receivers and antenna couplers. Likewise, I understood how to activate and operate the ship's older communications gear left over from World War II and Korea. Identical items had been in civilian radio hobbyists' hands for several years via the war-surplus electronics market.

Finally, unlike the regular Navy radiomen on my ship, I was enthralled with the physics and vagaries of Earth's atmosphere and the ways subtle changes in the ionosphere could make long-distance radio communications possible. I understood much of what was happening inside the equipment, too, as radio signals flew to and from distant locations at almost the speed of light.

In Club Kobe, "House of the Rising Sun" swung into its jazzy electric organ break again. Smoak and Carver now were out on the dance floor, swaying and moving around with two bar girls. A bar girl smiled at me and started walking toward the big booth. Nothing was wrong with my hormones. I was not going to say no.

Just at that moment, the jukebox music suddenly was drowned out by a shrill cacophony: Police whistles. Two beefy Shore Patrol petty officers and a Shore Patrol chief strode into the bar. They all wore white "SP" armbands on their left sleeves.

The two SP petty officers started pulling sailors off the dance floor and hauling them out of booths, while the Shore Patrol chief shouted: "Recall! Recall! All hands back to your ships on the double! Recall!"

He lifted his whistle and blew it again for dramatic emphasis. Meanwhile, the two SP petty-officers continued yanking drunken sailors away from Club Kobe's bar girls and shoving them toward the front door. Smoak and Carver were among the first two thrown out.

The bar now became a blur of confused and conflicting motions. A few sailors tried to keep dancing. Other seamen and petty officers in summer white uniforms put down their drinks and began to scramble or stagger toward the front door without asking why.

But that was *not* my nature. I was the son of a Little Rock newspaper's international news editor; I had been brought up to be curious about what was happening in the world.

I walked over to the grizzled SP chief just as he watched his men yank up two surly boiler tenders by the fronts of their white jumpers.

"What's a recall?" I asked sincerely. It was a term I didn't remember hearing in Naval Reserve training classes.

The SP chief glared at me and looked at the black, third-class petty officer's crow on my right sleeve. Now he stared at me as if I had just plopped down from the moon.

"*War*, shithead!"

"Who with?"

The Shore Patrol chief didn't answer. Instead, one of his beefy hands snatched the front of my jumper. His other hand swiftly reached around and grabbed the top rear of my bell-bottomed pants. He propelled me straight to Club Kobe's front door and out into the crowded street.

"Go back to your ship, Sparks! *On the double!*" he shouted.

Old-time Navy men often called radio operators "Sparks." The nickname was a holdover from the first few years of the 20th century, when huge, noisy, spark-gap transmitters and crude coherer receivers provided the first ship-to-shore radio communications for U.S. fleets.

Honcho Street quickly became a surging stream of white, blue, green and khaki uniforms. Other SP teams were spreading the alert. Hundreds of Navy and Marine personnel spilled out of the wall-to-wall night clubs and bars.

Some sailors and Marines jumped into taxis and shouted a completely unnecessary command: "*Haiyaku!*" Yokosuka's cab drivers almost always drove in "Hurry!" mode, even on the city's most cramped streets.

Fewer than 20 years had passed since the end of World War II, so some of the cabbies, it was rumored, had trained to be kamikaze pilots but never made it into the air before Japan surrendered. Their new mission was to scare Americans to death with their driving.

Once I got my bearings on the street, my first instinct was: *Run to the ship!* I had been a track letterman, a state-champion distance runner, in high school. In my first few strides on Honcho Street, however, I collided with a staggering seaman and a Marine lance corporal who took a drunken, irritated swing at me and just missed. I stopped running and hailed a taxi.

As my cab weaved and raced toward the *Higbee*'s pier, I kept hearing the Shore Patrol chief's *"War!"* cry echo in my head. I wondered fearfully: *Is the Cold War over? Who's our enemy? Russia? Red China? North Korea? All?*

No explosions were lighting up the night sky. No jet fighters screamed overhead.

Maybe we've invaded Cuba. I thought this now as I was tossed from side to side in the weaving cab's rear seat. It had been less than two years since the Cuban Missile Crisis.

Yet, if Cuba was the target, why were *we* being recalled so urgently? Ships from the Seventh Fleet would need weeks to get there. We would have to go through the Panama Canal.

Meanwhile, much of Asia would be left unprotected from the Russians, Chinese and North Koreans.

Within the next few minutes, I would discover that I had never even heard of the place to which we were being sent.

And, within the next few days, I would begin to suspect that those sending us there – the higher-ups in the White House, Pentagon and Congress – knew not much more than I did about…Vietnam.

The author, age 12, listening to a Silvertone shortwave
receiver, 1956. *(Photo by Silas Dunn)*

CHAPTER 2

The Radio Kid

"I'm Popeye the Sailor Man! (*Toot, toot!*)
I live in a garbage can!
I turned on the heater
And burned off my pee-ter!
I'm Popeye the Sailor Man! (*Toot, toot!*)"

-As sung on an elementary school playground, 1955

ARKANSAS
1955-1961

Nothing on Earth held much appeal for me in 1955. I wanted to ride thundering rockets to the moon and planets. I wanted to zoom through the sky in Air Force F-86 Sabre jets. I gave no thought at all to someday joining the Navy.

The year 1955 was a time when some astronomers still thought there might be intelligent life on Mars and Venus – super-smart civilizations building long, straight canals across deserts and mysterious cities beneath thick clouds. I was enthralled with those possibilities and often kept my eyes on the skies.

My parents had little money. My father was a hard-working editor at a low-paying Little Rock newspaper, and my mother was a housewife. They gave me things that were much better than cash allowances, however. I had plenty of unfettered time and almost complete freedom to pursue my imagination and dreams – as long as I stayed reasonably close to home and didn't get hurt or into trouble.

Sometimes I did roam around the city on my bicycle. But mostly, I stayed and played in my back yard. I liked to climb up in a peach tree, picked and eat some of the ripe fruit and pretend I was somewhere in outer space.

Other times, I mixed powders and liquids from my chemistry set and stuffed the gummy paste into stiff cardboard tubes removed from coat hangers. Then I glued paper fins and a nose cone to the tubes. And, when I was sure my mother wasn't watching, I struck a match, held it under my latest "rocket" and tried to make it take off. Usually, it just spewed a few flames, caught fire and toppled over onto the brick steps that served as my "launching" pad.

I also spent many hours building, flying, crashing and repairing balsa-and-tissue-paper model planes, while imaging myself flying the real planes some day. Adding fuel to that dream was the Air Force base at Jacksonville, just a few miles northeast of my home in Little Rock. Each day, many different types of military jets and prop-driven planes passed over our rented house on South Cedar Street.

For a young plane watcher, my back yard was an aerial paradise. I could see F-86 and F-88 fighter planes, B-47 bombers, RB-47 reconnaissance planes, B-36 bombers, and occasional relics of World War II, including P-51 Mustangs, F-4U Corsairs, C-47 transport planes, and B-17, B-24 and B-25 bombers. Civilian airliners and light planes also buzzed overhead, heading to or from Adams Field, Little Rock's main airport on the east side of town.

At night, after supper, I liked to return to my back yard for a few minutes. While firefly phosphorescence winked all around me, I swept the dark sky with a small, handheld telescope and wondered what the people on distant worlds were doing.

By age ten, I had developed a curiosity about electronics and radio communications, too, and now it was intensifying. At first, I was just a radio listener. My parents put a small table-model AM receiver in my room so I could hear baseball games, music and dramas such as "Sergeant Preston of the Yukon." But soon, I was turning the dial and discovering that I could hear stations far beyond Little Rock, as well.

One night, clear as a bell, an announcer said: "This is radio station KOA, Denver, Colorado." Soon, I heard another radio announcer say: "This is WBBM, Chicago." I was amazed – and hooked.

I looked up "radio" in my parents' 20-volume Collier's Encyclopedia set and learned that medium-wave AM broadcast signals could travel long distances after dark. Some of the signals followed Earth's curvature, and some of them reached the "F" layer of the ionosphere and somehow were bent back toward the surface, landing hundreds or even thousands of miles away.

This seemed wondrous to me, a mysterious blending of nature and technology. Right away, I became an enthusiastic "BCL" – broadcast-band listener. I started tuning into the weakest signals I could discern, and I kept a logbook listing details such as the call letters, frequency and location of each new distant station I heard.

For my 11th birthday in 1955, my parents gave me a subscription to *Popular Electronics* magazine,[1] which included articles about the hobby of "DX-ing," listening for radio signals from distant places. Soon, I also started tearing up discarded radios and TV sets and using some of their parts to build simple one-tube and two-tube radios. A few of the haywire receivers picked up a few local AM broadcast stations and an occasional shortwave signal. And some of them failed to work at all.

When I read a magazine article about astronomers using new devices called "radio telescopes," I tried to create one using a pair of earphones, a six-volt battery and pieces of an old Erector set as the antenna. When I pointed the antenna at the sun and connected the battery, the earphones instantly filled with crackling and hissing "cosmic" sounds. And the direct current passing through the earphones quickly overheated the electromagnets and burned them out. Little puffs of smoke floated out of my ears when I pulled off the ruined headset.

On Christmas Day while I was still 11, my parents gave me a stunning gift: a Silvertone multiband radio from Sears & Roebuck. It was hardly a sophisticated shortwave receiving set. Yet, as I sat cross-legged near the Christmas tree, I was completely mesmerized.

I turned its knobs and heard voices announce, in foreign-accented English, that I was listening to Radio Australia, to the BBC in London, to Deutsche Welle (the Voice of Germany), to Radio Netherlands, to station HCJB in Quito, Ecuador, and to broadcasts from other faraway cities.

Quickly, I developed a fascination for hearing broadcasts from distant countries, finding their capital cities on maps and logging everything new that I heard. I was now an avid "SWL" – a shortwave listener. By the time I turned 12, some of my listener reports were being published in Hank Bennett's "Tuning the Short-Wave Bands" column in *Popular Electronics* magazine.

But I was now getting eager to do more than just listen. A few of my schoolmates had uncles and fathers who were federally licensed amateur radio operators—"hams." I had visited their "ham radio shacks" (usually converted sheds or ex-chicken coops in their back yards) and marveled at their ability to talk – using Morse code or voice transmissions – with other "hams" in other states and other countries.

With help from some of Little Rock's hams, I began learning Morse code and studying Federal Communications Commission (FCC) rules and regulations that applied to amateur radio. I wanted to take the tests and become a "ham," too. In late January, 1957, I passed the Morse code test and the Novice Class written examination. Six weeks later, on March 20, 1957, four days before my 13th birthday, I received my first amateur radio license and FCC call sign, KN5JRN.

Using a *Popular Electronics* article as a guide, I wired up an eight-watt, one-tube radio transmitter, put an antenna wire up on my roof and began talking, via Morse code, with other Novices. Soon, I was reaching Mississippi, Texas, Kansas, Illinois and many other states.

I didn't give up my other hobbies. But the thrill of reaching farther and farther away by radio quickly intensified. A few months later, I went to the Little Rock FCC office and took another written test and a faster Morse code test in front of a stern federal radio examiner. I earned a coveted General Class ham radio license and dropped the Novice designator from my call sign. Now my station was K5JRN, and I had many new operating privileges.

My parents rewarded my progress by helping me purchase a used, 50-watt Heathkit[2] DX-20 transmitter and a battered, $20 Hallicrafters[3] S-40 receiver. The S-40 was at least 10 years old now but still much better for ham radio work than the Silvertone.

The new operating privileges and better equipment quickly helped extend my transmitting and receiving range. I began making contacts with ham radio operators in Europe, Africa, Oceana, Asia, Central America and South America. My interest and skills in radio communications continued to rise. But my dreams of flying and going into space soon crashed.

At Pulaski Heights Junior High School, I began having trouble reading blackboards and seeing distant objects without squinting. The school nurse told my parents I needed to see an eye doctor. Soon, I was wearing my first pair of glasses. I knew the Air Force would *never* put nearsighted pilots in its cockpits. And spaceships would not carry astronauts who had to wear big, black horn rims inside their bubble helmets. I would need some other way to serve my nation.

I didn't have to wait long to find that patriotic new calling. One night in early October, 1957, I stood in my backyard and watched in worried awe as a gleaming, gold-colored dot moved quickly and silently through the dark sky, crossing the backdrop of the Milky Way. It was the Soviet Union's Sputnik I satellite. The next night, as Sputnik 1 again passed overhead, I sat at my shortwave receiver and listened to Sputnik's weak, quavering "beep...beep...beep" signals on 20.005 MHz. Then I tuned into the loud, proud boasts of Radio Moscow as it hailed Soviet scientific "superiority" over the West.

The United States quickly reeled from the combined shock of more USSR satellite launches and the disheartening sights of U.S. rockets falling back onto their launching pads or tumbling out of control and exploding. Like many other Americans, I grew increasingly worried that we might be attacked soon, or even invaded, by the Soviet Union.

When the Eisenhower Administration put out an urgent national call for more scientists and engineers, I decided I would study electronics in college. But first, I had to grow up. And that still seemed almost an eternity away.

On summer Saturday mornings in 1958, I continued to wake up long before dawn, so I could spend an hour or two trying to reach Alaska, Australia, New Zealand or Japan by radio.

But now, I also had my first job. After breakfast, I would ride my bike to Wallach's Radio & TV Repair Shop on West 13th Street, across from Robert E. Lee Elementary School. Mr. Wallach had hired me to help fix his customers' broken televisions, radios and record players. Mr. Wallach ran the small shop by himself and typically paid me 50 cents a day for my fledgling efforts. I knew how to find bad tubes and replace some of the bad parts. And he showed me how to use some of his test gear. I also learned how to work the front counter and ask the right questions when a customer brought in a radio, TV or phonograph to be fixed.

Unfortunately, the shop was barely a block away from See's Variety Store, my favorite childhood shrine, and once my work day ended at noon, the two quarters quickly burned a hole in my pocket. See's stocked a nice selection Comet and Guillow model airplane kits, and fifty cents was more than enough to buy a 25-cent Spad, Fokker or Phantom Fury kit, a ten-cent tube of glue and a nickel candy bar.

Often, however, I also left Mr. Wallach's shop with something better than money. He let me salvage old vacuum tubes, resistors, capacitors and other parts from dead equipment that was being thrown away. Long after I returned to school the next fall and quit going to his shop, I used the parts to build an array of simple receivers and transmitters. Some of the projects worked, and some of them just sparked and belched noxious smoke. One even burst into flames when I tried to test it. Yet each time I built something new, I believed I was moving closer to helping America get into space.

I had some other lofty goals, as well. By the time I turned 14, I wanted to be suave and sophisticated; I wanted to play rock 'n' roll guitar; I wanted Patty L. to love me; I wanted to use radio telescopes and discover life on other planets; and I wanted to play major-league baseball. The year after the shock of Sputnik, all of these things still seemed somehow possible.

All of my close friends at Pulaski Heights now wanted to be space engineers, as well. All except one: Wesley. He had a more down-to-Earth goal. Sometimes, on Saturday or Sunday afternoons, I would pedal the mile or so to Wesley's house, which was located in a fashionable neighborhood just a few blocks from our school.

Wesley was, in his low-keyed fashion, Mr. Almost-Everything: editor of the school paper, president of the National Honor Society chapter, president of virtually all school clubs. He was polite, refined, handsome and not shy around young ladies. I envied him, of course, because I was painfully awkward and self-conscious in social situations. Often, I felt like a doofus, especially around Patty L. But I figured she might love me eventually, particularly if I overcame my shyness, learned to dance and discovered civilizations on Mars.

Wesley initially had seemed to share my goals about taking to the skies. But by eighth grade, he was talking openly about an Army career, a choice I could not fathom. My father, an Army captain, had fought in the notorious Battle of the Bulge and come home from occupied Germany at the end of 1945 with a Bronze Star, a second Bronze Star with an Oak Leaf Cluster, and a Purple Heart. He stuffed his medals into his sock drawer (where they remained the rest of his life) and immediately plunged into working hard to provide for his family.

Dad had told me only a few stories about the war, mostly funny moments from basic training or his trips across the Atlantic Ocean on troop ships. Sometimes, there were harsher tales about the hardships of infantry life but almost nothing about combat itself. He never insisted that I should join any particular branch of service. He just explained that, as an able-bodied young man, I would face pressures from the Selective Service System once I reached 18. And if I didn't volunteer, I might be drafted and get no choice at all in where I ended up.

He had joined the Army right after completing college and had tried to be a paratrooper. But, at jump school at Fort Benning, Georgia, his ankles were deemed "too weak" to withstand the stress of hard landings with heavy equipment. So he was sent back to the infantry.

Long after the war, however, he remained proud of his paratrooper boots and training. He marched four miles to work each morning, so my mother could use the family car. And he and happily wore his paratrooper boots any time he had to walk through snow.

Wesley and I talked about many things during those junior-high Saturday and Sunday afternoons. We both liked model airplanes and shared interests in space and astronomy. We were Boy Scouts, as well. He ranked somewhere near the top of its system, and I ranked somewhere near the bottom, with no hope of going higher.

The subject of military service frequently came up. We knew we both might be expected to enlist. But in which branch? Before I had started wearing glasses, I had badgered Wesley to join the Air Force with me, so we wouldn't have to crawl through mud and barbed wire. We could wear clean, cool flight suits and blast MiGs.

After Pulaski Heights Junior High School, Wesley and I went to separate high schools and soon lost touch. I attended infamous Little Rock Central High School, starting in 1959, while federal troops, sent there by President Eisenhower, enforced desegregation.

Wesley went to Hall High School, which also was desegregated, but with less drama and international media focus. He continued his ways as an academic leader, organized Hall's first swim team and eventually overcame several obstacles to win an appointment to West Point.

I ran on Central High's track team, worked as an assistant editor on the school newspaper, and eventually became president of the school's socially insignificant club for ham radio operators. It had six members. The student body numbered nearly 2,000.

I favored desegregation. Yet I was never brave enough to say so aloud at Little Rock Central. I feared angering some of my parents' openly racist relatives. More than that, I feared being ostracized by my classmates. Most of those around me seemed to just want to do "normal" high school things. So we attempted to ignore the civil rights drama unfolding inside and outside our school.

In the state's biggest high school, I seldom saw any of the Little Rock Nine, except in hallways as we hurried from one classroom to the next. I wanted to win an academic scholarship so I could study engineering. Yet, each time I took an aptitude test, the scores indicated I should teach English or pursue a "creative" endeavor. I rejected this. I still wanted to get into space somehow and maybe even become the first man on the moon.

But I was a "B" student at best in most subjects --smart enough to succeed, yet not disciplined enough to buckle down. I soon realized that many things were becoming more interesting to me than math, chemistry and physics. My mind now stayed full of thoughts about girls and athletics, as well as electronics.

I had shown some talent for running in junior high school, and now I was on Central's varsity track team. I began to hope that perhaps I could win an athletic scholarship, instead, and run my way to an electrical engineering degree.

Meanwhile, I continued getting up long before dawn and tinkering with ham radio until after sunrise. My mother tried to get me to eat a healthy breakfast, at least a bowl of cereal with some fruit, before I left for school. But often, I would just drink a Coke and chew two pieces of Wonder Bread before hurrying out to start the two-mile walk.

I could have strolled six blocks down South Cedar Street and waited for one of the electric trolleys that ran east along 13th Street. There was a trolley stop just a block from the high school's big campus. But the walk to school was part of training for the track team, which was coached by a young Baylor University graduate named Clyde Hart. (Years later, he would coach several Olympic gold medalists, including sprinters Michael Johnson and Jeremy Warner.) Coach Hart had us wear two pounds of lead weights on each ankle. The little slabs of lead were sewed into light canvas pouches that we could tie to our legs and stuff into the tops of our socks, beneath our blue jeans.

Track team members wore them all day in classes, and sometimes we joked that we had "bulletproof" ankles. When we finally took off the lead weights at the start of track practice, our feet felt light, and we believed, at least for a little while, that we could run faster. After a few of Coach Hart's quarter-mile conditioning laps, however, most of us began to feel as if our whole bodies were burdened with lead weights.

At home, I built a small modulator and added voice capabilities to my DX-20 transmitter. Now, in the evenings and on weekends, I could carry on vocal conversations other radio hams. But Morse code remained my first love.

27

The rhythmic "dit-dah" sounds of "CW" (as the code transmissions are known) could make it through fading, static and interference that made voice communications completely impossible.

One day in 1961, just after my 17th birthday, basic greed finally began to overwhelm my hopeless goal of outer space. I had a conversation via ham radio with a crusty old retired Navy chief radioman in Texas. He asked me how I was doing in school, and I responded that I was maintaining a B average in the 11th grade.

During his next transmission, he seemed very impressed. He told me that a special enlistment program created by BUPERS (the Bureau of Personnel) during World War II was still in effect. The Navy was desperately short of radio operators, he said, and the special program offered immediate benefits to FCC-licensed amateurs who knew Morse code and understood how to use transmitters, receivers, antenna tuners and other devices.

A few days later, the chief stopped his car in front of my house, knocked on the door and introduced himself to my mother. As he entered my "radio room," the chief grinned at my equipment – some of it homemade and decidedly haywire.

"You built this stuff? Son, you're *just* the kind of radioman the Navy needs!" he said.

Naturally, I was flattered. "Tell you what," he added. "I've got some old radio stuff in my car, and the Navy wants me to get rid of it. I bet you could put it to good use."

"What kind of radio stuff?" Already, I was hooked.

Fifteen minutes later, he carried in the last box, and my little radio room now was almost overrun. He had stacked up several pieces of war-surplus receiving and transmitting equipment, plus small cartons of electronic parts still in packages stamped "1944" and "1945."

"This is a TCS transmitter and receiver." He pointed to one pair of hefty, black metal boxes bristling with knobs and switches. "And this is an RAO shortwave receiver."

"Wow, you mean I can borrow this stuff?"

My mother looked suspicious and apprehensive as he replied.

"No, son. It's yours to *keep*. All you have to do is consider – just *consider* – joining the Navy someday. Share some of this with your buddies, too. And give them one of these cards." He handed me a small stack of business cards that identified him as a retired Navy chief radioman. "If any of you join up and show this card," he told me, "the Navy will give me a little bonus." He picked up one card and turned it over. "Be sure they see this." A handwritten acronym – "BUPERS" – was on the back, followed by a group of about six numbers and letters.

He gave one to my mother, too. She still looked skeptical. "Don't worry, ma'am," the Chief politely reassured her. "I'm not signing him up for anything. Anyway, he's still too young."

The Chief pulled a piece of paper from his pocket, unfolded it carefully and gestured at what he had just delivered to my room. "This receipt verifies that all of this is free-and-clear government surplus, and the Navy has authorized me to distribute it." He smiled at my mother. "Just think of it as the Navy giving back some tax dollars."

Now he grinned at me again. "Hey, I almost forgot to tell you the best part. If you do join the Navy, you'll get to skip being a one-stripe seaman recruit *and* a two-stripe seaman apprentice. If you show them your ham license and this BUPERS regulation, you can enlist with *three* stripes on your sleeve *and* a Radioman Seaman rating. No other branch of the service can give you this deal."

He shook my hand. "Okay, have fun with it. And thanks for letting me drop by. I still have to make a couple of stops on my way to Memphis." With that, he was gone. And I did "have fun with it." The old gear – some of it bearing small brass placards that said "Restored for Civilian Use" – all worked. And the war-surplus spare parts were pure gold for some of my unfinished electronics projects.

But I put the Chief's cards on a shelf and gave no more thought to joining the Navy. I was still a kid, and the future still seemed a long time away. The world that mattered most to me was right in front of me, in my youthful dreams and cluttered radio room.

Above: The author, age 19, in Washington, D.C., the day before reporting for active duty, June 1963. *(Photographer unknown).*
Below: RM3 S.T. Dunn, USNR, awaiting active-duty orders, Anacostia, MD, June, 1963**)** *(Photographer unknown)*

CHAPTER 3

Reservist

**Arkansas,
1962-1963**

In the final weeks of my senior year at Central High, I had to make a choice. The military draft was active, and I had received a letter in the mail. I was about to be classified 1-A, meaning immediately "available for unrestricted military service."

I did not want to be drafted, and I had seen enough war movies to know that I never wanted to crawl through mud and machine-gun fire carrying a rifle. Also, two of my uncles – one a Marine and the other a soldier – had fought the Japanese on islands in the Pacific.

After hearing some of their war tales, I had grown up with *no* desire to be a Leatherneck or dogface. And, I had discovered from bus trips and long car rides that I was prone to motion sickness. I was giving the Navy no thought, either.

Once my 18th birthday arrived, I was resigned to the reality that I might have to carry a backpack radio in an Army or Marine rifle squad. But as I rummaged around in my room, I suddenly found the business cards the Navy chief radioman had left behind a year ago. And I remembered his solemn promise.

If I enlisted in the Reserves, I recalled him saying, I would *always* remain on land and *always* work in clean, comfortable, *shore-based* communications facilities.

Naively, I dared to believe that recollection.

Two days after my birthday, I walked to Little Rock's Naval Reserve Center (NRC) about a mile from my house on South Cedar Street.

I felt no sense of irony as I took a shortcut through the grounds of a state mental hospital and then walked past the city's zoo. I figured I would just pick up a Navy Reserve information brochure and return home to think about it.

Two hours later, I was a sailor. The recruiters at the NRC had been *very* happy to meet me. Almost before I knew it, I had taken the oath of allegiance and received an immediate promotion from Seaman Recruit (E1) to Radioman Seaman (E3). The retired Chief had not lied, at least about that. The Navy, it turned out, truly *was* critically short of radio operators.

My first official act as a Navy Reservist was walking the mile back home, past the zoo and mental hospital, staggering beneath the weight of a sea bag full of uniforms and shoes that smelled strongly of mothballs and long-term storage. My second official act was wondering what the hell I had just gotten myself into.

Three weeks after high school graduation, I was sent to an accelerated, two-week boot camp at the Naval Training Center in San Diego, California. As a freshly minted E3, I outranked all of the other recruits in Company 5017 – indeed, nearly all of the hundreds of new sailors on the base. Unlike my friend Wesley, however, I quickly discovered that I was ill-suited for a military career.

I had always imagined that I would be noble and courageous under fire. I had won countless "battles" and killed entire "armies" while playing war games with neighborhood kids. Pine cones provided us an almost endless supply of grenades, and my cracked-and-taped Louisville Slugger baseball bat made a wonderful mortar, bazooka or machine gun. It could even switch firing modes instantly when some of the "enemy" kids tried a banzai charge.

In San Diego's surprisingly cold summer dawns, however, I quickly discovered that I had trouble mastering even the basics of military life. Right away, I couldn't seem to get "squared away" enough to pass inspections. Something always seemed to be wrong with my uniform, haircut, shoeshine or shave.

I could march about as well as anyone. But other aspects of my basic training did not go smoothly. Indeed, Company 5017's commanding officer, a chief petty officer named Gunter, often was in my face, yelling expletives that never seemed to end.

During a firefighting drill, for example, I suddenly moved the wrong way, took a full-pressure water blast in the back and was sent tumbling and sprawling. In the tear gas training chamber, I panicked, ripped off my gas mask and tried to fight my way out the door. But I was no match for the two beefy petty officers who grabbed me and kept throwing me back inside. Finally, I had to just stand there, breath the noxious stuff and feel my eyes burn and painfully water, while everyone else in Company 5017 finished their brief turns in the chamber and left. The gas, I learned, wouldn't kill me. But I spent the rest of the day marching with stinging eyes, blurred vision and tears streaming down my face.

On another day, I failed a white hat inspection. The inside of my "Dixie cup" had a slight stain caused by skin oil from my forehead. Chief Gunter ripped the hat from my head, turned it inside out, plopped it down over my face like a lampshade and made me march five paces in front of Company 5017 for what seemed like miles while we paraded past other boot camp companies and groups of Chiefs and officers. There was no shortage of laughter and jeers for me, the company "scrounge."

One of Chief Gunter's favorite punishments, however, was to make small groups of errant sailors run around the perimeter of the "grinder," the vast paved field where we and many other Navy recruit companies marched hour after hour. For most trainees, Gunter's punishment runs were painful drudgery. For me, they provided brief moments of respite and freedom from harassment. I had been both a letterman on Little Rock Central's state champion track team *and* a distance runner. While other recruits struggled and wheezed their way around the grinder, I lapsed comfortably into familiar strides and breathing patterns. I finished each punishment run feeling more a bit more refreshed than exhausted.

Eventually, however, I gave myself away. During one mass punishment run for all of Company 5017, I couldn't resist my natural sense of competitiveness. I pulled ahead of the pack, set a track-meet pace and finished far ahead of everyone else.

Chief Gunter realized his mistake and promptly gave me a special new punishment. That night, I was sent to stand guard over the company's wet laundry that was air-drying on clothes lines outside our barracks. I was armed with a heavy, 1902 Springfield rifle that had its barrel completely plugged with lead. As I marched back and forth in front of the clothes lines, a cold, thick fog rolled in from the ocean and chilled me to the bone. The hours passed very, very slowly as I moved with the Springfield and repeated the 16-count manual of arms each time I stopped to do an about-face.

At 4:30 a.m., when Chief Gunter arrived to turn on the barracks lights and wake up the company with a shrill police whistle, I was a walking zombie, desperate for sleep. He took away the Springfield and ordered me to go change uniforms and fall in.

Company 5017 spent that weary day marching to breakfast, then marching to the grinder and marching back and forth across the grinder until lunch. The commands came quickly and often were yelled out in sounds that were strange versions of familiar words.

By the left flank...harch! By the right flank...harch! Hup-toop-threep-fourp! Hup-toop-threep-fourp! Guide! Guide! Drive! Drive! Left turn...harch! After a quickly eaten lunch, we marched from the chow hall back to the grinder and moved in various formations until 3 p.m. Just when I thought I couldn't stay awake any longer, we were marched to another building and herded into a warm classroom for an hour-long lecture on "What to Do During an Atomic Attack." The officer delivering the talk spoke in a quiet, bored monotone, as if imparting the information for the thousandth time.

I must have somehow slept with my eyes open and without snoring. The class seemed to end quickly, and all I remembered was that it might be best to be in a subway when an A-bomb exploded. *And don't forget to breathe through a folded handkerchief if radioactive dust is present and you don't have a gas mask.*

The next day, following six exhausted hours of sleep and a heavy breakfast, I failed my Navy swimming test. It happened soon after we were herded into a huge facility with two large swimming pools.

"Undress!" a Navy swimming instructor ordered. "Take off everything, including your skivvies!"

Fifty of us, naked and shivering lined up and saw that we were going to have to leap off a 20-foot-high diving platform feet first, one at a time. Then, after we surfaced, we would have to swim across a huge, deep pool of cold water. That was the test.

I had never jumped off anything higher than a basic diving board. And I had never swum across anything wider than a small city pool.

When my turn came, I jumped, trying to protect my private parts with my hands, as instructed. I slammed into the surface at a bad angle, swallowed a lot of water as I went down and immediately panicked when I surfaced.

Coughing and thrashing my arms, I headed straight toward the nearest side of the pool, not the far end.

A long pole suddenly jabbed into the water just ahead of me. I grabbed it and clung to it for dear life as two cursing instructors yanked me out of the pool.

"What the HELL are you doing in MY Navy?" one of them bellowed in my ear.

I had no response. I was still coughing up water. But it didn't matter. The instructors each grabbed an arm and hustled me over to another, smaller, shallower pool.

There, about a dozen other recruits, all looking sheepish, were standing or bobbing in waist-deep water. They, too, had failed the test, including a pudgy young Navajo who had plunged off the high platform and stayed at the bottom until a rescue swimmer finally dove in and hauled him, gasping and gagging, to the surface.

I had been three jumpers behind the Navajo on the platform, and I saw him sink and struggle as I waited my turn. He also had swallowed a lot of water and was flailing his arms with palms upward, apparently fighting in confusion against his own natural buoyancy, when the rescue swimmer reached him.

A few more recruits were hustled over and shoved in to join us, and remedial swimming class soon began. One of the loud-mouthed instructors demonstrated how we could float on our backs and propel ourselves forward. We were to use our arms and hands to pull us along the surface and simultaneously spread our legs apart and pull them together again to provide additional propulsion. Seen from above, we would look like an "X" and then an "I" and then an "X" again, if we did things in the right sequence.

"Okay, now swim across this goddam pool!" Instructor Loudest-Mouth called out. He blew a whistle, and we started thrashing the water. As we began moving, we could see several other swimming instructors lining up along the edges of the pool. They held long poles that I assumed would be used to save us from drowning.

WHAP!

The instructors started slamming the poles against the water. The pole tips created painful concussions in our ears.

WHAP-WHAP-WHAP-WHAP-WHAP!

They also sounded their whistles – long, shrill blasts.

And another instructor bellowed over the cacophony: "Let's go, you goddam tadpoles! Your ship just sank! Swim for your lives! Swim! Swim! If you make it to the end of this pool, you're out of this class!"

WHAP!

WHAP-WHAP-WHAP-WHAP-WHAP!

Some of us didn't make it. We stopped swimming too soon and let our feet touch bottom. We were desperate for a rest. But too quickly, we were prodded with the damnable poles.

"You! Grab hold!" one instructor shouted at me.

I grabbed the pole, and two instructors hauled me out of the water just as a few lucky recruits made it all the way to the end and cheered.

"You're *dead*, dipshit!" one instructor yelled in my waterlogged ear. "But I have good news! You've just been resurrected! Now get your ass back to the end of the pool and start swimming. When you make it back here, you'll be out of this class."

After two more exhausting tries, I finally made it all the way across. And when I did, "out of this class" turned out to be a lie, of course.

Two hours a day for the next three days, starting at 7 a.m., all of us had to return for remedial swimming instructions.

We were lectured on how to jump into the ocean from great heights, such as the deck of an aircraft carrier. If we held our feet together just right, we *might* manage to save our private parts and not shatter our legs, we were promised.

We were shown – also in theory – how to swim beneath burning oil and come up for a gulp of air (or smoke) by sweeping our arms around wildly and creating a hole in the burning oil just as we surfaced.

We practiced using our white hats as basic floatation devices.

Just turn it inside out, get it wet, whap it down on the water to trap some air, and then hold it close to your chest as you float on your back and relax. Repeat as necessary.

We learned how to pull off our dungarees, tie knots in the pants legs and whip the wet pants over our heads to trap air, creating water wings. We also swam up and down the cursed pool on our backs while the long sticks again smashed near our heads, whistles blew, instructors cursed and shouted, and cold water surged into our ears. The goal of the mayhem was twofold, of course. The instructors wanted our swimming lessons to be unpleasant, so we would work hard to complete them quickly. And they wanted us never to forget what we had learned. It worked.

Once my highly compressed two-week boot camp was finished, I could swim on my back like a belly-up frog. I could march in step without turning the wrong way. And I could shoot an M-1 Garand rifle from my right shoulder and hit the outer rings of a paper target, even though I was a natural leftie.

And, of course, I knew to head for the nearest subway tunnel if the Russians attacked us with nuclear weapons.

Two months after Reserve boot camp, I enrolled as an electrical engineering major at the University of Arkansas in Fayetteville. At an orientation session for new freshmen engineers, an assistant dean told us: "Welcome, gentlemen, to pre-business. Most of you will flunk out of engineering school and change majors."

I snickered. I was sure I would be one of the survivors.

Meanwhile, in another part of orientation, there was a surprise. Being a Naval Reservist did *not* exempt me from having to join the campus Reserve Officer Training Corps (ROTC) program. And the only choices were Army or Air Force. I lined up with other freshmen males for a drawing from a box and pulled out a sheet that said "U.S. Army." I was horrified. "I don't want to be in the Army," I told another freshman. He looked at his sheet of paper and replied: "I don't want to be in the Air Force." So we quietly swapped and got in the lines for the two ROTC programs.

Once classes got underway, I wore an Air Force uniform to campus twice a week. And once a week, I ran home after my last class, changed out of ROTC clothes, put on my Navy uniform and walked a mile to Fayetteville's small Naval Reserve training center.

It did not take me long to flounder in math classes. And I loathed mechanical drawing, especially when ink dribbled out of my adjustable-width ruling pen, leaked beneath my T-square and splotched hours of work. I started skipping classes so I could play chess and eat donuts with my roommate. He was having an equally hard time with engineering school, and now was thinking of going into the ministry. By early December, we were both on academic probation and eager to flee Fayetteville.

I transferred to Arkansas State Teachers College in Conway at the start of the spring 1963 semester. Now I was much closer to Little Rock and home cooking, and I had decided to change my major to journalism. But soon, I was skipping classes again, this time to play cards and socialize in the Student Union building.

Conway did not have a Navy Reserve training center. So, once a week, I put on my wool blues and hitchhiked or took a Greyhound bus 35 miles to Little Rock. The drill sessions included some classroom time, and I soon passed a test. On March 16, I advanced from Radioman Seaman to Radioman Petty Officer Third Class. I now had a "crow" on my sleeve.

Ultimately, during my forthcoming two years of active duty, I would advance one more pay grade to Radioman Second Class and get to go first in chow lines, along with First Class Petty Officers and other Seconds.

Rank, indeed, had its privileges.

Meanwhile, my junior-high-school friend Wesley K. Clark Jr. would become an officer and gentleman at West Point, as well as a Rhodes Scholar in England.[1] Later, he would survive combat in Vietnam, rise through Army ranks and eventually become NATO's Supreme Allied Commander and a Democratic candidate for President of the United States.

The author in the *Higbee's* Operations Division berthing compartment, mugging with a broom, 1964. In reality, radioman petty officers seldom had to sweep compartments.
(Photographer unknown)

CHAPTER 4

Sailor

Early in June, 1963, I finally admitted that my civilian career hopes were in shambles, and I could not keep putting off the two-year active duty obligation hanging over my head.

I decided, reluctantly, it was time to grow up.

I packed my still-pristine sea bag, rode a bumpy Lockheed Electra flight to Washington, D.C., and reported to the Naval Receiving Station at Anacostia, Maryland, on June 20.

The next morning, I was interviewed by a sour-faced yeoman petty officer first class who grumbled: "So, what do you want? What kind of duty?"

When I told him I had been "guaranteed" shore duty by the recruiters in Little Rock, he smirked and started typing.

But if I *absolutely* had to go to sea, I added helpfully, I would prefer to be on an Atlantic Fleet aircraft carrier, hopefully in the Mediterranean. He nodded again, smirked again, and kept typing.

Shortly before that interview, one old-salt enlisted sailor waiting his turn had cautioned me sternly: "Don't *ever* tell them what you *really* want. Always tell them the exact opposite. They'll give you what you say you *don't* want. It's a game they play."

But I had been brought up to always tell the truth. Thus, like George Washington, I could not tell a lie, especially right there next to the nation's capitol, with God, the President, the Chief of Naval Operations *and* J. Edgar Hoover all looking over my shoulder.

Give me shore duty or give me an aircraft carrier, I had essentially declared, in my finest Patrick Henry voice.

Over the next week, while I waited anxiously to know my first active-duty station, I was assigned to base work parties and sent to perform a challenging array of national-defense tasks.

These included mowing an admiral's lawn, cleaning metal meal trays in the base scullery, hanging up and taking down ceremonial flags inside an unused aircraft hanger, and chasing tennis balls at an officers' tennis tournament.

One morning, a senior petty officer who appeared badly hung over forgot to give me a job assignment. After he wandered off in an early-morning daze, I asked a nearby second-class petty officer what I should do.

He just shrugged and said: "Hell, I don't know. Skate out until somebody catches you and puts you to work."

He outranked me by one stripe, so it was a lawful order. But before I could ask what *skate out* actually meant, he, too, walked away.

I thought about it for a few moments and finally divined it. If nobody knew what to do with me, it was up to RM3 Silas Theron Dunn III, USNR, to show some *military* initiative.

Furthermore, all of the work parties thus far had been inane drudgery, and none of their tasks had required the finely honed skills of a *radioman*.

I went back inside the transit barracks, found an unused clipboard and a few pieces of paper and scribbled some illegible notes on the top sheet. Then I carried the clipboard outside and started walking along a sidewalk.

Soon, I was striding purposefully, holding the clipboard in my left hand and saluting officers smartly with my right.

Within an hour, I had marched past and around all of the nearby buildings, and I was starting to get hot and sweaty in the muggy air. I decided I needed a new plan.

As I neared a base bus stop, I saw a battered battleship-gray bus rattling toward me. It stopped, and, instinctively, I hopped aboard.

The bus followed a circuitous route around the base, halting at various buildings and intersections to pick up or drop off passengers that included officers, enlisted sailors and an occasional civilian base worker. I had no idea where the bus line ended.

But I quickly figured it out when the bus driver suddenly stopped in front of one building and shouted "Bebop!" And everyone on the bus stood up to get off.

Clipboard in hand, I followed them.

"Bebop," it turned out, was the United States Navy School of Music.

As I walked past its small sign, I heard brassy musical scales and snatches of band music wafting from rehearsal rooms. Others from the bus went inside Bebop's front doors. But I remained outside and "consulted" my clipboard.

I studied the building's façade for a few seconds. Then I made a checkmark and wrote a note: "*Music school - No paint needed.*"

This would be my cover story, I decided. If anyone asked, I would say I was from the transit barracks, and I had been ordered by some second class named Williams or Wilson or Wilton – *Sorry*, sir, *I can't remember which* – to check building fronts for areas that need paint.

It sounded no worse than any of the other make-work assignments being handed out to transit sailors.

After a few moments, I went back to the bus stop, waited for the next bus and this time rode it to the base hospital. I got off, walked up to the front of the building, "inspected" it and wrote on the clipboard: *"Hospital - upper right corner – small area needs paint."*

Already, I felt better. If challenged, I now had something to report.

And heroically discovering paint flaws seemed just a bit more important to national defense than mowing grass or retrieving errant tennis balls.

For the rest of the day, I kept up the ruse and went from building to building, sometimes walking, sometimes riding the bus. My list of "paint defects" grew longer and longer.

Soon, I was "re-inspecting" buildings that I had already "inspected." And sometimes, I would walk toward a building and suddenly pretend I had forgotten something.

I would stride back to the bus stop, consult the clipboard, make a meaningless mark or two, and ride again to Bebop or the hospital or base headquarters.

The enlisted men driving the buses likely sensed I was skating, but none of them cared. They just drove hard and fast, especially when no officers were aboard.

The next morning, transit sailors again clustered around a second class to get their work assignments. He wasn't the same PO2 as yesterday. So I showed him my clipboard and said "I'm Dunn. I'm still on the paint-inspection detail."

He nodded, checked off my name and kept assigning others to work parties. Grinning at my own cleverness, I strolled over to the nearby bus stop.

This time, I kept up the ruse for eight straight hours. I looked at trim areas around front windows and made notes and small diagrams on my clipboard.

At long last, when my day's "work" was finished, I went back to the transit barracks – and discovered that early liberty had been granted.

The sailor stuck inside the building on fire watch told me that everyone else in the transit barracks had left the base four hours ago. Half of my day of clever deception had been a complete waste of time.

Two days later, I was handed orders. Shore duty.

I stood at the yeoman's desk and stared at him speechless – Ethiopia? *Ethiopia?*

What would I do in Ethiopia? *Why* Ethiopia?

The Navy, the yeoman told me, had a small radio relay installation in Asmara, Ethiopia (now Asmara, Eretria). Suddenly, he laughed at my stricken reaction and pulled the orders out of my hand.

"These are your *real* orders," he said, grinning. He handed me a different set of papers.

Sure enough, I was getting the exact opposite of what I had so honestly requested.

It wasn't shore duty, and it wasn't an aircraft carrier in the Atlantic.

I was being assigned to a rocking-and-rolling destroyer, one that soon would join the U.S. Seventh Fleet in "WestPac," the Western Pacific.

Above, a U.S. Navy helicopter hovers low over the stern of the
destroyer *USS Higbee* (DD-806) during operations
in the Tonkin Gulf, 1965.

Below, the aircraft carrier *USS Ranger* (CVA-61) steams toward its
next flight operations on Yankee Station, 1965.
(Photos by Si Dunn)

CHAPTER 5

Radioman

Yokosuka Naval Base
August 2, 1964

Yokosuka cab drivers could zip right through the Navy base's main gate and drop sailors off at piers close to their ships.

This was very handy for the ones who had consumed too much drink or were in imminent danger of overstaying liberty.

I had had only part of one beer, and I was deeply anxious to know why a sudden recall was underway. I paid the cabbie 200 yen, about 60 cents, and bailed out.

The Shore Patrol chief's *"War!"* cry at Club Kobe was still reverberatingd inside my head.

The *Higbee* was moored nearby in a nest of four ships. The others tied up with us side-by-side were the guided-missile destroyer *USS Joseph Strauss* (DDG-16) and two additional Gearing-class destroyers: the *USS Leonard F. Mason* (DD-852) and the *USS Joseph Orleck* (DD-886).

Several bigger ships were visible out in the harbor. I could see the aircraft carrier *USS Kearsarge* (CVS-33) and the cruiser *USS Oklahoma City* (CLG-5), flagship of Vice Admiral Roy L. Johnson, commander of the Seventh Fleet (COMSEVENTHFLT).

Other vessels were anchored in the harbor, as well. I could make out the dimly-lit shapes of a couple of support ships and an attack transport that could carry troops and amphibious landing craft.

At least one of the *Higbee*'s four boilers already was fired up. Smoke was rising from one of the two stacks. The other ships in the mooring cluster also showed visible signs that urgent preparations were being made to get underway. Something big definitely had happened. But *what*?

At the *Higbee*'s gangway and quarterdeck, there seemed to be little time for the traditional boarding formalities. Usually, as we stepped onto the gangway, we saluted the ensign—the American flag – fluttering above the fantail on the flag staff.

Then we stepped up and asked the officer of the deck (OOD) for "Permission to come aboard, sir."

This time, a sense of urgency was overriding tradition. *Higbee* crewmen popped quick salutes aft as they hurried up the gangplank. And they lifted only brief salutes to the Officer of the Deck (OOD) as they surged past the quarterdeck.

The OOD, meanwhile, returned the salutes almost in assembly-line fashion, not necessarily in synch with the salutes being rendered.

There were no strangers on a destroyer, at least at face level. We recognized each other as members of the crew, even when we didn't know each other's names and life stories.

Once I was aboard, I headed aft toward my tiny living space beneath the ship's fantail. I needed to change out of my liberty uniform and report quickly to Radio Central.

My rack (bunk) and two-foot-square footlocker were in the Operations Department's berthing compartment, directly beneath the aft 5-inch/38 gun mount. Its two guns were designed to fire shells five inches in diameter at targets up to 10 miles away, and their barrels were 38 calibers – just under 16 feet – long.

I also slept right above one of the ship's twin 12.5-foot, four-bladed screws and only a short distance from an ammunition magazine. I had the bottom rack in a tier of three.

Lying there when the ship was underway often felt like being wedged in a canvas coffin that was stuffed inside a careening boxcar.

The Operations Department's compartment was the living space for the ship's radiomen, signalmen, sonarmen, radar operators, and electronic technicians. There was little talk among the other crewmen as we stood next to our racks and hurried to change, in very narrow spaces, out of our liberty uniforms.

Some of the sailors were smelly drunk and openly angry that they had been dragged out of the bars and skivvy houses well before midnight. But most of us were anxious to know where – and *why* – we were being sent to sea in such a hurry.

I folded up my liberty uniform carefully, trying to keep it clean and unwrinkled as I put it away. Then I quickly pulled on the work clothes of a destroyer sailor: blue dungarees and light-blue chambray shirt.

We were supposed to wear a blue ball cap at all times when outside—"topside" – on the ship. But many destroyer sailors liked to stretch the rules.

My ball cap typically dangled from my right rear pocket, where I could pull it out quickly and slap it on my head if I saw an officer coming and needed to render a salute. (American sailors never saluted "uncovered.")

I closed and locked my footlocker and quickly stepped through a watertight door into the electricians' and machinist mates' berthing compartment.

From there, I ran up a steep set of steel stairs—a "ladder" in Navy parlance. The ladder led through an open hatch to "Broadway," the ship's main interior passageway.

Broadway had the ship's tiny "gedunk" store (mainly candy bars and uniform accessories), the even tinier post office, the barbershop and sickbay, manned by a chief corpsman and a couple of hospital corpsmen.

Halfway along the passageway, I turned right and went out the starboard watertight door to the main deck. Moving forward a few more steps, I reached another steel ladder and scrambled up one level to the O-1 deck, which we called the ASROC (anti-submarine rocket) deck.

The boxy ASROC launcher was armed with eight 1,000-pound ballistic rockets capable of firing conventional homing torpedoes or nuclear depth charges against enemy submarines. I passed by it, staying just outside the red warning circle painted on the deck.

Finally, I opened a watertight door next to the ship's forward stack. One step inside the watertight door, I knocked hard on a locked door marked "Radio Central."

As I waited to be admitted, I was grateful that I had an information advantage over most sailors. Particularly on small ships such as destroyers, most radio operators held secret or top-secret security clearances and had to be jacks of all trades when handling sensitive information.

Part of my job was to read through stacks of classified and unclassified messages and pay close attention to all new radio traffic coming in at 100 words per minute via the high-security Fleet Broadcast radio-teletype circuits. Often, I was the first to know the *Higbee*'s next destination or assignment when a new ship-movement order arrived from "Jehovah."

That was the not-so-secret tactical code name for COMSEVENTHFLT, the Seventh Fleet's commander.

Radioman Second Class (RM2) Lomax opened Radio Central's locked door and let me in.

Lomax was a "lifer" who had joined the Navy at age 17, just before the end of World War II. Now in his late thirties, he should have made it to chief petty officer long before now. But, as he had explained to me several times, he was perfectly content to stay where he was: nominally in charge of a radio room watch section – and nothing else, including his own life.

Tonight, however, he looked worried, an expression I had not seen on his face.

"What's going on?" I asked as I closed and locked the door behind me.

"Some kind of trouble. I don't know."

This was a typical Lomax response. He really did *not* want to know if something outside his secure world might affect him.

Radio Central was a smelly, noisy work space, and tonight it was noisier than usual. I could hear radio-teletype machines clattering away at top speed.

Also, in one overhead speaker, the Navy's Yokosuka Harbor Control frequency, 2716 kHz, was alive with voices as tug boats and other auxiliary craft reported their movements and destinations.

From another overhead speaker, I could hear a radio operator aboard a nearby ship sending an encrypted message to Yokosuka's naval communications station, NDT.

The five-character encryption groups flowed by in urgent, mysterious combinations of *dits* and *dahs*: *"XYHUT BVCXZ WEQAM HJROT..."*

Radio Central's main compartment was about 10 feet wide and 10 feet deep. But the electronic equipment bolted to steel racks on both sides narrowed the walkway and the work space to about five feet wide.

Higbee watch section supervisors such as Lomax spent most of their time working at a small desk in one corner of the radio room. Along with supervising one other radio operator and a watch section messenger, their main task was to check through and file all incoming and outgoing radio messages.

The desk also kept them close to the 21MC "squawk box" which linked Radio Central to the ship's bridge.

Another steel door was just beyond the watch supervisor's desk. It was supposed to be kept closed and locked at all times, but usually, we left it open for air flow and movement convenience. This heavy door led into the "crypto" compartment.

That's where I would be able to find out where and why we seemed to be going to war.

The crypto compartment was about 10 feet wide, six feet deep and packed with bolted-down radio-teletype (RATT) machines, shortwave receivers and small, rack-mounted oscilloscopes. Several heavy steel boxes also were bolted to metal racks or to shelves on the bulkheads. These were labeled "KW-7" and "KWR-37R."

The KW-7 and KW-37R boxes contained circuits that automatically encoded or decoded radio-teletype messages. They enabled us to send and receive messages classified Secret, Confidential or EFTO – Encrypted for Transmission Only.

Messages classified Top Secret, however, were still received or transmitted as five-character code groups. Those messages had to be decoded by hand within a small closet that had a steel door and a heavy-duty combination lock.

Only a handful of the ship's officers were authorized to open that door. And they had to lock themselves inside while they handled information dealing with the ship's nuclear warheads or other highly sensitive matters.

As I hurried into the crypto compartment, the Fleet Broadcast circuits now were hammering out a steady stream of high-priority radio messages. Indeed, the RATT machines seemed somehow to be running faster than their 100-word-a-minute top speed.

RM3 Stern, the radio operator for Lomax's watch section, and Radioman Seaman Apprentice (RMSA) Larkyns, the watch messenger, were both hovering over the machines, hurriedly tearing off long strips of teletype paper and separating out the messages that the *Higbee*'s Captain and other officers needed to read.

Other sights and sounds added to the tense, *we're-going-to-war* atmosphere.

Synchronization lights flashed rapidly on the blue-gray, top-secret KW-37R decryption devices. Eerie patterns of phosphorescent light danced up and down on small oscilloscope screens. And several radio speakers warbled out the *deedle-deedle-deedle* sounds of the incoming RATT signals from NPN, the Navy's powerful shore station on Guam.

Suddenly, I realized the RATT machines also were sounding out five quick, audible bell signals – *ding, ding, ding, ding, ding!* – and printing the precedence code *ZZZZ* at the beginning of almost every message.

I had handled FLASH messages in training, but I had never expected to see one in real life. Now, bulletins of the same precedence that announced the attack on Pearl Harbor were zipping across the pale-yellow message paper and spewing out from the two sleek, gray AN/UGC-6 teletypewriter machines that had been installed less than a year ago.

The FLASH precedence, according to the Navy's 1964 *Radioman 3 and 2* training guide, was "reserved for initial enemy contact messages or operational combat messages of extreme urgency."[1]

A FLASH took precedence over all other Navy message traffic, the guide stated, and was expected to be "[h]andled as fast as humanly possible with an objective of less than 10 minutes."

The highest-precedence messages I had ever handled until now had been IMMEDIATEs, which required delivery to their addressees within 30 minutes to one hour.

The noisy electromechanical chaos in the crypto compartment now left me convinced we were plunging straight into World War III. Hurriedly, I picked up some of the latest radio traffic and scanned it, trying to find the name of our new adversary.

The repeated references to "Tonkin Gulf" stumped me. *Where was that?* And who were the North Vietnamese? I had no idea.

My father had been an infantry captain in France, Belgium, Holland and Germany during World War II. So I had grown up with a natural focus on Europe, both at home and at school.

Geography had been one of my best subjects. I could find tiny Liechtenstein, Andorra, Gibraltar and San Marino on maps. Yet Asia – beyond Japan, Okinawa, China, Taiwan, the Philippines and Korea – remained almost a complete mystery.

One of the newest SITSUMs – situation summaries – finally revealed more of what I was seeking. At 3:08 p.m. local time in the Tonkin Gulf, three North Vietnamese PT boats had made an "unprovoked" attack on a Seventh Fleet destroyer, the *USS Maddox*, while it was on "routine patrol" in "international waters."

The fast-moving boats had fired torpedoes and 37mm guns at the ship. The *Maddox* had responded with her booming 5-inch naval guns. And four F-8E Crusader aircraft from the carrier *USS Ticonderoga* had swept down and unleashed Zuni rockets and 20mm cannon fire.

The U.S. forces, the summary stated, had sunk one PT boat and badly damaged the other two without suffering any casualties or significant damage.

I helped Lomax and the others get the most urgent and important messages onto the routing boards. These were heavy metal clipboards with steel covers that hid messages from unauthorized eyes.

One covered clipboard was painted yellow and marked "Secret." Another was painted green and marked "Confidential."A third clipboard, left unpainted, was marked "Unclassified."

When all of the boards were carried at once, they were a weighty handful for the radio messengers, especially at sea when they had to hang onto ladder handholds while lugging the boards up to the bridge or down to the wardroom or the officers' berthing spaces, known as "Officers Country."

Larkyns gathered up the boards and hurried off to take them to the *Higbee*'s captain, Commander J.J. Herzog, the executive officer, Lieutenant Commander T. J. Sullivan, the operations officer, Lt. (j.g.) Tim Jenkins, and other officers.

I rushed out behind Larkyns and followed him up the ladder. Then I turned another way and headed straight for the ship's tiny library.

The library was situated behind a water-tight door not far from the bridge. It was barely big enough for one person to stand inside, and only a few officers and enlisted men used it, primarily to borrow paperback novels.

Yet, befitting a ship assigned to the Seventh Fleet, the *Higbee* also had several books on Southeast Asian history and geography. I start pawing through them and soon solved my dilemma.

What I still thought of, vaguely, as French Indochina had been partitioned in 1954 into the Democratic Republic of Vietnam (North Vietnam) and the State of Vietnam (South Vietnam), after a bloody war that ended France's involvement in Southeast Asia.

I had been 10 years old when this happened, and no doubt it had made headlines in the afternoon newspaper my father brought home from work. But, apparently, I had paid no attention. I had been too fixated on Little League baseball games, model airplanes, tinkering with radios, and playing war with neighborhood kids.

The area had remained "French Indochina" in my mind and in my school textbooks, even in high school. And it had not grabbed my interest in 1963, when a publication I seldom read, *Time Magazine*, reported on "the pinprick war" America was fighting to try to help South Vietnam defeat the Viet Cong guerillas. The Pentagon, at that time, had even stated that "the corner has definitely been turned toward victory."[2]

Very few Americans apparently understood what now was happening in the former French Indochina. At the end of the 1946-1954 Indochina War, the Geneva Agreement had established North and South Vietnam as separate countries. Ho Chi Minh's Communist forces had some 90,000 troops occupying southern parts of Vietnam.

"With the signing of the Geneva Agreement, most of these troops were regrouped and evacuated to North Vietnam," according to the 1967 book *Area Handbook for North Vietnam*. "Nevertheless, Ho Chi Minh left behind about 10,000 men and caches of arms and equipment in hideouts throughout the remote jungles of the Mekong Delta and the mountainous region north of Saigon as insurance against Communist failure to win the 1956 referendum provided for by the Agreement."

These troops became known as the Viet Cong "and served as the nucleus of military and subversive efforts to overthrow the government of South Vietnam and seize control of the country."[3]

From the middle of Arkansas, Europe to me had always seemed just over the horizon, while Asia seemed far enough away to be on another planet. But now, I was on that "other planet," and I was trying to understand why and what these new events meant.

I did not know yet that the Navy quietly and sporadically had been operating ships in and near the Tonkin Gulf since 1961. President John F. Kennedy had dispatched them there to show U.S. support for Laos in its battle against the Communist Pathet Lao forces.

Laos straddled both Thailand and South Vietnam, and the Pathet Lao were backed by China, Russia and North Vietnam. The fear in Washington was that if Laos fell, Communist-backed forces then would push into Thailand, Cambodia and South Vietnam, and they would all fall like dominoes.

Indeed, on my 17th birthday, while I was still a junior in high school, Task Force 77 – three aircraft carriers and numerous support ships – had begun operating in the South China Sea off the coast of South Vietnam. It was the same area where we were now being sent – as part of Task Force 77.

The U.S. secretly had been poised for large-scale war in that part of Southeast Asia and had even contemplated the possible use of nuclear weapons, at least until 1962. But the failure of the Bay of Pigs invasion in Cuba, half a world away, threw the Laotian support project into chaos.

Instead, it became simply an annex to a new plan to start putting combat troops into South Vietnam, according to John M. Newman in his book *JFK and Vietnam: Deception, Intrigue, and the Struggle for Power*.

"The Laos Annex to the Vietnam report was the opening salvo of a drive initiated by the JCS (Joint Chiefs of Staff) to intervene in Vietnam, an effort born within hours of the Pentagon's realization that [President] Kennedy was not going to intervene in Laos."[4] In the White House, only Vice President Lyndon Johnson had supported the initial notion of letting U.S. troops fight in Laos.

My paucity of knowledge about Southeast Asia was not unusual. Indeed, it extended all the way to the top of the Kennedy and Johnson Administrations, as former Secretary of Defense Robert S. McNamara later conceded in his book, *In Retrospect: The Tragedy and Lessons of Vietnam*.

"I had never visited Indochina, nor did I understand or appreciate its history, language, culture, or values," he wrote. "The same must be said, to varying degrees, about President Kennedy, Secretary of State Dean Rusk, National Security Advisor McGeorge Bundy, military adviser Maxwell Taylor, and many others. When it came to Vietnam, we found ourselves setting policy for a region that was terra incognita. Worse, our government lacked experts for us to consult to compensate for our ignorance."[5]

Aboard the *Higbee*, we had no knowledge or understanding of this as we went to sea.

We just hoped – and trusted – that those above us knew what we were supposed to do.

Radio Central, the main radio room aboard a Gearing Class
destroyer. The encrypted radio teletype equipment and the
crypto compartment were behind the closed door.
This is the restored radio room of the museum ship *USS
Joseph P. Kennedy Jr.*, (DD-850)
(Photo by Si Dunn)

CHAPTER 6

Underway

More radiomen now had returned from shortened liberty, and Radio Central was crowded with chaotic activity when I came down from the ship's library.

Before the *Higbee* could get underway, we had to set more than a dozen transmitters and receivers to the newly assigned frequencies for Fleet Common communications, fleet broadcasts, destroyer squadron communications, and talking with aircraft and other ships. Many dials and switches had to be manually repositioned; many coaxial patch cables needed to be looped from one connector panel to another.

To keep everything straight, a status board had to be updated with a grease pencil, to show the circuit names, assigned frequencies and corresponding transmitters and receivers, once they were put on line.

Two of the most important entries on the status board indicated the equipment assigned to LOP1 and LOP2, the two local operating positions. The LOPs were the bolted-down desks positioned near the front entrance. At each LOP, a new, still-classified Collins R-390A receiver was securely fastened to a metal shelf right above an Underwood communications typewriter.

The special typewriters had no lower-case letters. But they did have fast-eject handles that enabled a radio operator to eject a piece of paper with one quick pull and move a fresh piece of paper into position with a second pull. A good operator could change sheets of paper in seconds, while memorizing the incoming Morse Code text. And he could type it in while mentally catching up to the flow of newly arriving characters.

Decoded radio messages then had to be typed onto color-coded forms that had built-in carbon paper to create duplicates.

Yellow forms were for messages classified SECRET, green forms were for messages classified CONFIDENTIAL, and white forms were for UNCLASSIFIED messages.

The classified messages, and messages rated UNCLAS EFTO (Unclassified Encrypted for Transmission Only), always arrived as five-character groups of what seemed to be gibberish.

The ship's Communications Officer had to manually decode the nonsensical letters and numbers while locked inside the small crypto compartment.

If a message was classified TOP SECRET, he had to paste the decrypted text onto a special red form and carry it himself to the Captain and other officers and then store it in his locked space.

LOP1, just to the right of Radio Central's entry, was the position I preferred when sending and receiving CW. At both LOPs, the telegraph keys were firmly bolted down, and this was an important safety feature.

During the Pacific crossing, I had discovered that if I sat at LOP1 or LOP2 and the ship suddenly leaned hard to port and rolled back to starboard, I could hang onto the telegraph key with one hand and keep sending, albeit awkwardly. Similarly, if I was receiving a message, I could hold onto the typewriter frame with one hand and keep typing one-fingered.

Sometimes, however, we had hit rough water so suddenly that the ship's movements had thrown me backwards out of the LOP1 chair, which was *not* bolted down. I had tumbled hard across the gray rubber mat covering the Radio Central deck and ended up bruised and wedged against the supervisor's chair near the crypto door.

If I had been sitting at LOP2, instead, I might have been thrown into, or behind, the seven-foot-high metal rack holding the ship's powerful new 500-watt Collins AN/URC-32 single-sideband (SSB) transmitter.

LOP2 now was getting almost no use – and not just for safety reasons. More and more messages were being sent and received via encrypted radio-teletype using the top-secret KW-7 and KW-37 systems.

In the new transition from well-honed analog to rudimentary digital communications, one CW operator's position now was proving to be enough, most of the time.

Copies of received and sent CW messages had to be put in separate tickler files and stored in a filing cabinet in Radio Central. Sometimes, in rough seas, the filing cabinet drawers suddenly would pop open and hit us hard before slamming back shut as the ship rolled.

Messages torn from the radio teletype machines were kept in a separate "tickler file" on their original pale-yellow paper.

Part of a radioman's job was to check all tickler files carefully. If, at any time, we knew or suspected we had missed a fleet-broadcast message, we had to contact another ship or a shore station and see if the missed message was intended for the *Higbee*.

Any radio operator who missed or overlooked a vital message, such as orders to move the ship to a new location, instantly would be in deep trouble with his captain, his operations officer, his communications officer *and* his chief radioman. Indeed, the errant radioman could be demoted and even transferred to a bad duty assignment once a replacement radioman was found.

Early the next morning, August 3, 1964, the final liberty stragglers returned to the ship. Some had been hidden away in Yokosuka's "honeymoon" hotels, and the Shore Patrol had missed them during the big recall.

Chief Linn gathered his radio gang in Radio Central and announced that we were going on a modified version of "port and starboard" watches. The day watch would run from 7 a.m. to 6 p.m. – nearly 12 hours. The other 12 hours would be split into two watch sections. The eve watch would run from 6 p.m. to midnight. And the tiring mid watch would stretch from midnight to 7 a.m.

After he announced the watch rotations, the next thing he said was: "Dunn will be on the mid watch."

Indeed, I would have the mid watch, and it would have me.

With a full workday still ahead of us, there would be almost no time for any sleep before midnight. I would have to stay awake all night and try to get a few hours' sleep during the next morning, when the day would be punctuated with crewmen working, loud announcements over the 1MC, shrill boatswain mate's calls, assorted bells, and the incessant noises and vibrations of the ship's propellers.

Then, after an early lunch, I would be expected to return to Radio Central, temporarily relieve the on-duty watch section supervisor for the noon meal, and stick around and help out on the busy day watch until time for dinner. After dinner, I would have the eve watch. Then, after less than six hours' sleep, I would have the day watch, with Chief Linn frequently hovering over me.

Once *that* ended, then I would get the evening off to try to take care of personal matters and grab a little sleep. But, by midnight, I would once again be back on the mid watch, yawning and fighting to stay awake until dawn.

As events in the Tonkin Gulf and South China Sea unfolded and continued to unfold, this sleep-depriving watch pattern quickly was about to become normal routine for radiomen below the rate of chief.

The sleep shortage would turn many radio-gang members into zombies and me into something scarier: a seasick zombie.

At about 9:30 a.m. on August 3, as other ships begin moving out of Yokosuka's harbor, a boatswain's mate aboard the *Higbee* blew his shrill pipe and made a new call over the ship's 1MC: *"Now set the special sea and anchor detail. Make all preparations for getting under way."*

One by one, the destroyers in the cluster cast free of the ship next to it and maneuvered slowly away from the pier and into the harbor.

Shortly after 11 a.m., in the Pacific waters just beyond Tokyo Bay, the four destroyers formed a single-file column, picked up speed and steered southwestward.

Designated "Destroyer Squadron 3" (DESRON 3), the column was led, at Station 1, by the guided missile destroyer *USS Joseph P. Strauss* (DDG-16), the DESRON 3 commander's flagship.

The *Higbee* was in Station 2, keeping 1,500 yards astern of the *Strauss*. Meanwhile, two other refurbished Gearing Class destroyers, the *USS Leonard F. Mason* (DD-852) and the *USS Orleck* (DD-886), were at Stations 3 and 4, and also keeping 1,500-yard separations.

Within minutes, the separation between destroyers was opened to "double standard distance," 3,000 yards, and DESRON 3 sped up to 27 knots, just a few knots below the *Higbee*'s flank speed (its absolute top battle speed) of 35 knots.

In the distance, farther out in the Pacific, other U.S. Navy ships also were visible, roughly paralleling our course in their own formations.

A mighty armada was on its way toward Southeast Asia, responding to a single, ¾-inch-diameter hole that had been punched into a metal plate on the *USS Maddox* by a North Vietnamese 14.5mm machine gun bullet.

Seasickness set in quickly for me after we left Tokyo Bay. The Pacific was being roiled by the worst typhoon season on record. As Desron 3 neared the East China Sea, waves started rising higher than 30 feet, and the *Higbee* dutifully leaped up, wallowed over and did stomach-churning drops into the troughs.

I fought nausea for as long as I could. But I got sick as I tried to keep reading radio-teletype messages in the crypto room's hot, closed confinement. Soon, I was on my hands and knees in the narrow passageway outside Radio Central, vomiting and gagging. I had not made it outside in time to reach to the port side lifelines.

Chief Linn opened Radio Central's main door and laughed at my misery. "Get a swab, Dunn. Clean up your mess!" he ordered.

I tried to reply, but now I was retching and writhing with dry heaves. I managed to get up to my hands and knees for a moment. Then I started shaking and jerking violently.

Suddenly, I added some bile to my vomit, and I collapsed into the putrid, soggy mess I had just made.

Chief Linn slammed shut the door to Radio Central and locked it.

Fifteen minutes later, when I could walk again, I staggered over to an inside ladder a few steps forward of Radio Central. I went down to Broadway and found one of the "deck apes," a Boatswain's Mate Seaman Apprentice, near the ship's Coke machine.

Carefully keeping my distance, I asked him to get me a bucket and mop – a "swab."

He found them and brought them to me, also carefully keeping his distance as he eyed the wet mess on my dungarees.

I had already learned, during underway training and the Pacific crossing, that my episodes of seasickness would repeat themselves every few hours and finally subside after three or four days at sea. By then, weak and dehydrated, I could start eating and drinking again and keep most foods and liquids down.

But if any big change occurred in the pattern of the waves, such as a sudden storm, or if the mess cooks tried to serve certain foods, such as boiled cabbage or mustard greens, I could get sick all over again, very quickly.

I also had figured out that as long as I could feel the wind on my face and watch the horizon while the ship undulated, I could keep my stomach down. So, whenever I was off duty, I often stood amidships on the ASROC deck, just above the wave-washed main deck, and clung to the steel lifelines that served as our railings.

Sometimes, I did this during my radio watches, as well, especially when Chief Linn was not around to stop me. My nausea always rose quickly when someone started smoking in a crowded space. In the radio gang, everyone smoked except me.

The 6 p.m.-to-midnight eve watch and the mid watch – midnight to 7 a.m. – were the best times for me to sneak out. My two watch section shipmates knew what I was doing and why.

I would step outside into the darkness, so I could feel the wind on my face and see the phosphorescent glow of the waves.

I was barely a 15-second walk from Radio Central, yet I felt guilty for leaving my post, and I tried never to stay outside longer than a couple of minutes – just enough to stave off the next bout of seasickness a bit longer.

Ironically, the spot where I felt safest and least nauseous was just a few feet from the *Higbee*'s ASROC launcher. It likely was armed with at least one small W-44 nuclear warhead capable of creating a 10-kiloton blast.

Whether we really had a W-44 aboard or not supposedly was Top Secret. Yet radio messages alluding to its existence or movement or maintenance typically were classified at the next-lower level – Secret – and handled by enlisted radiomen.

Before the *Higbee* could pull into any Japanese port, such as Yokosuka or Beppu, the warhead (or a W-44 decoy, if that was what we actually carried) had to be removed and ferried by highline over to an ammunition ship outside Japan's territorial waters. Once we returned to sea, we received another W-44 (or equivalent decoy) and reloaded it into the ASROC launcher.

The Japanese, for obvious reasons, wanted no nuclear weapons on their soil or in their territorial waters.

In daylight, when I felt better and had a little time to be by myself, I liked go further aft to the "DASH" deck. This was a small helicopter deck and storage hanger. It was positioned on the O-1 level between the ship's aft stack and Mount 52, the rear 5-inch/38 gun turret.

The DASH deck was supposed to be the launching and recovery pad for a Drone Antisubmarine Helicopter (DASH). This weapon system had been installed on the *Higbee* during its 1963 refurbishment.

A DASH vaguely resembled a large flying bug and was about the size of a small car. It was designed to be flown by remote control.

During takeoff and landing, the bug-like drone helicopter was maneuvered from a deck control station on the dwarfish flight deck. Once the DASH was a "safe" distance away from the ship, it was flown by a drone pilot in the Combat Information Center (CIC) near the bridge. The ship's radar was used to guide it to and from targets.

Supposedly, a DASH could carry and drop one or two antisubmarine homing torpedoes up to 10 miles from the ship.

But the DASH system proved to have serious problems, according to Jack L. Wells, a retired Navy commander who served aboard Gearing Class destroyers and other ships during the Vietnam War.

It was "a major maintenance headache and very difficult to fly," and it had "a tendency to just go flying over the horizon, ignoring radio commands, never to be seen again."[1]

Indeed, the *Higbee*'s DASH system had flown just twice, both times during underway training in early 1964. Since then, it had remained in storage, and the DASH hanger now was used as a small auditorium for training, showing movies or holding church services at sea.

The DASH launching and recovery deck now was a popular place to grab a folding chair and sit out in the sun. It was out of sight of the bridge and one level up from the cleaning and painting activities that kept the "deck apes" constantly busy on the main deck. If you had time to "skate," the DAS deck was the place to be.

By the second day out of Tokyo Bay, as we neared the upper edge of the South China Sea, I was finally getting accustomed to the ship's motions. I stood on the ASROC deck and stared at the many gray silhouettes moving along with us in the distance: destroyers, cruisers, oil tankers, transport ships, aircraft carriers.

It all seemed surreal.

Over and over, I kept thinking: *So this is war. So this is war.*

Scenes from the old black-and-white television series, *Victory at Sea*, and their Richard Rodgers soundtracks, played in my head.

As a young teenager, I had watched almost every episode of the World War II television documentary, never imagining that, in just a few quick years, I would be steaming into a combat zone aboard one of the ships left over from that era.

I tried to draw comfort and courage from the massive naval power that now surrounded my small ship. Yet, I remained worried.

Even with good access to information coming out of the Tonkin Gulf, the Pentagon and Jehovah's flagship, I had no idea what we might face next or what we might have to do.

I just knew that I was 20 years old and not at all ready to die for my country.

Above, the Gearing Class destroyer *USS Gurke* (DD-783) joins up with the *USS Higbee* during operations in the South China Sea.

Below, an aircraft carrier prepares to receive three A4 Skyhawks returning from a mission, while a destroyer provides protective screening. *(Photos by Si Dunn)*

CHAPTER 7

Attack

"For all I knew, our Navy was shooting at whales out there."

– President Lyndon Baines Johnson

South China Sea
August 4-6, 1964

As the *Higbee* steamed southward through typhoon-tossed waters, the now-infamous "second attack" occurred in the Tonkin Gulf, about a hundred miles off the coast of North Vietnam.

Shortly after 9:30 p.m., August 4, Tonkin Gulf time, the destroyers *USS Maddox* and *USS Turner Joy* engaged in a nearly three-hour sea "battle" against what they believed were North Vietnamese PT boats speeding at them through the darkness.

The two tin cans fired hundreds of high-explosive shells at fast-moving radar blips and swerved violently to avoid what seemed to be many torpedoes in the water.

Yet the Navy planes that swooped down to assist the ships could not spot any attacking boats to destroy.

Dutifully, they shot up the water around the phantom radar targets identified by the ships. Then, when their fuel ran low, they flew back to their aircraft carriers.

Aboard the ships still surging southward from Japan, the radio communications groups quickly were swamped with messages. And life was no easier in the Navy's Pacific shore stations.

Seventh Fleet communications circuits faltered and then failed amid the flood of queries, reports and updates, all bearing the startling precedence "FLASH."

As writer Eugene G. Windchy later noted in his 1971 book, *Tonkin Gulf*, "The…latest teleprinter equipment, speedy though it was, could not keep up with the demands of human curiosity. Messages…jammed the radio circuits so badly that a high priority item could take four or five hours to get through. It was unfortunate that nobody had thought to send a communications ship…."[1]

What had just happened in the Tonkin Gulf became less and less clear. Some of the SECRET and TOP SECRET radio messages now reflected growing doubt that the "second attack" had even occurred.

One message in particular stood out as I tore it from a radio-teletype machine and prepared to run it up to the bridge.

The dispatch was from Commodore John J. Herrick, the senior officer aboard the *Maddox*, to officials at the Pentagon, State Department and White House:

"REVIEW OF ACTION MAKES MANY RECORDED CONTACTS AND TORPEDOES FIRED APPEAR DOUBTFUL. FREAK WEATHER EFFECTS AND OVEREAGER SONARMAN MAY HAVE ACCOUNTED FOR MANY REPORTS. SUGGEST COMPLETE EVALUATION BEFORE ANY FURTHER ACTION."[2]

Other messages also questioned whether radar images attributed to North Vietnamese PT boats actually may have been false echoes created by weather anomalies.

Still, the naval armada pressed on, and those of us aboard the ships had little knowledge of the intense political debates now raging in Washington and the United Nations regarding the Tonkin Gulf.

I was puzzled and surprised the next day when I saw a FLASH message with the heading "OPERATION PIERCE ARROW."

It signaled that President Lyndon B. Johnson had just ordered retaliatory air strikes against North Vietnam.

Immediately, I was troubled that we were pushing toward war without making sure we were right. Other messages in the continuing stream indicated we still had no proof that a second attack had occurred.

Two aircraft carriers, the *Constellation* and *Ticonderoga*, launched a total of 64 planes, and the selected targets were heavily damaged. These included a PT boat base and an oil storage facility at Vinh, just a short distance north of the demilitarized zone that had been created in 1954 to separate South and North Vietnam.

Twenty-one years later, I would meet the pilot who had led the first mission, Commander (later Admiral) James Stockdale. He would tell me that he and other pilots had shared my shock at how the unsubstantiated "second attack" was used as a rationale for going to war.

In his 1984 book *In Love & War*, Adm. Stockdale recalled his reactions after he was awakened early and informed of his PIERCE ARROW mission. He had just spent the previous night, August 4, flying over the *Maddox* and *Turner Joy*, trying to find and shoot nonexistent targets given to him by "spooked operators and spooked equipment[.]"[3]

After he returned his F8 Crusader to the *Ticonderoga*, he had reported "No boats, no boat wakes, no ricochets off boats—nothing but black sea and American firepower"[4] and had gone to bed, confident that higher-ups would sort things out.

But Stockdale, who later would be awarded the Medal of Honor and four Silver Stars for his service in the Vietnam conflict, wrote:

"As I spattered my face with cold water and pulled on my khaki trousers, I felt like one of the few men in the world who really understood the enormity of what was going to happen. The bad portents of the moment were suffocating. We were about the launch a war under false pretenses, in the face of the on-scene military commander's advice to the contrary. This decision had to be driven from way up at the top."[5]

Meanwhile, on the *Constellation*, the other aircraft carrier operating near the Tonkin Gulf, Lt. (j.g.) Everett Alvarez likewise was experiencing misgivings as he was preparing to suit up and fly his A-4 Skyhawk in the PIERCE ARROW raid.

Just a few hours earlier, Alvarez and other *Constellation* pilots also had rushed to assist the *Maddox* and *Turner Joy* and likewise found no targets to shoot.

Once they returned to the carrier, he noted in his 1989 book, *Chained Eagle*:

"We sat around in our ready room, still stupefied at how hysterical they'd been on the *Maddox* and *Turner Joy*. We had been there to help yet they had shown little ability to coordinate in their wild disorder. None of us had seen any PT boats and it seemed the destroyers were battling phantom targets."[6]

Alvarez also pointed out:

"Nobody told us that the Joint Chiefs of Staff had ordered the *Maddox* to conduct electronic surveillance of special types of enemy radar in case we had to operate against North Vietnam. Nor was there a word about the *Maddox* steaming up and down the same route along which unmarked patrol boats from South Vietnam had sailed several nights earlier, arousing North Vietnamese radar and other defenses as the southern intruders blasted the enemy's military targets."

Alvarez's book continued:

"The operation marked a heightened level of warfare between the two Vietnams. It was the first time South Vietnam had opened fire on its enemy from the sea. Approval had come from the highest political level in Washington. President Lyndon Johnson had given the go-ahead for an escalating series of highly classified covert sea and air operations. The object was to strike back against North Vietnam and make it pay a price for infiltrating men and materiel into South Vietnam."[7]

As an enlisted radio operator with only an interim Top Secret clearance, I was not really supposed to know, nor understand, details of operations that involved North and South Vietnam, the U.S. military, the Central Intelligence Agency, the Pentagon, the State Department, and the White House.

Yet my job included carefully reading each message and making certain that key officers were made aware of events or actions that conceivably might affect the *Higbee*.

Consequently, I began piecing together an understanding that America's "sudden" involvement in South Vietnam was nothing new.

Nor was there anything new about U.S. destroyers maneuvering provocatively close to the North Vietnamese coastline.

Likewise, I soon figured out that a shadowy operation described only as "OPLAN 34A" in radio messages actually involved South Vietnamese boats attacking North Vietnam, with direct assistance from the Central Intelligence Agency.

And these "34 Alpha" incidents were happening near the same watery tracks as the so-called "DE SOTO" patrols that the *USS Maddox* had conducted.

Indeed, "[t]he first covert actions under OPLAN 34A [had] commenced on February 1, 1964" and three weeks later, President Johnson had directed that "[c]ontingency planning for pressures against North Vietnam should be speeded up," according to Earl Rice Jr., in his book *Point of No Return: Tonkin Gulf and the Vietnam War*.[8]

The stage had been set more than five months before the *Higbee* joined the Seventh Fleet.

Back in Yokosuka, I had been puzzled by tersely worded radio-teletype messages that referred to a mysterious operation called "YANKEE TEAM." Now, as we continued steaming south toward the South China Sea and Tonkin Gulf, I began to see a few revealing details in messages.

The "YANKEE TEAM" flights involved secret reconnaissance missions over Laos and southern North Vietnam.

What I didn't understand was *why* we were doing any of this. I had paid almost no attention to Southeast Asian history.

I didn't know or remember that America had been frequently involved in the region since World War II and particularly since 1954, when the French had been defeated at Dienbienphu and driven out of Indochina.

The PIERCE ARROW raid results now chattered across the RATT machines' pale-yellow paper.

Targets had been hit, but antiaircraft fire was intense, and two Navy pilots had been shot down.

One, flying a propeller-driven A1H Skyraider, likely had been killed when his plane dove straight into the water and exploded. The other, Lt (j.g.) Everett Alvarez, had ejected from his crippled Skyhawk.

Initially, incoming radio traffic indicated Alvarez likely was dead, too. He had bailed out at low altitude, and, as one now-declassified priority message reported: "FLT LDR (flight leader) OBSERVED WHAT APPEARED TO BE SPLASH OF AN ACFT (aircraft) STRIKING WATER 20-56N 107-08E. NO PARACHUTE WAS OBSERVED TO DEPLOY BY ANY PILOT IN THE AREA."[9]

Another message, however, indicated that Alvarez's AN/PRT-3 "beeper" signal had been heard for approximately one minute after he ejected.

The message added that the U.S. Air Force had dispatched a twin-engine HU-16 Albatross amphibian from its Aerospace Rescue and Recovery Service. I later learned that the Albatross had flown north from Da Nang for about 50 miles before being recalled.

I began to wonder if any other attempts would be made to find and rescue – or recover – Alvarez. The *Higbee* was still too far away to help.

And I suddenly realized that if more pilots were shot down near the North Vietnam coast and we tried to rescue them, I might be pushed directly into harm's way.

I might have to be the radio operator in a Navy landing party – a few lightly armed sailors hunkered down in a very small boat, trying to reach a dangerous shore.

I had a solid reason for this worry.

Just four months earlier, in U.S. coastal waters fully at peace, I had *volunteered* for it.

A starboard view of the *USS Higbee*, showing the ship's motor whaleboat (hanging near the after stack). Radio Central was located near the forward stack, just beyond the dark rectangular area forward of the box-shaped ASROC launcher (center).
(U.S. Navy, photographer unknown)

CHAPTER 8

Landing Party (Flashback)

"The practice of dispatching groups of sailors ashore to fight as impromptu infantrymen is a centuries old naval tradition that has, during the last fifty years, been mostly honored in the breech."

– Neil Sheehan, *The Arnheiter Affair* (1971)

"Do not climb heights in order to fight. So much for mountain warfare."

– Sun Tzu, *The Art of War*, circa 500 B.C., translated by Lionel Giles, 1910

Off the California Coast
May, 1964

We were somewhere off Southern California, steaming toward San Clemente Island for ship-to-shore bombardment practice. Our scheduled movement to Yokosuka, Japan, was still weeks away. We were now in our fifth month of underway training along the West Coast.

It was a bright, sunny afternoon, and I had just pulled rank on a 22-year-old Electronics Technician Seaman (ETSN) named Hayford. I had gotten myself assigned as the radio operator for the *Higbee*'s landing party, the small group of sailors who could be sent ashore to act as infantrymen or naval gunfire spotters during special situations.

The "U.S. Asiatic Fleet Regulations 1931" had established the following rules for ships' landing parties:

> *Art. 521. [General] Every ship of the Fleet shall have a landing force composing one or more complete units (squad, section, platoon, company, or battalion) depending on complement, organized in accordance with the Landing Force Manual.*
>
> *Art. 522. Emergency Force. When in port where conditions on shore are disturbed and when the necessity for a quick*

landing may arise, there shall be kept in readiness an emergency landing force consisting of one commissioned officer, one signalman, and a squad of eight men, one of whom shall be equipped with an automatic rifle.

Art. 523. Exercise Frequency". [Landing parties will be exercised frequently.] [1]

In the days before World War II, a landing party communicator typically was a signalman who carried semaphore flags for daytime signaling. He also had a small, battery-powered lamp for nighttime Morse code communications between the shore party and ship.

"Radio outfits, and the necessary personnel" and "field radio sets, when obtainable" were mentioned as early as the 1920 edition of the Navy's *Landing-Force Manual*, but only "for brigade headquarters"[2]—a meaningless designation, except for ships big enough to carry hundreds of Marines or U.S. Army troops. In those days, military radio equipment was still too bulky and unreliable for use by small ground units or sea units. Indeed, when America entered World War I, the components for "portable" field radio sets had to be carried to the frontlines aboard special "wireless trucks" or on the backs of mule teams or horses.[3]

By World War II, however, portable radio transmitters and receivers had become compact enough to be carried in backpacks – *if* the radio operator was hefty and strong. Some of these portable sets became available on U.S. ships, and Navy radiomen sometimes replaced signalmen in small-scale landing parties.

Nonetheless, the Fleet Marine Force, established in 1933, already had sounded the death knell for sailors going ashore as infantry. The Leathernecks had their own radio operators, who were trained in warfare, as well as handling electronic equipment.

Throughout the Korean War and afterward, there had been little use of naval landing parties. Their jobs had been taken over not only by small units of Marines but also by helicopters and spotter planes. Still, "organized infantry capabilities" – naval landing parties – would continue to be required, even on small ships such as destroyers, until the 1970s.[4]

All I really knew about landing parties, of course, was what I had seen in war movies. Typically, a small unit of Americans sneaked onto a Pacific island and tried to assess Japanese strength or rescue a pilot or spy. Then, predictably, they were ambushed and pinned down by enemy fire.

That was when the radioman saved them. He handed his radio handset or walkie-talkie to the landing party's officer and heroically stood beside him while the beleaguered officer shouted firing instructions to the Navy ship waiting offshore in the darkness.

In moments, the big guns opened up, the enemy ambush was plastered, and the Americans broke through to safety and victory.

Once I learned about the landing party training for the *Higbee*, I immediately started my campaign to pull rank on Hayford. I wasn't seeking glory. In truth, what I really wanted was an opportunity to "skylark," to get off the ship and away from Chief Linn for most of a day. But I also figured it might be interesting to play "commando" at the target range on San Clemente Island. We were not at war with anyone. So the training just seemed a convenient opportunity to go ashore, loll about in the sun and tinker with some different radio equipment for a change.

Unfortunately, there usually is wisdom behind the old adage: "*Never* volunteer." A landing party radioman, I soon would discover, was little more than a glorified pack mule. It was his job to carry and operate the "Angry 9," the heavy, outdated AN/GRC-9 landing party radio that filled up a big backpack.

Hayford actually was the better choice for the job. He was bigger than me, and he had been trained in operating and taking an Angry 9 apart and possibly fixing it if something simple went wrong. I was convinced, however, that I knew enough about radios to fix an Angry 9 or anything else left over from World War II. And Ensign Lee, the ship's young communications officer, was won over easily by my specious argument that a landing party's radioman should be a *real* radioman.

ETSN Hayford got mad, of course. He had wanted a day off the ship, too. But I outranked him, E-4 to E-3.

So he was ordered to get the radio ready…for me.

Naturally, I trusted that he would do the job right.

Early the next morning, we three "commandos" – Ensign Lee; Gunner's Mate 3rd Class (GM3) Richard Smith; and me – regally rode ashore in broad daylight aboard the *Higbee's* 26-foot motor whaleboat. The big, throbbing vessel had an eight-knot cruising speed, perfect for outrunning enemy rowboats.

Ensign Lee was in his mid twenties and had been out of the Naval Academy for less than two years. Ship's communications officer was his first seagoing assignment. And, thus far, he had been little help in my frequent conflicts with Chief Linn, who was old enough to be his father.

Mr. Lee sometimes resembled a thin, freckle-faced high school senior dressed up in officer's khakis.

I didn't know much about GM3 Smith except that he was muscular, heavily tattooed, seldom talked, and had been in the Navy nearly 20 years. At some point in the recent past, he had been busted down two pay grades, from GM1 to GM3. One tale was that he had been convicted of drunk and disorderly conduct and slugging two Shore Patrol guys. Another tale was that he had single-handedly destroyed the inside of a bar "just for the pure hell of it." Both tales, I figured, were reasonably correct.

Two bored enlisted Marines met us at a San Clemente Island pier and helped us load ourselves and our gear into the bed of a gray military pickup truck. Then they drove us about a mile up a hillside to the firing range.

It was a rough ride but one I greatly welcomed. Along with the Angry 9 radio, I carried a World War II Browning Automatic Rifle (BAR) that I did not know how to load, nor shoot. Together, the radio backpack (about 40 pounds, with batteries), the BAR (17 pounds), and the ammo belt weighed half as much as I did. I literally staggered beneath their combined poundage when I tried to walk.

GM3 Smith could have carried the BAR without much effort. He could have given me the much lighter M1, which I *did* know how to load and shoot. But he didn't offer. And, considering his record, I wasn't about to ask. GM3 Smith also carried our "combat rations," a brown paper bag full of peanut butter sandwiches.

Mr. Lee, meanwhile, was armed with spiffy new binoculars and a holstered .45 that flapped awkwardly against his thigh when he walked. He didn't know how to pull the holster around toward his hip, so it would droop a bit and give him more of a gunslinger look.

Viewing us objectively, I figured Gunner's Mate Smith would be our only hope of survival if we ever got into real combat.

San Clemente Island had been purchased by the Navy in 1934 and soon became America's only active ship-to-shore live firing range. About 65 miles offshore from San Diego, it is the southernmost of the California Channel Islands.[5]

Atop the high ridge at the gunnery range, we climbed out of the truck, hiked a short distance over rocky terrain and set up our spotting position in an area where there was absolutely no cover. Snipers, had there been any, could have nailed us from a mile away.

I was doubly grateful to finally put the radio backpack and the BAR on the ground. I unfolded the BAR's tripod legs, aimed the barrel toward the firing range, draped the ammo belt over the barrel and promptly forgot about the gun while I got the radio out of its backpack and turned it on. *It* I knew how to work—or at least I thought I did.

Right way, I encountered a different problem. The rugged ground had patchy areas of cholla cactus. I stepped into some of its sharp needles, and two of the hard slivers penetrated the side of my right shoe, stabbing painfully into my skin. When I sat down to remove the needles, I tried to brace myself with my hand, and two more needles jabbed into my right palm. The cactus needles also had barbs that made them difficult and painful to pull out. Already I was a casualty, and the first shot had not even been heard.

Behind and below us, the *Higbee* now was floating off shore, guns up, ready to fire. The ship's two mounts would be shooting over the ridge at targets no one aboard the ship could see. The main job of the *Higbee*'s three "commandos" was to radio the initial firing coordinates, then call out corrections, so the shellfire could be "walked" onto designated targets.

The target range was a surreal sight. At its back, a big, cratered hill blocked errant shells from flying over to the inhabited east side of the island. Meanwhile, our targets were spread out in a bowl-shaped valley in front of us.

Wrecked cars scattered among the rocks served as "enemy tanks." Herds of feral goats grazed near the cars. They were "enemy troop concentrations."

I expected that the goats would scatter when the first shell hit the range. But I soon would learn differently.

I used the Angry 9 to call the Marine blockhouse that controlled the firing range.

"Range Control, this is Truck One, over." The heavily protected bunker was less than a hundred yards away.

"Read you five by five," a Range Control radio operator responded. Over the distance of a good stone's throw, our signal was strong and clear.

Now I called the *Higbee* for a signal report. "Truck, this is Truck One, over."

No answer.

From the top of the ridge, I could see the ship clearly, sitting barely a mile or so out in the calm, blue water.

"Truck, this is Truck One, over."

Again, no answer. I pressed the push-to-talk button and asked the Marine blockhouse to contact the *Higbee*.

The ship responded immediately and reported that they could not hear our signal.

I was mortified. The Angry 9 weighed a ton and had cost thousands of dollars. The ship had just gotten shiny new communications technology, yet the landing party radio had been left in storage and ignored until now.

I pawed over the radio for a while, checking switch settings and antenna connections. Nothing seemed amiss. I thought about opening it up. Maybe Hayford had cut a wire or unplugged the final amplifier tube. But there wasn't time.

Ensign Lee picked a target, an "enemy tank," and I gave the Marines his first guess at its firing coordinates. I listened and nodded as they relayed the numbers to the *Higbee*.

Mount 51, the ship's forward 5-inch/38 gun turret, fired a single shell. Before the sound reached us, the shell exploded at the top of the ridge, close enough to jolt us and the blockhouse with a thunderous *boom* and shower us with small pieces of rock.

My radio handset quickly filled with expletives from the Marines in the blockhouse, and Ensign Lee gave me a hasty firing correction: "Up 500!"

He figured we were at least 500 yards short of reaching the target area.

KA-BOOM! Mount 51 fired another single shot.

This shell roared in, passed over the ridge and exploded close to a wrecked car—well away from the one we were aiming at. It also hit near the edge of one herd of goats.

Pieces of the wrecked car flew into the air. So did two goats, killed instantly. A few other goats fell in their tracks, victims of shrapnel. Yet, the remaining goats barely flinched. They kept grazing like animal fatalists.

Later, I would find out that wild goats had been roaming free on San Clemente Island for hundreds of years, possibly since the days of early Spanish explorers. And, since 1934, the goat herds had been under shellfire so often that violent explosions now were just another part of their normalcy.

If you kept grazing and didn't die, you were having a good day.

"On target! On target!" I radioed.

Both mounts on the *Higbee* boomed repeatedly. Shells rained down inside the valley. More "tanks" flipped into the air, and more "enemy troops" fell where they grazed. The slaughter now seemed stupid and senseless. *We shouldn't be killing innocent animals*, my conscience told me.

But our original target still was not being hit. We gave the ship new coordinates and killed more goats.

The blockhouse Marines finally grew tired of relaying our target coordinates, and I was completely frustrated that I still could not directly reach the *Higbee* by radio. Looking around, I suddenly noticed a ship signal light mounted on a short pole about a hundred feet away on the ridge. I ran over to it, pointed it toward the harbor and started working the awkward lever that opened and closed the light's shutter.

"*D6*," I sent in very slow, flashing-light Morse code. I had seen ships send that signal, a truncation of "DD-806," to the *Higbee*.

Someone on the signal bridge pointed a light up the hill toward me. "*AA*," he sent. "*AA*."

He was asking me to identify myself. Clearly, I was no Navy signalman.

Finally, I remembered to send a long flash indicating that I had seen his signal and was ready to reply. He stopped his "*AA*" signals and waited. With much effort and movements of the rusty shutter lever, I spelled out: "DUNN RM3."

After a few moments, I saw a long flash. He was ready for my message.

"DROP 100," I spelled out with awkward effort. If I had been trying to do this under enemy fire, we would have all been dead many flashes ago. I had no authority to order the ship to shorten its firing range by 100 yards. The *Higbee*'s shells were successfully blowing up "enemy" cars and goats. But they weren't dropping close to the "tank" we had picked out as our primary target. Meanwhile, Ensign Lee and GM3 Smith both were watching the explosions, eating some of the sandwiches and paying scant attention to what I was doing.

A few moments later, two more shells soared in and exploded much closer to our designated target. My message had gotten through. One small piece of fender, hit by a stray bit of shrapnel, fell off our "enemy tank."

I grabbed the radio microphone and called the blockhouse. "Relay! Drop 50! I say again, drop 50!" Just one more slight adjustment and we would be right on target.

The radio channel fell silent for a few seconds. The receiver's squelch circuit automatically shut off all incoming hiss and static. Now the blockhouse keyed up again. "Negative, Truck One. Break with you. Truck, this Range Control, cease firing. Repeat, cease firing. End of exercise. Range Control, out."

In my handset, I heard: "Truck, roger. Out."

The *Higbee* slowly stopped moving and dropped anchor in the harbor.

I ate a sandwich and surveyed the carnage. A few dozen "enemy troops" now lay scattered on the field of battle, while their fellow goats grazed around them without visible concern.

The two bored Marines showed up again with their pickup truck. We threw our gear into the back and climbed in beside it.

The three of us bounced around like ping pong balls in the truck bed as the Marines drove us – fast – down the hill. They dropped us off at a small pier and took off again in a cloud of dust, clearly glad to be rid of us.

After a few minutes, the *Higbee*'s motor whaleboat arrived at the pier to pick us up. I stepped unsteadily from the pier into the bobbing boat and nearly toppled into the sea with the Angry 9 and the BAR. One of the motor whaleboat crewmen saved me by grabbing one of the radio pack's shoulder straps at the last moment.

As we motored back to the ship at five knots, I knew I would now be considered – at least on paper—one of the ship's trained commandos. But I felt no sense of accomplishment. Every muscle was aching and trembling from lugging the radio and BAR.

I suspected Hayford had gotten back at me by detuning the transmitter so it would not reach the ship. And I was sad about the dead goats. Plus, the fantasy inspired by war movies was completely finished.

As I felt the motor whaleboat's gentle motions and diesel throb, I wished I had let Hayford lug the gear. And I fervently hoped I would *never* have to be the radioman in a real naval landing party.

A radar picket destroyer, the *USS Ernest G. Small* (DDR-838), keeps watch for North Vietnamese and Chinese planes and patrol boats in an area where the South China Sea merges with the Tonkin Gulf, 1965.
(Photo by Si Dunn)

CHAPTER 9

Dark Signals

"Fighting with a large army under your command is nowise different from fighting with a small one: it is merely a question of instituting signs and signals."

> – Sun Tzu, *The Art of War*, circa 500 B.C., translated by Lionel Giles, 1910

"Historically, naval men have been slow and unimaginative with respect to signaling."

> – Eugene G. Windchy, *Tonkin Gulf*

During the Tonkin Gulf incidents, the U.S. Navy's problem was *not* a lack of signals, nor a lack of imagination. It was the opposite: too many radio signals feeding too many overly active imaginations.

In August, 1964, many – but not all – Seventh Fleet combat ships were equipped with some of the latest naval communications hardware and some of the world's most sophisticated sea-search and air-search radars.

The aging *USS Maddox* was still waiting its turn for communications upgrades when it came under fire from North Vietnamese PT boats. It did not yet have the new encrypted radio-teletype gear that allowed messages simply to be typed and sent. *Maddox* officers and radiomen still had to encrypt or decrypt messages by hand and send encoded messages using Morse code.[1]

The *USS Higbee*, meanwhile, sported an almost completely new complement of radars and radios. It also had the highly classified KW-37R and KW-7 systems that automatically processed sensitive radio messages.

The KW-37R in-line teletype decoder, code-named "JASON," had been created in the 1950s by the National Security Agency. The system solved what had been a vexing problem for the U.S. Navy since well before World War II.

Ships at sea needed to maintain radio silence as much as possible, to prevent an enemy or potential enemy from locating them by using radio direction finding (RDF) equipment. Yet huge numbers of radio messages, including new ship movement orders, had to be sent to thousands of Navy vessels around the world. And many of those messages required acknowledgements or replies. So a fleet broadcast system had evolved that transmitted an almost continuous stream of information into a dozen broadcast zones around the planet.

The Tonkin Gulf was on the ragged edge of the Philippines broadcast zone, in a realm of generally poor shortwave radio reception. ("That whole Southeast Asia is generally a poor propagation area," Commodore Herrick later commented.)[2]

Prior to the KW-37R system, fleet broadcast messages had been sent out via Morse code, and each classified message for a particular ship or command had to be encoded by hand prior to transmission. The received messages likewise had to be decoded by hand, using cumbersome code books and manual decoding devices.

Navy radio operators had sat at shortwave receivers and monitored fleet broadcasts hour after hour, always listening for messages addressed to their ships or commands.

Meanwhile, the KW-7 in-line teletype encoder system, code-named "ORESTES," enabled Navy radiomen to send messages classified SECRET, CONFIDENTIAL or UNCLAS EFTO just by typing them into their radio-teletype machines. The outgoing text immediately was scrambled for transmission, then automatically decoded at the receiving end and printed out as plain text.

The KW-7 and KW-37R devices made sensitive and secure communications much faster and easier to maintain. But their quickness and relative ease of operation also would prove to be an Achilles heel for the Navy during the Tonkin Gulf chaos.

Not all of the *Higbee*'s radio gear was new. Along with the Angry 9 landing party radio, the ship retained a few other pieces of equipment that had been used during World War II and the Korean War. The TCS-12 transmitter-receiver combination was a prime example.

In some parts of the Navy, the TCS-12 had been stricken from service and declared war-surplus junk. The one I had been given in Little Rock was still sitting in my hobby room at home. Yet, during the *Higbee*'s Fleet Rehabilitation and Modernization process in 1964, someone had decided to keep the ship's old TCS and move it to Emergency Radio.

Emergency Radio was a small area in the aft part of the ship. In theory, if Radio Central was blown away by an incoming shell, any surviving radioman could go to Emergency Radio and use the TCS to maintain at least a minimum level of communications with other ships. Unfortunately, the blend of new and old equipment proved challenging for many destroyer radio operators. Some of them were inadequately trained on the new equipment, and many did not know how to use the old gear, either. It had not been covered in Navy radio school.

Marginal training and the mixture of old and new communications equipment were only two parts of the "perfect storm" that afflicted the Seventh Fleet in the Tonkin Gulf and helped draw the United States deeper into the Vietnam conflict. But they were significant factors.

Eugene G. Windchy, in his 1971 book *Tonkin Gulf*, recounted a meeting where several officers and enlisted men from the destroyers *Maddox* and *Turner Joy* were hauled aboard the carrier *USS Ticonderoga*. They were scheduled to meet with Admiral Thomas H. Moorer, Commander in Chief of the Pacific Fleet (CINCPACFLT). But first, a member of Moorer's staff, a Navy captain, lined them up and chewed them all out. "I haven't had any sleep in 48 hours," the captain complained. "During my whole career in the Navy, I've seen something like *two* flash messages. Now I've seen seventy-five! I've been called out of bed for all sorts of ridiculous reasons."[3]

Sleep shortages quickly became epidemic among Tonkin Gulf sailors and were particularly intense in short-handed radio gangs. My eyes burned and sagged almost constantly while I was on watch. During the precious few hours when I could slide into my rack, I fell into unsatisfying twilight sleeps in which I dreamed in Morse code, answered phantom calls to NHLL and mentally typed incoming strings of never-ending gibberish.

Tensions remained high during the first weeks of operations in the Tonkin Gulf, and one particular incident did nothing to sooth our nerves. I was on radio watch one afternoon near mid-August when another FLASH message suddenly arrived from the Commander of the Seventh Fleet: "ENEMY AIR ATTACK IMMINENT." I tore the message straight from the teletype printer, slapped it onto the yellow SECRET message board and raced to the bridge to give it to the Captain.

He signed it quickly and called out to the Officer of the Deck (OOD): "Sound general quarters!"

The OOD turned to the boatswain's mate of the watch and ordered: "General quarters!"

As I raced back to Radio Central, I heard the 1MC general address system click on. The boatswain's pipe sounded a quick, shrill "All Hands." Then, as I knocked on Radio Central's locked door, the boatswain's mate's voice boomed out over the decks and throughout the ship's passageways and compartments: "Now general quarters! General quarters! All hands man your battle stations! This is *not* a drill! Set Condition Zebra throughout the ship!"

As crewmen hurried to close and secure watertight hatches, the electronic general-quarters alarm sounded: *"Blang! Blang! Blang!"*

Gunners scrambled into gun turrets and ammunition magazines. Still other crewmen started watching radar and sonar screens intently in the Combat Information Center and watching gauges in the engine room as the ship surged ahead, accelerating toward battle speed.

The fear inside Radio Central was palpable, even as we tried not to show it.

Ten of us now were packed inside. We had no view of the outside world, except what arrived by radio. We would have to wait until the 5-inch/38 mounts to start firing to actually know if we were being attacked.

Mentally, I tried to remember what equipment and documents to destroy if the ship got hit and was threatened with capture. Deeper inside, I was panicking. I was ready to leap over the side. Gearing Class destroyers were designed for speed and maneuverability, not survivability. They were thin-skinned and loaded with fuel oil, ammunition, torpedoes, hedgehog rockets, anti-submarine rockets, depth charges and nuclear warheads.

I put on a lifejacket, then grabbed and loaded the old .45 that was supposed to help protect the crypto room from intruders. As I struggled to strap on the weapon, Chief Linn saw me and laughed. Yet this time, his laugh was more nervous than scornful. "Dunn, what the hell are you doing?"

"Going to my battle station, Chief!" I replied.

He didn't try to stop me as I rushed out the door, stepped across the narrow passageway and shut myself inside Radio II. The small compartment was packed with several rack-mounted, 500-watt high-frequency and low-frequency transmitters, plus a short-range GRC-27 ("Greek 27") UHF transmitter. If the *Higbee* opened fire or was hit by enemy fire, it was my task to make sure that the shock did not knock the radios off frequency. The job was left over from World War II and was now mostly useless, because the ship's new radio equipment was electrically and mechanically very stable.

I had grabbed the .45 in a moment of war-movie bravado. I didn't want to die alone, unarmed, cooped up inside a hot metal coffin. If somebody shot at us, I wanted to shoot back.

I made quick, perfunctory checks of the gear. Everything was on frequency and working. Now my job was to sit, wait until the guns started firing, and check everything again.

I found the compartment's sound-powered headset and slipped it on. I could hear a few random sounds from places inside the ship. But there was none of the joking and network chatter that sometimes ran rampant during battle-stations drills.

"Control, Radio Two manned and ready," I reported.

"Control, aye."

I had no idea who or where "Control" was. In compartments and gun positions all over the ship, crewmen designated as "phone talkers" now were wearing sound-powered headsets, ready to accept orders and report battle damage and casualties. And everyone on the circuit was keeping quiet. *We're all scared*, I realized.

I had two plans firmly in mind if MiGs attacked. One, I would step outside on the ASROC deck and fire hot lead into the sky. I might get lucky with a shot. Or, two, if we had to abandon ship, I would use the pistol to try to fend off sharks.

As I held the gun in my hand, thumb ready to click off the safety, the Captain took the 1MC microphone and informed the ship's officers and men what the brief radio message said. "For the first time since World War II and Korea," he announced, "the *Higbee* may have to fire in anger at an enemy. We don't know yet if we will be facing North Vietnamese or Red Chinese MiGs. But if an attack does come, I know you will do your duty to your country, your ship and your shipmates. Godspeed and good luck!"

It was a speech worthy of any war movie I had ever seen. I gripped the gun tighter and felt sweat dampening my palm.

The tension remained high for another half hour. But no planes attacked. Finally, the signal was passed to secure from general quarters.

I relaxed my death grip on the .45, re-holstered it, and stepped across the passageway into Radio Central.

I took the gun back into the crypto room and tried to act nonchalant as I hung the holster on its hook on the starboard bulkhead.

"What happened?" I asked Heflin.

With a quiet smile, he showed me new messages that had been ripped from a teletype machine and rushed to the bridge for the deck officers' signatures.

One message said that a flight of our own planes returning from North Vietnam had been misidentified by radar operators on one ship. Another message blamed false radar images. In either case, a nerve-wracking alert had flashed throughout the Seventh Fleet and all the way to the Pentagon and White House.

We had come within minutes, perhaps moments, of disaster. If air-defense missiles had been launched by some of the ships, several Navy or Marine jets might have been brought down by "friendly" fire. Hands had been waiting tensely, ready to press firing buttons, when the mistake finally was sorted out.

Aboard the *Higbee* and other ships, days passed to night and back to daylight again, and more false radar images sent crews scurrying to battle stations. The worst alarms came in the middle of the night, disrupting the troubled rest of those who already were sleep-deprived and growing irritable.

Mistakes on the job and minor injuries became more common. Shipmates got into grumpy arguments. Sometimes there were brief fistfights. Meanwhile, the *Higbee* continued running anti-submarine warfare (ASW) screens for carriers or following in their wakes, ready for search and rescue if someone fell overboard or a plane or helicopter hit the water.

Several times, the *Higbee* also was dispatched on independent missions to investigate possible submarine contacts, rusty freighters bound to or from China, or strange areas of discolored water that usually turned out to be schools of fish feeding near the surface. Sometimes, we also recovered odd objects from the sea, including unmarked life jackets and glass floats from fishing nets.

At the end of August, after nearly a month of screening assignments and independent patrols, the *Higbee* received a welcome message. We were ordered to steam "home" to Yokosuka, for rest, recreation and repairs.

But, just as the ship departed Yankee Station, there was other news. Typhoon Ruby now was sweeping through the South China Sea. We would first have to detour to the Philippines, to the U.S. Navy base at Subic Bay.

COMMANDER DESTROYER SQUADRON THREE
CARE OF FLEET POST OFFICE
SAN FRANCISCO, CALIFORNIA

From: Commander Destroyer Squadron THREE
To: DUNN, Silas T. III, ███████, RM3, USN

Subj: Commendation

1. The Squadron Commander takes pleasure in commending you for outstanding performance of duties as set forth in the following:

"For meritorious achievement in your performance of duties while serving on board U.S.S.HIGBEE (DD 806) for the period 11 through 19 August 1964 during contingency operations in the South China Sea. Your constant attention and devotion to duty, patience, initiative, and proficiency in copying the GOLF ROMEO broadcast and maintaining an almost continuous ORESTES termination with NAVCOMSTA Guam resulted in HIGBEE achieving a vastly superior flow of communications. To quote from NAVCOMSTA Guam message 142229Z of September 1964, ... "It has been noted that during the same period the U.S.S. HIGBEE was very proficient in copying the GR broadcast and working hi-priority ship to shore circuits, a proficiency equalled by few other commands." This proficiency resulted in HIGBEE being able to supply NAVCOMSTA Guam with valuable information by relaying to them your techniques in maintaining the best possible GOLF ROMEO copy. To quote again from the NAVCOMSTA Guam message, "Communications information provided by your command for the period 11 through 19 August has contributed immeasureably in the analysis of communications in the South China Sea area recently completed by this station and NAVCOMMSYSHQ representatives... Your assistance is expected to contribute to improved communications in WESTPAC and is greatly appreciated." You have set an excellent example for others to follow. Your skillful application of professional abilities and devotion to duty have been in keeping with the highest tradition of the United States Naval Service.

2. This commendation will be made a permanent part of your service record.

U. P. Healey

V. P. HEALEY

Copy to:
BUPERS

Above: A commendation received by the author in 1964 for "meritorious achievement" as a radio operator during "contingency operations" early in the Vietnam War.

CHAPTER 10

Rough Rider

The ship's "liberty hounds" got excited once word of the new destination filtered through the compartments. Some of them went straight to their foot lockers and started checking the conditions of their tropical white uniforms.

Right outside the Cubi Point Naval Base's main gate, some of them told me, a small bridge crossed over "Shit River," a sluggish stream that stayed ripe with sewage. If you tossed coins from the bridge into the foul water, Filipino kids would dive in, pull them up from the bottom and then tread water and beg for more. Some of my shipmates thought this was funny. The image horrified me.

What really excited them, however, was just across that bridge: the town of Olongapo. Sailors were restricted to its main street. But what a main street it was, they exulted. "Wall-to-wall bars, wall-to-wall bar girls, and wall-to-wall hotel rooms you can rent by the hour!" one radarman said as he shined his liberty shoes.

That picture had plenty of lurid appeal for me, too. I was convinced the weird conflict in Vietnam soon would explode into a full-scale war that included sea battles, possibly with the Chinese and Russians. I did not want to die without having had at least a little more experience with "life." I opened up my foot locker and started checking my liberty uniform, too.

Higher authorities, however, had different plans for our first visit to Subic Bay. As we neared the Philippines, rough seas slowed our progress. The ship finally reached the outskirts of the harbor just before 2200—10 p.m. And the word that passed over the 1MC was *not* what the liberty hounds wanted to hear: *"Now set the special sea and anchor detail."*

The ship dropped anchor in 21 fathoms of water and stayed there through the night.

Shortly after reveille, the liberty hounds once again started checking their tropical whites and spreading hopeful rumors. Liberty call would be announced soon, they claimed. Suddenly, a new alert sounded from the 1MC:

"Now set the special sea detail. Make all preparations for getting underway."

Anguished cries rose in the Operations compartment and elsewhere. We thought we were being called back to sea. Instead, the ship simply weighed anchor, moved slowly toward a pier and moored in a cluster of other destroyers now that docking could be safely accomplished. The fuel tanks were topped off, and fresh food was brought aboard. Later in the day, after all work parties were completed, liberty call finally was passed for one section – a third of the crew, including Chief Linn.

I was not in that section, and tonight I had the eve watch. So I would hit my rack and fall asleep at about the same time the Chief would return to the ship, drunk. If I couldn't go ashore, the next best thing I could hope for was a quiet, uneventful radio watch without Chief Linn. Anyway, I figured I might get to go ashore tomorrow.

Later that night, a new radio message arrived, changing our orders again. The *Higbee* steamed out of Subic Bay early the next morning and held a long day of gunnery exercises in rough seas. Early on, I kept a bucket beside me as I sat slumped on the deck in Radio II. I kept the door locked, too, so Chief Linn couldn't barge in on me without knocking or getting the keys. After a couple of hours at sea, I threw up my guts and fell asleep at my battle station.

This was a serious offense, but I was too sick to care.

Sometimes, the 5-inch/38s woke me when they boomed. And sometimes, they were just noisy elements in strange dreams. No one knocked on the door. I finally woke to the shrill sounds of the boatswain's pipe and a voice booming from the 1MC:

"Now secure from general quarters. Sweepers, sweepers, man your brooms! Give the ship a clean sweep-down fore and aft. Now mess gear, mess gear! All hands stand clear of the mess decks 'til pipe down!"

I thought it was lunch time, but my watch showed it was now time for dinner. Anyway, I had no desire to eat anything except salty crackers. The way my stomach felt, I could easily stand clear of the mess decks forever. As I emerged from Radio II, ready to wash out the bucket, Chief Linn unlocked and opened the Radio Central door. He started to give me an order.

"Dunn – "

He looked at my blanched, gaunt face. Then he looked down at the bucket and realized it had just performed a valuable service. I figured he would launch into another tirade about Naval Reservists. Instead, he just blew out his breath, shook his head and closed the door. It locked with a loud, solid *CLICK!*

The ship now turned toward the remnants of Typhoon Ruby and began the 1,800-mile roller coaster ride toward Yokosuka, Japan. Soon, the *Higbee* joined the screen for the carrier *USS Ticonderoga*, along with the destroyers *USS Leonard F. Mason* (DD-852) and *USS Orleck* (DD-886), all bobbing up and down in the angry sea.

For part of two days, the formation mostly ploughed straight ahead, smashing into and riding up and over an endless procession of big waves. I ate nothing, gagged incessantly and clutched desperately at my belly as I worked the radio equipment. Every chance I could, I went outside to the ASROC deck's lifelines and took deep breaths of damp, cool air. This time, however, the outside world offered little solace. Angry green waves rose higher than the ship's upper decks. They dwarfed the *Higbee* and seemed poised to crush us as they swelled, surged forward and collapsed beneath *whoosh*-ing whitecaps that swept along the vulnerable main deck.

In the midst of the storm, the *Ticonderoga* suddenly radioed an urgent warning: *"Man overboard! Man overboard! Starboard side! Starboard side!"*

The *Higbee*'s 1MC quickly repeated the alert, and the ship's horn blew six times, a low, mournful moan that could be heard in almost all compartments.

On all four ships, sailors raced to their rescue-and-recovery stations. But those on the destroyers faced a stark and dangerous reality.

In this weather, many of their Man Overboard stations placed them directly in peril of the sea. With waves sloshing up and along the main deck, they could not stand at the railings and help watch for the hapless sailor – if he had survived the fall from the carrier.

Radio gang members were not assigned Man Overboard stations. If we were not already on watch, we were supposed to report to Radio Central and Radio II and help keep communications running during the search. In reality, three or four radiomen could handle everything, and the other five or six radiomen just stood around and got in the way in the cramped spaces.

I was scheduled for the mid-watch, and Chief Linn had decided to return to the chiefs' quarters after ensuring that we had things under control. I told Heflin I needed some air and would be on the ASROC deck, just steps from Radio Central.

I did need the air, but I also hoped I might be the one who spotted the missing man. Falling overboard and being left behind is one of a sailor's deepest fears, especially when the water stretches from horizon to horizon in all directions and downward for hundreds, even thousands, of feet. I knew I could swim and float for a few hours; I had not forgotten the water-wings lessons of basic training. Yet, anyone falling overboard here would be hundreds of miles from the nearest land and totally at the mercy of sea currents and winds. And sharks.

No matter how much you struggled and prayed that a ship would pass close enough to see you, the moment likely would come when you would have to let the sea take you. Or, a moment would come when something in the sea would give you no other choice.

Either way, no one would know what happened to you. You would be listed as missing, and relatives would hope against hope for many months. Then, finally, the Navy would declare you dead. But some of those who loved you would not accept it.

For years afterward, they would keep hoping for a letter, a phone call, a telegram, a knock on their door confirming, against all odds, that you had survived the sea and were coming home.

In the big waves now rising around the *Higbee*, I could see fish swimming frantically just beneath the swelling surface. They rose with the water, and then disappeared in the foam of the breaking white caps. I reasoned that a swimmer could be seen in this storm, too, but only if someone happened to look in the right place at the right time, and his head or an arm happened to bob up as he was lifted by a rising wave. *The more eyes on this water, the better.*

After a few minutes, the boatswain's pipe sounded, and an announcement blasted from the 1MC speaker on the ASROC deck: *"Now secure from man overboard stations."*

"Did they get him?" I asked Heflin when he let me in to Radio Central.

"False alarm," he replied. "Somebody thought an airdale got blown over the side. They took muster, and nobody was missing."

The next evening, at about 8 p.m., the *Ticonderoga* sent out a new alert to its screening ships. A single-seat A-4E Skyhawk jet had crashed in the water. Apparently its engine had failed just as the plane was catapulted, and the pilot did not have time to eject. This time, it was *not* a false alert.

Again, a dreaded message sounded over the *Higbee*'s 1MC: *"Plane crash, port side! Now set the special rescue and recovery detail, section one!"* And again, the ship's horn sounded six mournful blasts.

Section one crew members assigned to rescue and recovery stations raced to their positions, ready to rig additional topside lights, break out rescue and recovery equipment and get the motor whaleboat ready. Numerous sailors in the other two crew sections also prepared to help or watch.

The carrier and screening ships all slowed, changed course and began searching the grim, dark sea. The *Higbee* and the *Mason* quickly commenced an "expanding rectangular" search pattern in the area where the plane went into the water.

Some of us not on duty took positions along the rails and on upper decks. A few had battle lanterns and flashlights. Up on the signal bridge, the highest manned position, bright spotlights flared on and were aimed out at the water.

Big disks of yellow light now danced and slid over the rough, green swells. But all of the lanterns and spotlights together seemed pitifully small against the infinity of blackness now surrounding us.

I held a battle lantern borrowed from Radio II. It created a pale yellow disk perhaps four feet in diameter on the undulating surface. I swept the tiny beam back and forth across the water that flowed slowly along the port side of the hull. The light penetrated perhaps a foot into the seawater that extended downward hundreds of fathoms beneath us. I could see nothing except an occasional small fish and small bubbles and bits of plankton flowing by.

One of the big spotlights, however, soon located a small, dark object floating in the waves. Other lights quickly converged on it and kept it illuminated while the ship's motor whaleboat was lowered with a rescue-and-recovery crew aboard.

What they recovered, after a hazardous run through the rough seas and an equally dangerous return to the ship, turned out to be a bag of garbage. Likely, it had been thrown overboard from one of the dozens of freighters that moved in all directions through the China Sea each day.

The searchlights soon located another, much brighter, object. This time, the rescue-and-recovery crew fished out a hollow glass ball about half the size of a basketball. It was a stray glass float from a Japanese fishing net.

The boat crew remained on station and did their best to search the nearby water while bucking up and down, hard, on the big waves. The search continued through the night. Soon after midnight, the guided-missile destroyer *USS Joseph D. Strauss* caught up with the formation and joined the SAR effort.

By dawn, however, nothing else had been found. Either we had searched the wrong area or the sea had swallowed up every trace of the Skyhawk and its pilot. We had no way to know. The destroyers slowly moved back into anti-submarine screening positions around the *Ticonderoga*.

Soon, the formation picked up speed and continued slogging toward Yokosuka.

From the carrier, a message began making its way through the Navy network to the pilot's family somewhere in the United States, half a world away. He was missing and presumed dead.

We had made our best efforts to try to find him. But the darkness and the ocean were both too big. Very likely, he had not survived the crash when his plane ripped into the sea. None of us wanted to think that we might have left him floating in a lifejacket, at the sea's rough mercy, while we steamed away.

About 24 hours later, the five ships entered Tokyo Bay and headed toward Yokosuka. As the *Higbee* slowed and maneuvered to moor alongside the *Mason* at the Yokosuka Naval Station, a Navy band marched along the pier toward us, heavy with brass, cymbals and drums. In a scene that reminded me of a movie about World War II, the band suddenly halted, turned to face us, and struck up a loud, stirring rendition of "Anchors Aweigh."

I grinned, and tears leaked from my eyes. We had survived our first combat patrol and made it "home" alive. Now we were just a mile – and one liberty call – away from the neon signs and siren songs of Honcho Street.

Anyone eligible for liberty was eager to get off the ship *now*. But first, we had to muster on the ASROC deck in our dress blues. "Probably another goddam VD lecture," one sonar operator groused quietly as we stood in ranks.

"Or a surprise inspection," I replied with dread. I never did well in inspections. Something always was wrong with my shoeshine or haircut or uniform.

"Ship's company, attennnn-HUT!"

As we straightened up in ranks, the Captain, the executive officer and several other officers strode onto the deck and faced us.

"It is my pleasure," the Captain announced, "to read the following commendation from the Commander of Destroyer Squadron Three to three *Higbee* radiomen: Chief Linn, RM3 Rodriguez and RM3 Dunn." The Captain pulled a letter from an envelope. Out of my peripheral vision, I saw heads turning slightly toward me.

How could Dunn *be getting a commendation?*

"The squadron commander," the Captain intoned, "takes pleasure in commending you for outstanding performance of duties as set forth in the following: For meritorious achievement in your performance of duties while serving on board *USS Higbee* for the period 11 through 19 August 1964 during contingency operations in the South China Sea. Your constant attention and devotion to duty, patience, initiative, and proficiency in copying the Golf Romeo broadcasts and maintaining an almost continuous Orestes termination with NAVCOMSTA Guam resulted in Higbee achieving a vastly superior flow of communications."[1]

I could see some of my shipmates beginning to smirk and grin as the long commendation's reading wore on. Some of the liberty hounds also were getting visibly restless and shifting from one foot to the other.

The Captain, however, continued quoting enthusiastically and emphasizing the statements about our "proficiency equaled by few other commands" and how we had "contributed immeasurably in the analysis of communications in the South China Sea area" and "set an excellent example for others to follow." At the end of the reading, the three of us stepped forward, saluted and received copies of the commendation.

I was proud of the moment, proud that I had done something valued by others beyond the ship. Deep in my thoughts, however, I remained confused and troubled by what had transpired in the Tonkin Gulf and South China Sea.

Still, the commendation came with a comforting new realization. Chief Linn could keep complaining about Naval Reservists, and continue criticizing me as a sailor. But the squadron commander had just declared me one of the best radiomen in the Seventh Fleet. It was a significant "protection," one that could carry some weight all the way from the *Higbee*'s wardroom to the Chief of Naval Operations, if necessary.

The commendation came with one other benefit, as well. In Yokosuka, all sailors in the liberty sections were granted overnight liberty. But the Captain rewarded the three of us the highly coveted "72" – three days and nights away from the ship.

Once we were dismissed, some of the crew offered good-natured sarcasm about our awards. *"Higbee* heroes," one of them called us. But the glory didn't last. The 1MC sounded an announcement: *"Now liberty for sections one and two!"* Sailors in dress blues rushed to the quarterdeck, popped salutes to the OOD and the flag and jogged off the ship, heading for Honcho Street.

After my many bouts of seasickness, I desperately needed food. I looked pale and felt weak. Also, I needed to get used to moving on solid land again. My inner ear kept telling my brain that we were still at sea.

I staggered like a true drunken sailor once I was down the gangplank. Sometimes, a foot stopped at too high in the air. Other times, it plunked down too hard, trying to reach a lower surface as I walked along base sidewalks and streets that seemed to sway beneath me.

My first stop was on base, at the Enlisted Men's Club. I went into its dining room and ordered the biggest steak dinner on the menu, along with two slices of apple pie a la mode. My wallet felt fat with cash. For weeks, there had been no place to spend any pay, except on candy bars at the ship's store. After the second piece of pie and a second vodka screwdriver, I began to feel human – and full – again.

I went next door to the EM Club's casino and played slot machines with a $2 roll of nickels.

With the last coin in the tube, I hit an $80 jackpot. I traded the massive pile of nickels for four twenties, finished off another screwdriver and felt truly glad to be back "home" in Yokosuka.

Once I was outside again, the alcohol and the phantom sea motions got into a major new battle. But the gaudy neon signs just outside the main gate kept flashing my name – in Morse code.

Swaying and still off balance, I headed for Honcho Street.

The author plays his guitar in the *Higbee*'s Operations compartment after a radio watch, 1964. Note the indentation pattern in his hair left by headphones. *(Photographer unknown)*

CHAPTER 11

Sea Ghosts

Being moored to a pier for an extended stay was the next best thing to shore duty. Radio watches were easy and almost always uneventful.

Most of the crew, including radiomen, left the ship in the afternoon for overnight liberty. A lone RM3 or RM2 and a messenger could maintain the watch, perform administrative and maintenance duties, and keep the KW-37R systems online and synchronized to receive fleet broadcasts.

The radio gang on a nearby moored ship also could be convinced to watch out for messages addressed to the *Higbee*. In return, we stood radio guard for them on another day.

In port, few messages needed to be transmitted or routed for officers' signatures. So the messenger usually had little to do except nap, help with the cleaning duties, route an occasional message for signatures, and find late-night snacks.

Fresh food was plentiful in port. We never ran out of meat, chocolate milk or fresh rolls. And we were hooked up to fresh water lines. So we could take Hollywood showers without a master at arms yelling at us and threatening to put us on report.

Liberty call usually came early in the afternoon. And two days out of three, I had overnight liberty. Like others on the ship, I spent a lot of my free time and money on Honcho Street. But I seldom hung out with anyone else from the *Higbee* crew, unless I happened across them in a bar. I was a loner, mostly. And a wanderer.

Sometimes, from outdoor vendors and tiny shops in the bar district, I bought souvenirs to mail home to Arkansas: mostly scenic postcards and small examples of delicate Japanese art.

One afternoon, at a Honcho Street store that sold musical instruments, I bought a $20 guitar and carried it back to the ship. It was much too big to fit in my footlocker. And I endured some "Elvis" razzing at the quarterdeck as I carried it aboard. But I figured I might at least be able to store it behind some of the equipment in Radio II.

I was right. It hid very nicely behind the "Greek." And some of the heavily insulated power cables would keep it from rocking around in heavy seas.

When my money ran low between paydays, I started spending some of my liberty hours inside the cramped, cell-like privacy of Radio II. I strummed the few chords I knew and tried to plunk out parts of "Malagueña." I knew I had no future as a guitar virtuoso.

Music, however, was becoming a partial counterpoise to my fears that we would soon go into all-out war. I had a harmonica, too, and taught myself how to play "Shenandoah", "Moon River" and "Turkey in the Straw."

Radio II hardly qualified as a spiritual retreat, even in port when the equipment was turned off and the only noise came from fans blowing in cool air. The cramped compartment smelled strongly of rubber, metal and insulation. And the residual odors of stack gas and fuel oil never went away. Yet it was one of the few places where I could sit alone and simply think.

I was disillusioned now and depressed. I had grown up with naïve, idealized notions about America and its place in the world. I knew we had played decisive roles in defeating Nazi Germany and imperialist Japan. And we had fought communism in Korea. I had spent my youth hearing and trusting that we were the virtually flawless champions of freedom and democracy.

So, what we were now doing in Vietnam and along its coastline made no sense to me. The August 4th "second attack" in the Tonkin Gulf had been discredited in classified communiqués. We seemed to be pushing toward war without justification. Many years later, I would learn that a variety of factors, along with the Tonkin Gulf incidents, had led the United States to go to undeclared war with North Vietnam.

But one of the key triggers had been the one-sided, nighttime naval battle involving the *Maddox* and *Turner Joy* and the ghostly radar images that later were identified as "Tonkin spooks."

As Edward Moïse explained in his book *Tonkin Gulf and Escalation of the Vietnam War*, "Tonkin spooks" are radar ghost images "characteristic, not of Asian waters in general, but of certain limited areas in Asia...The phenomenon generates radar images that are much smaller and more clearly defined than those normally generated by weather...Not even the most experienced radar operator can simply look at a Tonkin Spook on a radar screen and realize from its appearance that it does not represent an actual surface vessel."[1]

Tonkin spooks were implicated in a lesser-known "third attack" involving two destroyers in September, 1964. Other encounters with Tonkin Gulf phenomena also occurred within the Seventh Fleet. The *Higbee* had had its own encounters with Tonkin spooks during August and September. Several times, we were rousted out of our racks and called to battle stations when radarmen saw solid images of what appeared to be PT boats preparing to attack in the night.

Unfortunately, the lessons of these false encounters were not quickly learned, and lives ultimately would be lost.

Over a three-night period in June, 1968, for example, U.S. Air Force jets attacked what they thought were North Vietnamese helicopters flying in darkness over the Tonkin Gulf. Two of the targets turned out to be U.S. Navy Swift boats. Both were sunk, and five sailors were killed.

Air Force jets also fired at the Australian destroyer *HMAS Hobart*, killing two of her crewmen. And an American cruiser, *USS Boston*, was hit. Several other ships and small craft likewise were damaged.

"Unusual atmospheric conditions prevailing in Vietnamese waters at this period have been commented on by U.S. Air Force officers," according to a report of the Naval Historical Society of Australia.[2]

It is now widely accepted that Tonkin spooks and excited imaginations were responsible for the August 4, 1964, "second attack" that led to the Tonkin Gulf Resolution and escalated America's long involvement in the Vietnam War.

Ironically, sea birds also may have played a role. Some 22 species of sea birds have been identified in the Tonkin Gulf,[3] and a few U.S. Navy officers with experience in the region have postulated that sea bird flocks—which could show up on powerful radar screens and move at PT-boat speeds—may also have been culpable in the phantom sea battles.[4]

Radarmen aboard the *Higbee* told me, in 1964 and 1965, that they could see groups of sea bird moving on their screens. And often, when I stood out on the ASROC deck trying to fight seasickness, I watched long, narrow flocks of small, dark seabirds that resembled auks or small ducks flying low and fast as they flowed past the ship. The birds flew along for a few minutes, and then they landed to rest. After a short time, they took off again and swept along just above the waves, furiously flapping their short, stubby wings. When they were airborne, they flew faster than a destroyer moving at top speed.

Were these the mysterious "PT boats" that surged through the night?

September 18, 1964. The *Higbee* now had been moored at the Yokosuka Naval Station for nearly a week and a half, gently bobbing up and down in a nest of three destroyers that included the *USS Orleck* and the *USS Leonard F. Mason.*

Most of the crew and some of the officers were out on the town on liberty, once again drawn like moths to Honcho Street's garish neon signs.

I was out of cash, so I had spent part of the morning helping several *Higbee* crewmen paint buildings at a Yokosuka orphanage. Now I was starting another mid-watch in Radio Central, with nearly long seven hours to go until relief.

Nothing much was happening on the ship. The decks in Radio Central had been swept clean and would be swept again just before dawn. The incoming messages from earlier in the day had been checked and double-checked, just to be sure nothing directed at the *Higbee* had been overlooked.

J.L. Davis, my watch messenger, was somewhere below, trying to "borrow" some crackers and peanut butter from the mess decks. Neither one of us could stomach the overly salty, faux-chicken soup that usually was available for "mid-rats" (midnight rations).

I turned up the volume control on a big, rack-mounted transceiver tuned to the harbor control frequency, 2716 kilocycles. The radio channel was quiet except for an occasional tugboat or auxiliary craft briefly reporting its movements and some infrequent static bursts caused by distant lightning.

I was sitting alone at the encrypted radio-teletype machines, reading the fleet broadcasts coming in via rock-solid signals from NDT, the nearby U.S. Naval Communications Station in Yokosuka, as well as from NPO at Subic Bay.

Events in the South China Sea and Tonkin Gulf seemed to have quieted down and were staying quiet once again. A few messages of IMMEDIATE precedence were moving through the fleet circuits. But these high-priority reports of ship movements and reconnaissance flights seemed almost routine after the previous month's massive flood of FLASH messages.

At times like this, I did not dislike being a Navy radio operator. Nor did I dislike the unpopular mid watch. In port, it provided relative freedom and long moments of solitude.

Officers seldom came into Radio Central after midnight. And most of the other radiomen either were off the ship or asleep in their racks.

Best of all, the Chief was not hovering nearby, waiting to jump me for some "boot" mistake.

All of the ship's radio equipment was adjusted and working. And now I had time to reflect that I was seeing at least a little bit of the world, as well as a lot of its seawater.

On one recent liberty, before my money ran out, I had ridden a crowded train about 50 miles into Tokyo with five other shipmates. We had eaten Kobe steaks in a very fancy restaurant atop a tall building overlooking much of the city. Then we had strolled through the Ginza shopping district and bought some souvenirs, amazed at both the blinding displays of neon lights and the massive selections of cheap, enticing goods. Finally, we had taken in a strange stage show composed of Kabuki theater scenes, comic musicians who sang in Japanese and English while playing traditional and Western instruments, and a chorus line of tall, Caucasian women who managed somehow to take off all of their very skimpy costumes while they danced.

We were puzzled why no one was applauding after each act in the show. When the dancers finished, we couldn't help ourselves. We cheered and gave them a standing ovation – then realized we were the only ones clapping in an audience of many hundreds. Even the dancers seemed startled by our outburst. We sat down meekly and waited quietly until the last acts were completed. Then, once the performances ended, the audience strongly applauded the entirety of the show.

Some of the Japanese audience members glared at us as they left the auditorium. My shipmates apparently neither noticed nor cared. But I had read the 1958 book *The Ugly American* by Eugene Burdick and William Lederer. Also, just a year earlier, at a movie theater in Hollywood, I had watched the film version of *The Ugly American*, starring Marlon Brando.

I felt embarrassed by my poor understanding of where we were. I wanted to know more about the cultures and geography of Asia. I hoped we would visit Taiwan, Thailand and Hong Kong, where my Arkansas English might not be completely foreign. And I relished any hope or rumor that we someday might cross the equator and go all the way south to Australia and New Zealand.

These thoughts floated through my mind as I sat on a stool and rested my cheek against the top of one of the radio-teletype machines. In that position, I could feel its warmth and vibrations and idly watch its roll of yellow paper unspool.

The fleet broadcast suddenly stopped dead for several unnerving seconds, right in the middle of a PRIORITY message marked CONFIDENTIAL.

Immediately, I began worrying. If the KW-37R receiving system lost synchronization, it would have to be re-started. And that was a nerve-wracking process which required pushing and holding certain buttons, then releasing them at an exact moment – while listening to a badly fading time-tick signal from National Bureau of Standards station WWVH in distant Hawaii.

Until the start of the next atomic-clock minute, when the buttons could be let go, the RATT machines would run wild and spit out long sheets of gibberish that represented missed messages. Once the KW-37Rs were back on line and the signal was printing out, I would then have to check with nearby ships or shore stations and find out if any of the missed messages had been addressed to the *Higbee*.

This time, however, the KW-37Rs were *not* going down. Suddenly, a shore station operator manually keyed in some line feeds and moved up some blank paper at all receiving stations. Then he placed a punched paper tape into the automatic tape reader on his teletype machine and started the message running.

I sensed what was coming next. I had heard it dozens of times in August.

The RATT machines sounded out the unnerving bell signal – *ding, ding, ding, ding, ding!* – and printed the dreaded precedence code ZZZZ.

A new FLASH message for the Seventh Fleet started rattling across the paper. The destroyers *USS Morton* (DD-948) and *USS Richard S. Edwards*, (DD-950) now seemed to be in big trouble in the Tonkin Gulf.

Joseph C. Goulden recounted the incident in his book *Truth Is the First Casualty: The Gulf of Tonkin Affair—Illusion and Reality*:

"The night of September 17-18, 1964, destroyers *USS Morton* and *USS Edwards* went into the Gulf of Tonkin on another DeSoto patrol. Late in the evening they frantically reported action: The *Edwards* was 'holding radar contacts' with several enemy vessels, and the *Morton* was firing at them – ultimately 170 rounds of five-inch shells and 129 of three-inch shells. This 'engagement' was also at night, but, unlike the blackness of August 4, it was under a half-moon, with scattered clouds and visibility of up to four miles."[5]

Once again, nothing was hit. And three days later, according to Goulden, a board of inquiry at Subic Bay investigated the incident and concluded that "although the *Morton* and *Edwards* held numerous radar contacts, and had a 'running battle' with them, they had *not* been attacked by North Vietnamese patrol craft."[6]

The board of inquiry criticized "communications problems" involving the two ships and their task group commander and stated: "Response to queries from higher authorities were delayed because of inadequate communications equipment and insufficient personnel....The patrol unit was unusually slow with action messages from higher authorities and was unable to handle the volume."[7]

When this criticism later was read by radiomen aboard other Seventh Fleet ships, it seemed misdirected. Aboard the *Morton*, Capt. E. E. Hollyfield, the task group commander, had believed – but could not prove – that his two ships were in a running sea battle in pitch darkness with North Vietnamese PT boats. In the midst of the incident, he had been bombarded with FLASH messages from higher-ups demanding immediate SITREPs (situation reports). Yet he had nothing definitive to report. Also, he was aboard a destroyer that had not yet had its radio gear modernized. Its incoming and outgoing messages still traveled via Morse code at a top speed of 20 to 25 words per minute. And they had to be decoded or encoded by hand, further compounding communications delays.

Washington's frustration with the difficulty of getting messages into and out of the Tonkin Gulf also was noted in a previously Top Secret "Memorandum for the Record," titled "Chronology of Events of 18-20 September 1964 in the Gulf of Tonkin," dated Jan. 15, 1965.

The memorandum stated that during the incident involving the *Edwards* and the *Morton*, "circuits were overloaded and a backlog existed at several stations. The additional load of high precedence traffic, equipment failure, and poor atmospheric conditions resulted in unusually difficult communication problems." The memorandum emphasized: "In some instances, IMMEDIATE items took as long as 27 hours to reach Washington and FLASH items took 6-7 hours."[8]

It quickly was clear that the *Morton*'s and *Edwards*' engagement had yet been another "battle" with false radar echoes, which unofficially were being called "Tonkin spooks."

I feared that we still might be sent straight back to the South China Sea and Tonkin Gulf at 25 knots. But somewhere, cooler heads were beginning to prevail. The *Higbee* spent the next two days in port, then left Yokosuka at an unhurried pace for three days of gunnery exercises southeast of Japan.

On September 24, the *Higbee* pulled back into Yokosuka, and the Captain briefly left the ship to attend a change-of-command ceremony for another ship's captain. A few of us even got Cinderella liberty – we had to be back aboard by midnight. Meanwhile, the ship was reloaded with food, ammunition and others supplies, and by 6 a.m. the next morning, we were underway again in the company of other destroyers and the aircraft carrier *Ticonderoga.*

This time, our destination was a three-day courtesy call at Beppu, a port city in southern Japan. Along the way, the formation steamed at a modest pace, and we had more drills: battle stations; man overboard; engineering casualties in the engine room. We also had a couple of hours of booming naval gunfire as Mounts 51 and 52 took aim at a target sleeve towed (well) behind a jet and a target sled towed (well) behind a small ship.

Soon after the exercises ended, Chief Linn had RM2 Lomax take over my portion of the current radio watch.

"Dunn, go to the DASH hanger for small-arms refresher drills," the Chief ordered. "And don't shoot anybody." He made no effort to hide his sarcasm.

I left Radio Central and hurried down the ladder from the ASROC deck to the main deck. I could hear small-arms fire raggedly POP-pop-popping from the starboard side as I rushed along the main deck on the port side. I wondered how we could shoot at targets on a ship, and I saw the answer when I topped the ladder leading up to the DASH hanger.

Several enlisted men were standing along the far safety rail, happily blasting away at the Pacific Ocean with various small arms.

"Dunn, RM3!" a Gunner's Mate Second Class (GM2) announced out as he handed me a World War II-era, Colt semi-automatic .45-caliber pistol.

A Gunner's Mate Seaman (GMSN) nodded and found my name in the list on his clipboard.

"Forty-five, M-1 and .30-caliber machine gun!" the GMSN replied.

I walked up to the safety rail and pushed a clip into the magazine well in the .45's handle. To chamber the first round, I moved the pistol's slide back and released it. Now I aimed, fired three times and made splashes in the water with each shot.

The GM2 carefully took the .45 from me, and another Gunner's Mate handed me a World War II-era M1 Garand rifle and an eight-round clip. I opened the bolt and inserted the eight-round clip. I aimed the M1 and fired three rounds at a small wave breaking about a hundred yards from the ship. The first round hit the wave, but the two other rounds made puny little splashes farther out in the massive expanse of water.

I handed the M1 to the GM2 and walked over to another World War II-era, .30-caliber weapon, a tripod-mounted, belt-fed M1919A2 machine gun. It was already set up, so all I had to do was sit down on the deck, grip the handles and pull the trigger. I fired a burst of about ten rounds into the water a couple of hundred yards beyond the ship. The bullets made unimpressive little white splashes in the blue water.

"Cease fire!" the GM2 ordered.

I got up from the machine gun and returned to Radio Central as my name was checked off on the GMSN's clipboard.

Later that day, a note was added to my training record: I was a *Higbee* marksman. I had *not* missed the Pacific with a single shot.

On October 1, 1964, the *Higbee* hoisted anchor and left Beppu to join Task Group 77.5, which now consisted of the carrier *USS Ticonderoga* (CVA-14), the guided-missile destroyer *USS Strauss* (DDG-16) , and the Gearing-class destroyers *USS Orleck* (DD-886) and *USS Leonard F. Mason* (DD-852). We were returning to the South China Sea and Tonkin Gulf, and this time, we were a bit more prepared for the possibility that we might see some action.

A few days later, as we neared Yankee Station, a message arrived stating that everyone aboard the *Higbee* had been awarded the Armed Forces Expeditionary Medal for meritorious actions in the Tonkin Gulf and South China Sea. I took the message to the Captain, and he made a rousing speech to the crew over the 1MC, congratulating us on our outstanding service.

The next day, after we were on station behind an aircraft carrier, a helicopter delivered a bag of mail for the ship. About an hour later, the boatswain's mate of the watch piped "All Hands" and called over the 1MC that those not on watch should "lay aft to the ship's store" to pick up our new medal and campaign ribbon.

Lomax took my place in Radio Central, and I went aft through the inside corridor and joined a small line of sailors queued in front of the ship's store. Two wise-ass radarmen grinned at me as they walked past carrying small, thin, rectangular blue boxes. "Hey, look," one of them said, nudging the other. "Even Dunn gets to be a *Higbee* hero."

"For meritorious puking in a combat zone," the other radarman responded.

When I reached the counter, the storekeeper put a small blue box on the counter and quietly told me: "That'll be 75 cents."

I waited for him to laugh, but soon I realized he was serious. To get the war decorations we had just earned, we had to buy them.

"How much for a Navy Cross?" I asked sarcastically as I handed him a dollar.

He slapped my change on the counter and glared past me. "Next!"

Once we were operating again in the South China Sea and Tonkin Gulf, the *Higbee* began having more encounters with "Tonkin spooks," including one event that might have become known as "the fourth attack" had we opened fire.

Late one night in mid-October, we were suddenly was awakened by a quick, shrill "All Hands" call over the 1MC. The boatswain mate of the watch intoned: "This is not a drill! This is not a drill! General quarters, general quarters! All hands man your battle stations! Set condition Zebra throughout the ship!"

The ship's general alarm sounded its nerve-wracking *blang! blang! blang!*, and off-duty radiomen, radarmen, signalmen and sonarmen bailed out of their racks. We bumped into each other and cursed as we scrambled to pull on uniforms in the compartment's dim red light. As we finished dressing, the overhead lights flared on brightly and snapped our eyes shut.

Moments after I reported to Radio Central, the bridge sent down an order via the 21MC. "Send a radioman to CIC!" The Combat Information Center (CIC) was directly aft of the bridge. I was closest to the door, so I stepped out and went up the inside ladder to the next level.

In CIC, while radarmen and sonarmen worked tensely at their display screens, I stood by in case we needed to send out a FLASH message that we were under attack.

The night was moonless and cloudy, a perfect example of "pitch dark." But three radar contacts now were showing just a few miles ahead of us, all moving toward a fourth, seemingly stationary, radar blip.

Tensions heightened in CIC as the Captain entered to check the SPS-10 screen and talk with the Weapons Officer.

The targets were within range of the two gun mounts. And both were manned and ready, the Weapons Officer confirmed.

There was palpable fear now that the radar blips might be North Vietnamese PT boats linking up with a *swatow*. *Swatows* were fast, Chinese-made motor gunboats. They were a few knots slower than PT boats, but armed with 37-millimeter and 14.5-millimeter guns and depth charges. And they had surface-search radar.

It was easy to imagine that the blips indicated a cluster of boats getting ready to attack us. The targets remained solid and grew closer together with each sweep of the screen.

While we watched and waited, one of the officers in CIC handed me a draft message. It specified our approximate position and stated we were under attack by at least four unknown vessels.

If the Captain gave the word, I would race down to Radio Central and send it to COMSEVENTHFLT, the Pentagon, the White House and any U.S. ships in the vicinity.

The tension grew tighter as the three contacts reached the fourth. With any movement toward the *Higbee*, we would open fire, and then race toward the nearest destroyer, while hoping for help from one or more of the aircraft carriers.

At all-out battle speed, we could make about 33 knots. Swatows had a top speed of 28 knots or so. But North Vietnam's ragtag assortment of Chinese and Russian PT boats could exceed 50 knots and quickly gain on us.

Just as tension peaked in CIC, the newly merged blip began to lose some of its shape and intensity. Now, with each new radar sweep, its phosphorescent echo grew weaker and weaker.

The radar operators visibly relaxed. Sonarmen leaned back in their chairs and smiled. After a few more sweeps, the target vanished. The Weapons Officer took the message from me and tore it up with a wan smile.

We, too, had just been suckered by the Tonkin Spook. But at least we had not opened fire and wasted hundreds of shells on seawater and hapless sea birds.

Above: The Gearing Class destroyer *USS Leonard F. Mason* (DD-852) races across the wake of the *Higbee* during operations in the South China Sea, 1964. *(Photo by Si Dunn)*

CHAPTER 12

Wearing Out

Machines and men both began breaking down as the Seventh Fleet continued steaming in the South China Sea and Tonkin Gulf.

At one point, a rumor circulated aboard the *Higbee* that we had been at sea longer than any previous crew, outlasting even the ones who had been on combat patrols in World War II and the Korean War. Most of us believed it might be true.

Boredom and the effects of isolation took hold of many of us. There was nothing to see except seawater stretching in all directions to the horizon and the occasional, distant silhouette of another ship.

Often, I was too seasick, too sleepy and too busy as a radio operator to stay depressed for long about other matters. I had almost full access to information, so I had a good sense of what we were supposed to be doing – and why. But other crewmen were not nearly as fortunate. They had no access to the details that I was required to keep secret. Many of them also had less complex jobs and often worked in cramped spaces with little or no moving air.

The ship's air conditioning started failing periodically. And, often, it simply could not overpower the tropical heat. Compartments became hot metal boxes, and we sweated heavily as we slept through our exhaustion. Sometimes, completely against regulations, a few of us went topside to the ASROC deck or DASH deck. We took off our uniforms and stretched out in darkness on the steel, hoping the ship's forward movement would create enough airflow to cool us down.

The engine room spaces, which usually seemed too hot for sane human existence, became even hotter in the South China Sea, causing heat exhaustion among some of the snipes. A few cases of scurvy also cropped up.

Taking long, cool showers would have helped morale immensely. But the old saying, "Water, water everywhere and nary a drop to drink," was especially true aboard Gearing Class destroyers. The ships had eight water tanks situated in the boiler room next to the hull—four on the port side and four on the starboard side. And only four of the tanks held water for drinking, showering and cooking. The other four stored non-potable "feed water" for the ship's boilers. Two evaporators converted sea water to fresh water, but they barely produced enough to meet basic needs.[1]

When *Higbee* crewmen showered, a Master at Arms always stood ready to play "water cop." He listened carefully to how much water was being run in each stall. We were supposed to use just enough water to get wet—barely. Then we soaped up and shampooed and ran just enough water to rinse off—barely.

The moment the MAA decided a sailor was using too much water, he would pound the stall with his truncheon and shout: "Turn off that water, or I'll write your ass up! No Hollywood showers!" Hollywood showers could only be taken in port, when the ship was hooked up to fresh-water lines. Or, when you could go into town on liberty and rent a hotel room.

In port, the *Higbee* and other destroyers always stocked up with as much fresh food as possible. But those provisions usually were consumed within a couple of weeks at sea. Meanwhile, the Seventh Fleet's replenishment ships were hard-pressed to keep busy destroyers and other vessels supplied with new food. Powered eggs, dried beans, chipped beef on toast (the proverbial "shit on a shingle"), and freeze-dried chicken noodle soup were frequent staples on destroyer mess decks. And morale invariably dropped once these items appeared.

One day, the *Higbee*'s bakers tried to give us a morale boost by making big rolls. Unfortunately, they happened to be out of a couple of key ingredients. The rolls looked great, but they were somewhat flat and felt as hard as bricks.

A few of us tried to soften them up by dipping them into soup, but it was no use. A few sailors cursed, threw their rolls down and stormed off the mess decks, their morale lower than ever.

After chow, three of us gathered up some of the ultra-hard rolls and took them to the ship's fantail. There, we had a discus-throwing contest. We sailed the rolls into the sea and watched to see if sharks would bite them and maybe break their teeth. The rolls, however, just hit, bobbed and floated away toward oblivion, riding the waves fanning out from each side of the ship's wake.

In late fall, with the tropical heat still wearing us down, a clothing rebellion gradually took hold. Many of us began wearing dungaree shorts, shower shoes and no shirts while we were off duty. We ignored the "Uniform of the Day" directives that called for dungaree trousers, short-sleeved denim shirts and black dress shoes. Basic decorum also specified that we wear underwear and wrap ourselves with our towels when we walked the main deck to the ship's small shower facilities and when we trudged back to our compartments to put on fresh uniforms. But the savage heat lingered, and soon the towels simply were carried. After a while, some sailors no longer bothered wearing anything except shower shoes to and from the shower.

This lax attitude was stopped, however, soon after I stubbed a bare toe against a water-tight door and suffered a small cut that I did not immediately report to the ship's "doctor," the chief hospitalman. I tried to take care of it myself, using Aqua Velva aftershave as a disinfectant. When I woke up the next morning, my right foot was painful and swollen. And I had red streaks running up some of my leg veins.

In sick bay, Doc took one quick look at my foot and leg and chewed me out. "Dunn," he said, "infections set in quickly and easily in the tropics. You should know that. You have cellulitis, and if you had waited much longer, I would have had to evacuate you off the ship." Angrily, he jabbed a penicillin shot into my right arm, then gathered up some penicillin tablets and a packet of Epsom salts. "Take these as directed and get yourself a bucket."

"I've got bucket," I said.

"Yeah, I bet you do. Well, be sure it's clean. Soak your foot in it three times a day with warm water and Epsom salts. You'll have to wear a shower shoe until the swelling goes down."

I was not able to wear a regular shoe again for nearly a week. I hobbled and limped up and down ladders and through compartments, moving carefully so I wouldn't hurt my toe again. Even when I tried to rest, the toe ached and throbbed and made sleep difficult. The slightest touch sent pains shooting up my leg.

The first time Chief Linn saw me sitting in Radio Central with my foot in a bucket, he turned purple with anger. But there was little else he could do. The Doc had assigned me to light duty for a week. I sat at LOP1, wore earphones and sent and received Morse code messages while my foot soaked.

On a few of the other ships that spent long periods in the Tonkin Gulf and South China Sea, there were episodes of sabotage that forced emergency returns to port. Racial tensions also occurred, especially on big warships with large crews. Small groups of sailors sometimes stuck together and ganged up on other groups loosely formed along racial, ethnic or religious lines. The problem seemed to be much less prevalent on small ships with small crews.

Sometimes, I heard racial slurs aboard the *Higbee*, but the problems tended to stem from disagreements between two or three individuals, not groups of sailors. I had grown up in completely segregated neighborhoods and never socialized or worked with people of any other race until I joined the Navy.

President Harry Truman formally had desegregated America's armed forces in 1948.[2] Sixteen years later, the *Higbee*'s crew was a cross-section of American society: whites, blacks, Hispanics, American Indians, Asian-Americans. Aboard the *Higbee*, we were divided into small groups by operational specialty, and we lived and worked together in very cramped spaces.

Our lives and the survival of our ship, our home, depended on us at least nominally getting along and doing our jobs.

There was little room for error or conflict aboard a destroyer that was only 400 feet long and 40 feet wide. Still, the ship's log recorded a few fistfights, usually over petty matters that briefly loomed too large when two or three sleep-deprived sailors got crosswise.

There also were tales of suicides at sea. One story making the rounds told of a Seventh Fleet sailor on another destroyer. He decided suddenly that he had had all of the South China Sea he could stand.

"To hell with this! I'm walking home!" he reportedly shouted. Then he leaped into the water, started swimming away and was lost by the time his ship could turn around and retrace its wake. True or not, the tale became easier to believe the longer we stayed out. Ships mustered their crews each morning to verify that there were no "absentees." If you were absent from morning formation, someone verified that you were on watch or sleeping after the mid-watch. Otherwise, there were only two other possibilities: You were hiding somewhere, shirking duty, or you fell or jumped overboard during the night.

If you were gone, there would be no going back a hundred miles to search for you. A Navy radio operator would be instructed to pull down a BUPERS manual, open it to a specific page and start drafting a fill-in-the-blanks casualty message: "The Secretary of the Defense regrets to inform you that your son...."

Against this grim backdrop, three of us—ET3 Frank Schley, RMSA J.L. Davis and I—decided to try to become the Kingston Trio of the Tonkin Gulf. For several weeks, I had managed to keep my guitar practice sessions hidden away in Radio II. The cramped compartment was alive with loud exhaust fans, so I barely could hear myself play. The constant noise also covered up the fact that I was messing around with music instead of Navy radios.

One day, ET3 Schley suddenly came into Radio II to fix a problem with one of the transmitters. He caught me mid-strum.

I tried to put the guitar away, but Schley grinned. "What can you play?" he asked.

"Nothing," I replied. It was very close to the truth.

"Yes, you can. I heard you playing something when I came in. What do you know?" he demanded.

"I can strum a few chords," I finally admitted.

I put my fingers to the frets and fumbled my way through a ragged rock 'n' roll chord run from the late 1950s: C-Am-F-G.

Schley nodded and looked happy. "Hey, Davis and I have been talking about forming a music group. We need a guitar player."

Until now, I had never known Davis liked to sing.

"I have a record player in the ET shack," Schley said. "We can move it to the ECM shack and practice there."

The ECM shack was a small, air-conditioned, unmanned compartment near the DASH hanger. It was packed with transmitting and receiving equipment that provided the ship's electronic countermeasures (ECM) and electronic support measures (ESM) capabilities.

One piece of ECM gear in the shack, the ULQ-6 "deception repeater," was designed to generate a false radar target. For example, if a Soviet-made AN-1 or SS-N-2 anti-ship missile was fired at the *Higbee*, the ULQ-6 was supposed to use the incoming missile's target-tracking radar signal to create a false target. Then, the missile would, in theory, lose its target lock on us, plunge into the sea and explode a safe distance away.

The ESM equipment, meanwhile, included the AN/WLR-1 "water surface countermeasures receiver." It was supposed to provide over-the-horizon detection and analysis of enemy radar signals well before the *Higbee* showed up as a blip on enemy radar screens.

The ECM shack turned out to be an excellent place to practice. No one else entered it on a routine basis except ETs or officers conducting scheduled inspections. Any radiomen caught there could claim "training" or "technical interest" as worthy defenses while being run out. Furthermore, Davis and I both had high-level security clearances.

Schley owned a few 45 and 33-1/3 RPM records that could be played on his record player. He had the Kingston Trio, Joan Baez, and Peter, Paul and Mary.

The first song we started working on was Peter, Paul and Mary's rendition of "500 Miles."

We were much more than 500 miles from our homes – half a planet away, in fact. And we felt it now as we sang along with the recording, and I tried to find, and keep up with, the chords.

Schley was from Southern California. Davis was from Virginia. And I was from the geographic center of Arkansas. Until I joined the Navy, I had never been more than 400 miles from home.

Another favorite we tried to master was the Kingston Trio's version of "Where Have All the Flowers Gone?" Its antiwar lyrics also stirred feelings within us. But we were not protesting our miniscule shares of the Vietnam War. Our roles in the conflict so far made little sense and left us confused. All *Higbee* crewmen now were drawing combat pay – a couple of extra dollars per day. Yet we were witnessing almost none of the real horrors of war.

Schley, Davis and I also attempted to develop a rendition of Joan Baez's "Don't Think Twice, It's Alright." But it soon became clear to me that we had little hope of becoming a professional group. Schley had a good natural singing voice; Davis's was also good but not quite as strong. And mine was simply unimpressive. I could hit most of the right notes, but I had little volume. My only musical training had been in choir class in 7th grade. Basically, the three of us sang the same notes and couldn't harmonize. And I could strum only the simplest chords.

When the seawater was rough, we also had difficulty singing along with the recordings. The ship's motions made the record player's tone arm skip across and scratch the vinyl tracks or get stuck in one groove.

There was no escape from the reality that we were sailors on a destroyer in a war zone. Schley worked whenever electronics equipment failed, and our radios, radars and other devices now were breaking almost all the time as days stretched into weeks at sea. Davis and I were in the same watch section, so we were always on duty at the same time. And the long working hours for radiomen were wearing us down. Sleep became much more of a priority than singing.

Sometimes, I still hid out in Radio II for a few minutes and tried to learn new chords. I tried to improve my singing. And I wanted to believe that someday others might wish to hear it.

Late one afternoon, however, I had a new fit of frustration and weariness over being at sea. I carried the guitar out onto the ship's starboard side, near the fantail. No one else was out there. In the shadows of Mount 52's guns, I strummed a few chords, barely able to hear them over the noise of the ship's screws and the water boiling and surging in the ship's wake.

A few seabirds were following along behind the ship, floating overhead or swooping down to feed on pieces of fish kicked up in the white wake.

Suddenly, I clutched the guitar's neck like a spear and heaved the instrument off the fantail, into the sea. It landed flat, bobbed a couple of times, then caught the ship's wake and rode it like a surfboard. Several sailors saw me throw it, and the aft lookout alertly and dutifully reported "Guitar overboard!" to the bridge. The Officer of the Deck quickly sent a messenger to the fantail to ask me why I had done it.

"Because I can't play it. I'll *never* be able to play it," I told him. The messenger smirked and headed back to report.

I expected to be summoned to the bridge, perhaps to face the Captain. But nothing happened. The guitar, meanwhile, quickly became a black speck in the vast sea and soon was lost from sight.

Afterward, I had some remorse. I could have sold the guitar or given it to another sailor; dozens might have wanted it. But the thought hadn't crossed my mind at the time. I was just sick of the sea, sick of the ship, sick of speaking in never-ending acronyms and expletives, sick of not being able to eat or sleep, sick of not having any time to goof off, sick of being so far from home.

Peter, Paul and Mary's "500 Miles" barely expressed it.

A few days later, the ship was cruising slowly on radar picket duty, moving in squares about two miles on a side. I climbed up to the ASROC deck, hoping for a few moments of solitude before starting the afternoon radio watch.

Seagulls and other sea birds swooped, cried and whirled overhead.

One bird, an albatross, was noticeably bigger than the rest and seemed never to flap its long, narrow wings. I walked over to the starboard railing and watched it glide gracefully on unseen air currents. Barely two years earlier, in a high school English class, I had slogged through part of Samuel Coleridge's poem, "Rime of the Ancient Mariner," and I remembered how an albatross had been considered a bird of good omen, until the Ancient Mariner inexplicably killed it with his cross-bow and brought disaster and death to his crew.

As I watched, Coleridge's poem suddenly seemed start repeating itself. The Captain stepped out onto the starboard wing of the bridge and looked up. He watched the albatross swoop around for a few seconds. Then he raised a carbine, aimed it into the sky and fired one shot. The graceful albatross – our bird of good omen – instantly stiffened amid a puff of feathers. Then it plunged into the water like a kamikaze plane falling short of its target.

The lingering boredom only deepened as the ship cruised between the southern part of the Tonkin Gulf and the northern waters of the South China Sea, sometimes trailing behind aircraft carriers and sometimes steaming independently. My mind wandered to World War II history, what little I could remember without a textbook in front of me. A "sitzkrieg" – "sitting war" – had filled the gap between Germany's invasion of Poland in September, 1939, and the invasion of France in May, 1940. We now seemed to be caught in a type of "floatskrieg" off the coast of Vietnam.

More of the *Higbee*'s radio equipment began breaking down, and it became harder to get repairs from the electronic technicians, because of the growing outage backlog and shortage of parts. More than once, our two main 500-watt long-range transmitters were down at the same time, temporarily leaving us with no radio-teletype capabilities and no high-power Morse code capabilities.

When that happened, I carried messages aft to Emergency Radio and used the World War II-era TCS setup to contact NPO, the Subic Bay naval communications station.

The *Higbee*'s TCS had a power output of just 12 watts — barely enough to light up two incandescent Christmas tree bulbs. But that was good enough to send messages several thousand miles when atmospheric conditions were reasonably good and a skilled operator was receiving at the shore station.

My affinity for Morse code had drawbacks, however. No one else in the radio gang shared it. Indeed, they were now mostly using the KW-7 and KW-37R systems to send and receive messages via radio-teletype. Naval communications still were in the transitional phase between old and new — well-honed analog and newly minted digital.

Sometimes when I was in my rack, trying to catch a few precious hours of sleep, a hand suddenly would shake me, and I would squint into the painful glare of a red-filtered flashlight shining in my face.

Usually, it was one of the watch messengers gleefully waking me. Davis, Bill Carver and Mike Larkyns, the ship's three radioman seaman apprentices, generally disdained notions of rising higher in rank and responsibility. They seemed to regret having chosen to be radiomen, and they took little interest in working the ship's communications equipment. Their main pleasure was getting to leave Radio Central with the message boards, so they could stroll about the ship for a half hour or so and track down officers.

They especially liked waking ensigns and junior-grade lieutenants late at night or an hour or two before reveille, to have them read and sign the latest dispatches about potato shipments or urgent weather warnings for storms hundreds of miles away.

When one of the messengers woke me, it usually meant one of two things. Chief Linn was raging mad at me again, or somebody was having problems with CW, the Navy's oldest form of radio communication.

One instance stands out. After a tiring day and evening on duty, I was sleeping fitfully, dreaming I was trapped inside a runaway boxcar.

Suddenly, I started seeing bright-red blood everywhere and hearing my name echoing strangely: "Dunn! Dunn! *Dunn!*"

Larkyns was blinding me with his red flashlight. "We need you in Radio on the double!"

"What's wrong?" I was startled and fully awake now.

Larkyns quickly was gone without answering. His red flashlight bobbed in the darkness as he disappeared through the compartment's watertight door.

The ship, I now realized, was steaming fast in rough water, bucking up and down and rolling side to side. *Damn! It's something bad!*

I yanked on my dungarees, socks and shoes and hustled out of the Operations compartment, still buttoning my blue chambray shirt as I scrambled up the steel ladder to Broadway.

The main passageway was empty and dark except for a few widely separated red bulbs intended to preserve night vision. I staggered and weaved forward, trying to keep my knees loose and arms out, so I could brace against bulkheads as the ship swayed. Very soon, I felt queasy. But the urgency of the wakeup kept me pushing forward. Finally, I reached the ladder that led up to the narrow passageway outside Radio Central. I held on tightly with both hands and fought gravity's rise and fall as I worked my way up the half-dozen steps.

Once I got into Radio Central, I found RM3 Richard "Rod" Rodriguez standing just inside the door, holding an outgoing message in his hand. Another radioman was hunched over the LOP1 typewriter, pressing earphones to his head. Meanwhile, an overhead speaker was alive with static and a jumble of distant CW signals. One faraway station suddenly keyed up and sent a quick string of letters and numbers. It was NPN, the Navy shore station on Guam, sounding unusually weak because of "long skip." Much of the signal was coming back to Earth in greater strength somewhere else, maybe hundreds of miles from us.

"He won't slow down," Rod said. "What's he saying?"

I took the other radioman's place at LOP1, grabbed the message and clicked out "*INT ZBD*" (please repeat what you sent) on the telegraph key.

The Guam shore operator replied with "*R 091338Z*" sent at a rate of more than 25 words per minute, a pace exceeding two Morse code characters per second. He clearly didn't give a damn what the radio world sounded like at the other end of his weak and battered signal. I typed his response, looked down at the message in my hand and smirked.

"He's telling you that he received what you sent him. He's roger'ing the message."

While Rod looked relieved and Larkyns laughed, I grabbed the key again and tapped out: "*NPN DE NHLL ZNN AR*" – "Guam, this is *Higbee*, we have nothing more for you. End of transmission." (NHLL, the *Higbee*'s radio call sign, fostered another nickname for the ship: "In Hell.")

Barely two minutes after entering Radio Central, I was heading back toward my rack, again fighting gravity and this time cursing Samuel F.B. Morse, Guillermo Marconi, *and* the retired Chief Radioman who had suckered—then *flattered*—me into joining the Navy so he could earn a recruitment bonus.

None of this rage did any good, of course. Radiomen—good, bad or indifferent—remained in short supply in the Seventh Fleet. We were now one of the most critical of all "critical" rates. Ships, as well a shore stations, could not function long without skilled communicators. That is why, despite my repeated pleas for shore duty and the numerous entries in my medical records about strong motion sickness, I was stuck in the Western Pacific on a destroyer. The needs of the Navy's combat ships indeed came first.

Along with many different military radio channels, Navy ships also monitored the 500 kHz international calling and distress frequency that had been in use by commercial shipping since the early 20th century. The distress channel was fed into one overhead speaker in Radio Central. Mostly, it just crackled with static; we seldom heard any signals. Late one afternoon, however, a weak but persistent pattern suddenly caught our attention:

"*SOS...SOS...SOS...*"

One of the other radiomen heard it first and rushed to LOP1. He answered the freighter's distress call with a series of Navy "Z" signals requesting the freighter to identify and give its location.

The confused civilian radio operator responded with *dididahdah-didit*, repeated three times. *Three question marks.* It meant he had no idea what we were asking. Commercial ships used international "Q" signals, not Navy "Z" signals.

"Let me talk to him," I said.

I sat down at LOP1 and keyed: *"QRA? QTH?"*

Some of the other radiomen gave me strange looks. "What does that mean?" one of them demanded.

The distant radio operator responded to *QRA* by sending his ship's name and to *QTH* by sending the vessel's geographical coordinates. He added that his ship was a freighter.

It had run aground on a reef and was taking on water.

I responded with *"RRR"* (Roger, roger, roger) and *"QRX 2."* That meant I would call him back in two minutes.

I carried the information over to the 21MC squawk box and pressed the call lever.

"Bridge, radio!"

"Bridge, aye."

"Bridge, radio, we have received an SOS distress call from a freighter that has hit a reef." I read off the ship's geographical coordinates.

After a few moments, the bridge officer responded: "That's too far away for us to help, but we'll notify COMSEVENTHFLT. Send up a messenger."

"Radio, aye!"

Davis hustled up to the bridge, and I called the freighter's radio operator and told him the Navy was getting ready to help.

When Davis returned with the outgoing traffic, I went into the crypto area, sat down at the radio-teletype machine assigned to the Fleet Common circuit and typed "*BVKG DE NHLL K.*" I also sent two BELL characters to ring the receiving machine and alert its operator.

The Commander of the Seventh Fleet's flagship was the guided missile cruiser *USS Oklahoma City*. BVKG answered immediately, and events happened quickly after that. A Yankee Station carrier launched a jet to locate the stricken vessel and assess its situation. And the nearest Navy ship was instructed to render aid and help route civilian ships to the site. The crew soon was rescued and put aboard another commercial ship.

The next day, COMSEVENTHFLT sent a message commending the *Higbee*'s radiomen for alertness and professionalism. Chief Linn scowled at me after he read it. But soon, he had to force a smile. The ship's communication officer came into Radio Central looking pleased and said the Captain was impressed with the radio gang's performance.

As our longest stretch at sea began winding down, one of the ship's officers had the grand idea that the *Higbee* needed a newspaper. And who better to create it than RM3 Dunn, who, his service records indicated, had been assistant editor of his high school newspaper and had taken "Introduction to Journalism" as a college freshman?

The idea was approved, and *news gatherer* was added to my duties. The ship's two postal clerks were assigned to help me, on the theory that they didn't have much work to do between the infrequent arrivals and departures of mail at sea.

I began spending part of each radio watch tuning shortwave broadcast bands, trying to find news reports, sports scores and other items of interest. Unfortunately, the Tonkin Gulf and South China Sea continued to be an American shortwave listener's worst nightmare. Almost no stations within range broadcast in English.

I could hear virtually nothing from the United States, and even when I did, signals were very faint.

The Australian Broadcasting Corporation had one of the few intelligible strong signals in the region. So the first mimeographed issue of the *Higbee News* included Australian soccer and rugby scores, someone's clumsily drawn cartoon, and a couple of news items from London and Paris, by way of Melbourne. I managed to hear a few American college football scores, as well. Then I gave what I had to the postal clerks, and they typed it, mimeographed it and distributed the copies.

The complaints were quick to arrive. *Where* were the other sports scores, and the crossword puzzle, the national news summaries, the comics, and the latest bulletins from the 50 states?

It was hard for me to be Reuters and the Associated Press while seasick and weary. But I gave it a harder try and did a little better with the next few issues. Unfortunately, creating the newspaper also kept cutting into my already-marginal sleep time. And the postal clerks quickly grew unhappy with their role in the product. They were getting their share of the complaints, too.

We were creating the newspaper on the ship's only available typewriter that could produce both capital and lower-case letters. All of the other machines were communications typewriters whose letters were upper-case only. Blocks of text in all-capital letters quickly fill up space and make lengthy passages difficult to read. So the newspaper got priority use of the standard typewriter, which apparently belonged to one of the ship's divisions and had only grudgingly been loaned out.

As the postal clerks and I grew less and less enchanted with seaborne publishing, someone sympathetic to our unhappiness quietly loaned the typewriter to another division and got a signature for it. Then the typewriter magically was "loaned" to another division, and another signature was obtained. I have no idea what happened next, but the typewriter disappeared one night. A ship-wide search failed to locate it, and several divisions accused each other of losing it. One rumor was that it accidentally jumped or fell into water that, purely by happenstance, was 10,000 feet deep.

In any case, the *Higbee News* suddenly ceased publication. Forever.

Above: A U.S. Navy Seasprite helicopter flies low over calm waters in the South China Sea, 1965.

Below: In a posterized view, a Navy HU-2 Seasprite approaches the *USS Higbee*, 1965. *(Photos by Si Dunn)*

CHAPTER 13

First Casualties

"And ye shall hear of wars and rumors of wars…For nation shall
rise against nation…"

– Matthew 24:6-7

August through December 1964 was a time of tenseness and
fear for several ship crews in the South China Sea and Tonkin Gulf.

It also became a time of deaths and injuries. And I would be
among the early casualties.

During August especially, soon after the first Tonkin Gulf
incidents, Seventh Fleet sailors were called to battle stations many
times, day and night. We sat at our consoles and guns for hours,
waiting expectantly for combat. But each time, nothing happened,
and word finally was passed: "Secure from general quarters."

By September, calls to general quarters were less frequent.
But trouble was still expected. Aboard the *Higbee*, we remained
ready to shoot it out with any North Vietnamese PT boats or
swatows that dared to show up.

During September, October and November, 1964, the USS
Higbee participated in several search-and-rescue (SAR) missions in
the South China Sea. A number of carrier-based jets, propeller
planes and helicopters crashed into the water, and several sailors fell
or were swept into the unforgiving typhoon-roiled waters.

No pilot or crewman was recovered alive during our
searches. In most cases, the sea quickly swallowed up their aircraft
and their bodies. All the *Higbee* crewmen found were wheels, small
pieces of wreckage, bloody flight helmets and bits of human
remains. I wrote this several years ago about one incident that
remains an indelible memory:

The ship, now dead in the water, corked to port, then to starboard, and jerked up and down in rough swells while signalmen swept the water with big searchlights and crewmembers lined the rails with battle lanterns and flashlights. Near the starboard side, where I stood with a battle lantern, tiny circles of yellow light darted across the waves, surrounded by a deep blackness that seemed to go everywhere.

"Object in the water, starboard side!" a signalman sang out. A dozen lights converged on what he had found: an awkwardly bobbing, black-and-white nose wheel.

The "ship's swimmer," a young sonarman who had competed on his high-school swim team less than two years ago, dove in to retrieve it.

I moved my battle lantern away from the wheel and closer to the side of the ship. Soon, I illuminated something white and clean seemingly swimming past me about fifteen feet from the side. At first, I thought—I hoped—it was just a jellyfish. But as I held my light on it, I realized its motions came from the water, not from any form of life. I called out, surprised at the harsh strength in my voice: "Human remains in the water!"

Spotlights converged on the large and small intestines and other viscera until the swimmer gingerly scooped them into a plastic bag.

I aimed my light again, and this time, I saw flakes of flesh, gleaming, turning. The swimmer tried to catch a few, to put them into the bag. But they drifted apart.

Later, in Radio Central, I looked at a message sent to us from an aircraft carrier. It contained the Navy pilot's name and service number and the contact information for his family. I pulled down a Bureau of Personnel manual jokingly known as "the radioman's Bible" and opened it to an example message format. Then I sat down at one of the radio-teletype machines and started typing and filling in the blanks as I created a punched tape for transmission: "The Secretary of Defense regrets to inform you..."

I was creating the pilot's casualty notification telegram, the one his parents would think had been sent to them personally by Robert McNamara. I double-checked and triple-checked my typing, to be sure everything had been entered correctly. That was all I could do for the pilot and his family. Then I punched the KW-7's synchronization button, contacted NPN Guam, and sent the tape.

In just a few hours, the family would get the devastating telegram I had sent. As Guam ROGER'ed the message, I imagined the military funeral that would follow in a few days. I hoped the pilot's parents would never know that their son's sealed casket probably contained little more than a small plastic bag and some lead weights.

The air crews attacking targets in North Vietnam faced the greatest risks of death or injury. But there also were fatalities and injuries almost daily among the dozens of Seventh Fleet ships operating in the Tonkin Gulf and South China Sea.

Aboard the "small boys," the destroyers, casualties sometimes happened while the ships were racing to perform SAR searches for missing pilots or sailors who had fallen overboard.

Especially in rough water, just one wrong move or one momentary lapse of judgment could get someone killed or badly hurt.

Indeed, one incident in November, 1964, occurred with terrifying suddenness, and it left two sailors dead and two injured, including me.

A bit of background first.

The *Higbee* had just spent a week anchored in Hong Kong harbor, serving as "Station Ship Hong Kong." And each crewman had gotten at least one day ashore to enjoy the city's scenery and fantastic shopping just miles from Communist China, a nation that we feared was both helping the North Vietnamese and getting ready to attack us in the Tonkin Gulf.

Now we were steaming south, moving back into more typhoons.

Our assignment was the usual: Screen aircraft carriers from attacks by enemy submarines. The North Vietnamese had no subs, but the Russians and Chinese did have a few operating in the area.

As we made the transit into the South China Sea, news arrived on November 16 that I had been promoted to Radioman 2nd Class (RM2).

This meant a new "crow" with two chevrons on my sleeve, a few more dollars each payday, and, if I felt up to eating, I could step to the head of the chow line with the PO1s and the other PO2s.

Rank, indeed, had its privileges.

I also became one of Heflin's watch section leaders, a post I was filling already, at least unofficially.

Lomax recently had been transferred off the ship for missing a message and causing the *Higbee* to be two days late for an important assignment. The Captain had received a stern complaint from COMSEVENTHFLT, and Lomax's initials had been found on the unrouted message.

After Lomax was gone, the rumor persisted that he had been exiled to very grim radar picket ship stationed somewhere well above the Arctic Circle.

A week and a half later, during a night of especially rough seas, the *Higbee* and the three other destroyers in the anti-submarine warfare (ASW) screen suddenly received an urgent voice transmission from the *USS Ranger*.

"Man overboard!"

Almost immediately, the crews on the four screening destroyers were alerted.

While two destroyers held course, maintaining minimal protection for the carrier, the two other small ships – the *Higbee* and the *USS Bausell* (DD-845) – quickly veered, blowing their horns and moving into positions to start a search.

Within a minute, the *Ranger* canceled the alert.

The airdale had *not* been blown off the flight deck. Instead, jet blast had thrown him down an open aircraft elevator shaft. But those few seconds had taken a high toll.

From the *Higbee* deck log:

Wednesday, 25 November 64

20-24 Steaming as before. 2009 - Man overboard stbd side Ranger. 2010 - Man fell on elevator. 2012 - Bausell has two men overboard her starboard side. 2022 - Higbee detached from lifeguard station and proceeding to assist Bausell. 2025 - Maneuvering on various courses and various speeds in search of men overboard. Dunn ST RM2 USN received possible fracture of proximal end of 2nd and/or 3rd metacarpal bones of right hand when hatch closed on hand; not due to his own misconduct. Treatment administered by chief corpsman. Disposition: Placed on sick list. 2112 – Captain has the conn. 2113 – JO of D assumed the conn.

The night's toll had arisen from a very quick cascade of circumstances and decisions aboard three ships.

The *Ranger* had sounded the initial "Man overboard!" alert before verifying that the sailor actually *was* in the water. But every second counts when someone falls from a fast-moving ship.

Aboard the *Bausell*, the *Ranger*'s urgent *"Man overboard!"* alert immediately was repeated over the smaller ship's 1MC general-address system. And sailors responded within seconds, as they were trained to do.

Inside a water-tight door on the *Bausell*'s main deck, three sailors, including an experienced boatswain's mate second class (BM2) petty officer, were working in the ship's paint locker, beneath the bridge on the starboard side. That was their normal watch station during plane-guard operations with aircraft carriers. All three men were supposed to be wearing kapok life preservers while on watch.

Jim Checkett, who was the *Bausell*'s 2nd division officer and a newly minted ensign just out of the U.S. Naval Academy, recalled what happened next to the three men.[1] "Upon receipt of the 'Man overboard' communication, they immediately rushed out of the paint locker and ran out onto the focs'le and headed for the bow of the ship....none of them wearing life vests."

They were headed toward some of the ship's rescue gear, he explained, but they apparently never made it.

At that moment, the *Bausell* turned hard to starboard, toward the *Ranger*, and immediately slammed "into an enormous wave that broke over the bow of the ship and swept (the three sailors) off the bow…and up onto the O1 level, smashing them into the number two 5-inch 38 (gun) mount."

Two of the sailors from the paint locker then were pulled off the ship by the receding water. But the third sailor incredibly survived, with several broken bones. The sea had wedged him beneath the gun mount rather than washing him over the side.

At almost the same moment the wave hit the three *Bausell* sailors, *"Man overboard!"* was sounding on the *Higbee*, and I was rushing toward Radio Central. One of my shipmates decided to take a shortcut. He opened a hatch normally kept tightly shut. It led out onto the main deck. Without thinking, I followed him up the ladder, hoping to get topside fast. As he held the hatch open for me, a wave hit the ship hard and made him lose his footing. He also lost his grip on the hatch. It fell just as I thrust my right hand forward to grip the opening at the top of the ladder.

My first thought was that my hand had been chopped off. I fell down the ladder and hit the deck hard. I rolled over and gripped my right hand with my left. It was still there, yet I could feel nothing. Then the pain hit.

"I broke my hand!" I cried out. I started writhing as intense pain exploded in my hand and surged up my arm.

Three crewmen quickly grabbed me and held me down. One pushed my arm against my chest so I would quit moving my broken hand around.

"Get the Doc! Dunn's hurt!" I heard someone say.

I heard someone else hurry out of the compartment and call out: "Corpsman! We need a corpsman on the double!"

Now I could see a large, ugly welt forming across the top of my hand. Pain shot through it again and up my arm.

The chief corpsman arrived quickly. "Help me get him to sick bay," he told some of the gathered sailors.

Two of them helped me get back to my feet and walked me up the ladder to Broadway. The climb was tricky. The ship was bucking hard in the rough water, and I had to go up without using my hands. I had to keep my right hand supported with my left forearm. One sailor pulled me up by my belt, while the crewman behind me kept a hand pressed against the small of my back.

In sick bay, Doc took a closer look at my hand. Then he splinted it.

The Captain stopped by to check on my condition.

"I think he has some fractures," the chief corpsman told him. "He needs X-rays."

The Captain nodded and left. The *Higbee* had no X-ray machine, of course.

The Doc jabbed my arm with a needle. "Morphine. It'll help you sleep."

Indeed, by the time some shipmates got me back to my rack, I was barely conscious. The next thing I knew, reveille was sounding. The 1MC was blaring: *"Sweepers! Sweepers! Man your brooms! Give the ship a clean sweep-down fore and aft!"*

And Davis was shaking me. "Dunn! Wake up! You're going to the *Ranger*."

I felt enormously drugged and barely could move. But somehow, I managed to roll out of my rack. I was still in my dungarees and didn't need to get dressed.

"The *Ranger*? When?" I asked. My hand throbbed, and my mouth felt like it was stuffed with very dry cotton.

"Now! The helo's on its way!"

I thought he was joking. But as I stepped out onto the main deck, still halfway in a stupor, I saw the *Ranger* paralleling us about three miles to port and a Navy Sea Stallion helicopter turning to approach the *Higbee* from the stern.

The chief corpsman grabbed me. This time, he had a big pill and a small cup of water for me. "It'll help the pain," he said.

I swallowed the pill, and he helped me up the ladder to the DASH deck.

The helo was too big to land. So, roaring loudly, it hovered about twenty feet overhead and lowered a horse collar.

The chief corpsman and a boatswain's mate helped me into it while we were buffeted by the downdraft. The horse collar was supposed to fit snuggly under my arms. But I was so skinny that, as soon as the helicopter lifted, I began slipping through its grip.

The helicopter's winch operator apparently was not paying close attention. And the pilot had no desire to wait and hover while I was reeled in.

The Sea Stallion rose to about 300 feet and swung toward the *Ranger* with me dangling over the Tonkin Gulf. Now the horse collar was slipping up over my arms, and I was just hanging on with my one good hand and feeling woozy.

Halfway to the *Ranger*, the helicopter's winch operator suddenly realized what was happening. He shouted something into his microphone and started reeling me in quickly. At the last moment, before I lost all strength in my good hand, he grabbed my arm and saved me from a long plunge that surely would have been fatal.

Once I was aboard the *Ranger*, another corpsman gave me a shot – apparently more morphine. In moments, I was unconscious.

When I woke again, three days had passed, and the world looked bright pink. I had been given an overdose. My right hand now was in a heavy cast.

Directly across from my bed in sickbay, two other sailors were almost completely encased in casts. One, I later learned, was the *Bausell* sailor who had survived the killer wave. The other was the airdale who had fallen, or been blown, into the open aircraft elevator shaft.

A week later, when the same Sea Stallion crew took me back to the *Higbee*, the winch operator made sure the horse collar was tight, and he waited until we were right over the ship's DASH deck before he helped me out the door and lowered me gently down.

People kept getting injured or killed almost daily in the South China Sea and Tonkin Gulf – mostly in accidents. And the naval forces seemed to be operating virtually in limbo, except when launching or recovering aircraft.

I remember one afternoon when the *Higbee* was on a lonely watchdog station, drifting through water that was dead calm, and so flat it reflected clouds like a mirror.

The radar antennas circled and whirred restlessly as I carried the latest radio messages up to the bridge for signatures.

Out on the starboard wing, the OOD, a lieutenant (j.g.) was looking through his binoculars at a horizon devoid of anything except seawater and sea birds.

An ensign was standing beside him.

"What are we supposed to be doing?" the ensign wondered aloud, gesturing vaguely at the water. "Why are we here?"

The OOD shook his head without looking away from his binoculars. "Damned if I know," he said.

They both suddenly clammed up and tried to look "official" again as I arrived with the message boards. The OOD opened the yellow "Secret" folder first and found only a single routine message related to ASROC warhead maintenance.

The contents of the "Confidential" and "Unclassified" folders were just as routine and uninteresting.

The Seventh Fleet's communications networks seldom carried any summaries of U.S. or world news events. In large part, the content was simply "all Navy all the time."

Big ships such as aircraft carriers and cruisers often had at least a few other communications links to the outside world and sometimes published their own newspapers or news summaries of selected events back in the USA.

Aboard the *Higbee,* we had a single 60-wpm press teletype machine that could be connected to a receiver if anyone had the time or interest to try to find out what was happening beyond the endless blue water and blue sky that surrounded us. Sometimes, I did try. But the South China Sea and Tonkin Gulf remained notorious propagation "holes" where worldwide shortwave radio signals mostly disappeared.

Sometimes, I could find an English-language teletype broadcast from a commercial news service. Yet the news tended to be about Asian business or political affairs or the results of rugby matches in Australia.

It was much easier to just live inside our isolated bubble and trust that someone, somewhere, knew what we were supposed to be doing.

Gradually, I realized that a few officers and shipmates quietly shared some of my misgivings about our undefined mission off the coastline of North and South Vietnam.

Yet, aboard the *Higbee,* we were much too isolated to know that many others outside the Seventh Fleet now shared our concerns.

Indeed, in Washington and beyond, some political leaders and private citizens were growing openly hostile to the Johnson Administration's policies and responses in Southeast Asia.

In the South China Sea and Tonkin Gulf, most of us had no knowledge at all that "a large number of voices ...understood already in 1964 the essential futility of what the United States was trying to do in South Vietnam and who believed that Vietnam was in any case not crucial to American or western security."

These "voices," Fredrik Logevall stated in his book, *Choosing War: The Lost Chance for Peace and the Escalation of War in Vietnam*, "included most allied governments as well as key members of the Senate Democratic leadership, numerous second-tier officials in the State Department, the National Security Council, the Central Intelligence Agency, and dozens of editorial writers and columnists across the United States."[2]

Aboard the *Higbee*, we were merely one tiny fraction of the pawns now being tossed around haphazardly in an international game...of dominoes.

With the *Higbee* on routine patrol, three off-duty sailors soak up some sun while waiting to go back on watch inside the ship, 1965. *(Photo by Si Dunn)*

CHAPTER 14

R & R

As we continued our return to Yokosuka, I had my first encounter with "imitative deception."

Navy training manuals sternly warned against falling victim to fake radio signals sent by a cunning enemy. The right ways to deal with "imitative deception" had been one of the questions on my written test for promotion to Radioman 2nd class. Now, suddenly, it came alive in my headphones.

A few hundred miles south of Tokyo Bay, I needed to send several routine messages to NDT, the Yokosuka Naval Communications Station. I sat down at LOP1 and tapped out "NDT DE NHLL K".

Immediately, I was answered by a flood of Morse code radio signals, all signing *NDT.*

The *Radioman 3 & 2* training manual had cautioned: "An enemy may attempt to enter communications nets used by the Navy in order to confuse and deceive our forces."[1]

Indeed, seven or eight phony stations now were in the mix, along with the real NDT. The fakes were Chinese, Russian and possibly North Korean military stations. The trick was to pick out the right signal and stay mentally focused on its exact tone and Morse code rhythms while the others kept trying to break in and disrupt.

To separate the real NDT from its pretenders, I first used the Navy's simple but effective signal authentication method. I positioned an "authenticator," a small piece of metal that had a few holes in it, over a page full of letters and numbers. The pages were changed daily, to keep characters random.

I picked two of the random characters selected by the authenticator and sent a challenge out to any and all of the stations claiming to be NDT. The challenge in essence said: "Authenticate TZ" (or some other two-character combination). The holes in the piece of metal showed me the only valid responses to "TZ." Then I listened very carefully as the various operators gave their replies at almost the same time.

Some of the signals were easily dismissed when I heard them again. They had rough tones caused by badly regulated DC voltages. Or they made chirpy tones characteristic of unstable oscillators. Or they had fluttery echoes characteristic of radio signals bouncing off the ionosphere, which meant they likely were some distance away in China, North Korea or Siberia.

We were close enough now to Yokosuka that the real NDT's signals arrived via "ground-wave propagation." These radio waves followed the Earth's curvature over land and water and exhibited few of the characteristics of the imitators. A radioman with a good ear could hear the difference.

The real NDT's authentication response checked out. But just to be sure, I made him authenticate a new two-character combination. After that, I sent him the messages and kept his signal straight in my mind, even though the "NDT" pretenders kept pestering us by breaking in and asking for certain character groups to be repeated.

Late that evening, I had an strange "going home" sensation as we neared Yokosuka, a port I barely knew except for the Navy base and bar district. Davis was away, routing the message boards, and another radioman, Smith, a recent transfer from shore duty, was working in the crypto area. I decided to find some music on the ship's entertainment receiver and pipe it down to the crew's mess decks.

We had had almost no music to listen to for many weeks. The Voice of America, the BBC and Radio Australia all beamed programs to Asia, using very powerful transmitters and big antennas. But their shortwave signals generally skipped over the South China Sea and Tonkin Gulf.

The *Higbee*'s entertainment receiver mostly had just crackled with static and finally had been turned off and ignored for the past few weeks.

I tuned into a very strong, English-language transmission from Radio Tokyo. Soon, "Sakura," a 17th or 18th century Japanese folk song celebrating cherry blossoms, began to play. A koto and flute brought its simple, haunting melody to life in a way that suddenly reached far inside my mind and soul. In moments, tears were streaming down my cheeks and blurring my eyes. I felt as if we had just survived a long and dangerous journey, and now we were nearly *home*.

Honcho Street had changed little in our absence. A few of the bars had new names and new *jo-sans*. As soon as I was given a 72-hour liberty, I took a train to Tokyo with two other *Higbee* sailors who also had three-day passes. We lost ourselves in the glare of the Ginza, in noisy pachinko parlors, and in the dizzying heights of the Tokyo Tower, which had been completed and opened to tourists just six years earlier and resembled the Eiffel Tower, except for its orange-and-white, aviation-safety paint scheme. We ate thick Kobe steaks that had been cooked in beer and watched fancy floor shows performed partly in English and partly in Japanese. For a few days at least, we were about as far from the sea, mentally, as we could get.

Once we returned to the ship, however, it was my turn to stand in-port radio watches. And I started seeing brief, terse secret messages reporting something called *Operation Barrel Roll*. I had hoped the troubles in Vietnam would subside. But *Barrel Roll*, which had started on Dec. 14, signaled the use of armed reconnaissance flights over southern Laos, and it was classified Top Secret.

By fits and starts, the war in Southeast Asia was still heating up. And now it was threatening to explode and spread.

As Christmas neared, snow sometimes fell over Yokosuka. The flakes fluttered and swirled like millions of glowing moths drawn down to Honcho Street's neon signs. Occasionally, a brief icy slush built up on the decks, turrets and gun barrels. But the weather did not seem harsh, and neither did the world, now that we were no longer at sea. Barring any upsurges of combat in the Tonkin Gulf, we were scheduled to stay in port until the end of January.

Christmas Day 1964 and New Year's Day 1965 both passed quietly. The ship remained moored, with much of the crew gone on liberty or leave.

About this time, I entered a sort of moral period. I began reevaluating my life. I felt guilty now that I had dropped out of two colleges and wasted the money my cash-strapped parents had borrowed to pay my tuition. I had not honored their sacrifice. Also, I began feeling guilty about the time and money I had thrown away in Yokosuka's bars and skivvy houses.

When I could get off the ship for liberty, I started spending more time inside the base and trying to save up part of my meager petty officer's pay, so I could return to college next summer. Each payday, I now began taking some of my cash straight to the ship's postal clerks. I bought money orders and immediately mailed them home, so my parents could put the money into my savings account.

I could have saved more. But the Yokosuka Navy Exchange was a shopping paradise, particularly for Japanese cameras at cheap prices. I bought another Pentax 35mm camera and a small telephoto lens. And I began improving my film-developing and printing skills in the base's free photo lab for hobbyists.

I ate cheap steak dinners at the Enlisted Men's Club and sometimes won or lost a few dollars playing the EM Club's slot machines.

At night, when I finally left the EM club, I could see the beckoning signs outside the main gate.

It was difficult, but I remained mostly a loner now and continued to minimize my visits to Honcho Street.

For some reason, I began reading Ayn Rand's novels, including *The Fountainhead* and *Atlas Shrugged*. I didn't concern myself with her philosophical statements, such as "man's ego is the fountainhead of human progress." Likewise, I didn't worry about *Atlas Shrugged*'s discourses on the role of man's mind in American society and the repetitious question "Who is John Galt?"

In my 20-year-old mind, *The Fountainhead* and its protagonist, Howard Roark, and *Atlas Shrugged* and its protagonist, John Galt, simply provided a few hours of mental escape from my miscast life in the Navy. Roark's efforts to build buildings, and Galt's involvements in an independent economy within a futuristic America seemed to have no bearing whatsoever on anything I was doing in the Seventh Fleet. And I liked that. They were just escapism. When I finished the books, I gave them away without further thought and found other paperbacks and authors to read.

Sometimes, when it was our turn to stand in-port radio watches, Davis and I talked about Ernest Hemingway's novels and short stories by several other writers. He had dropped out of high school and joined the Navy, he said, to avoid reform school. Yet he was much better read than I was.

At sea, of course, I had found it almost impossible to read almost anything except radio messages. We worked under great pressure until the end of each radio watch. Then we crawled into our racks and tried to get a few hours' sleep.

If I tried to read anything longer than a few pages while we were surging through water, nausea quickly swept over me.

The stillness and relative tranquility of the extended port stay gave me more chances to think and to try to plan for my future beyond the Navy.

And, on a more practical level, I was able to eat regularly once again and regain some lost weight.

I wrote away for college catalogs and held them like treasures once they arrived. I signed up for a freshman sociology course offered by correspondence from one university and tried to get enthusiastic about the scientific study of society.

I also sent away for a lengthy electronics course offered by the Cleveland Institute of Electronics and begin its lessons. I still thought I might try to become an electrical engineer. But images of being a writer sometimes floated up, as well. The end of my enlistment still seemed an eternity away, yet it was now supposed to be up in about 150 days.

I could have kept a diary or at least written down a few reflections about the changes and challenges now taking place in my young life. But, other than sending "I am fine, how are you?" letters home, virtually the only writing I did outside Radio Central involved making a single mark on a small piece of paper. At some point in late 1964, I had begun carrying a "short-timer's sheet" in my dungaree pocket. Now, every morning, as soon as I could get to it, I unfolded the small piece of paper and added one more mark to the groups of four vertical lines and diagonal slashes that signified groups of five days.

A few other sailors carried their own short-timer's sheets. But on mine, each new day was considered finished the moment it began.

When Chief Linn was not around, the in-port work days usually went smoothly for the radio gang. We often had plenty of time to skate – to goof off and talk – while doing general message filing, sweeping the flooring and making minor adjustments to transmitter, receiver and antenna tuner settings.

Periodically, whether we were in port or underway, we also had to perform preventive maintenance on our equipment. This involved cleaning air filters, carefully dusting inside metal cabinets, verifying voltages and initialing lengthy bureaucratic check-off sheets. It tended to be hot, boring work.

And the Navy, of course, had a fancy acronym for it: POMSEE – "Performance, Operation, Maintenance of Shipboard Electronic Equipment."

"POMSEE" was one of Chief Linn's favorite terms – and another of his special punishments for me: "Dunn will do the POMSEE."

While others went ashore for New Year's Eve celebrations in the bars on Honcho Street, I stayed aboard ship and handled the overnight radio watch. Once I finished the POMSEE and the message filings, I still had several hours to fill – and kill – until my relief arrived at 0700.

I decided to indulge again in a hobby of my recent childhood. I tuned one of the R-390A receivers away from its Navy frequency and began listening to international shortwave broadcasts.

Most of the strong signals were from Asia. But soon, I found a few modestly audible stations transmitting in English from Australia, Canada and the United States. I also tuned across the 20-meter (14 MHz) amateur radio band and heard weak stations with W6 and K6 call signs – California. I longed to fire up one of the *Higbee*'s transmitters and make contact again with civilian America. But it would have been a serious breach of Navy regulations and a violation of Federal Communications Commission statues, as well. So I just listened and longed.

On Earth, being half a world away is as far from home as you can get.

I was, it now seemed, exactly that far away.

Screened by destroyers, the aircraft carrier *USS Ranger (CVA-61)* steams through calm waters near Yankee Station in the Tonkin Gulf, 1965. *(Photo by Si Dunn)*

CHAPTER 15

Back on the Line

By Seventh Fleet standards, the *Higbee*'s Yokosuka respite had been quite long: more than six weeks in port, including Christmas, New Year's and the entire month of January.

I was not ready to go, of course, when we were ordered to return to the South China Sea and lower regions of the Tonkin Gulf. This time, when we left Tokyo Bay, the *Higbee* "steamed independently," meaning alone instead of in a formation with other ships.

I was painfully seasick for the next four days, almost the entire transit time. And, in the midst of that misery, I had to keep performing my duties as a radioman and watch section supervisor, always with a bucket at my side.

The "dry heaves" were the worst. As the ship rose and fell and swayed side to side, I found it almost impossible to eat or drink anything. And nothing could stop the waves of nausea once they started. At their most violent, I would retch and gag and writhe on the deck, long after there was anything left to throw up.

Shipmates who had once kidded me about my affliction now gave me wide berth when I suddenly turned green and grabbed for my bucket or tried to make it to the lifelines outside. There was nothing they could do for me now except feel sorry for me. When the Dramamine tablets repeatedly offered by the ship's corpsman had no effect, there was nothing else he could do, either.

Often, I wondered if it were possible to die of seasickness.

On the day the *Higbee* left Yokosuka, President Johnson approved yet another level of escalation of the Vietnam War. An Air Force F-105 fighter squadron was transferred from Okinawa to Da Nang.

Meanwhile, *Operation Barrel Roll* had entered its sixth week of bombing operations. Air Force jets from Vietnam and Navy jets from the carriers on Yankee Station sped across South Vietnam's border into southeastern Laos and attacked parts of the Ho Chi Minh Trail. This North Vietnamese supply route relied on trucks, bicycles and human carriers to smuggle arms and ammunition through the Laotian jungle to the Viet Cong in South Vietnam. Ultimately, the bombing missions would continue for another nine years.

Barrel Roll was supposed to be one of America's most highly classified missions in Southeast Asia at the time. But I was able to discern what it involved just by reading the bare details laid out in a few SECRET radio messages and briefly overhearing one officer tell another that the targets were in the Laotian kingdom. Years later, I would better understand the reasons for the high secrecy. Officially, Laos was a neutral country; its neutrality had been guaranteed by the Geneva Conventions of 1954 and 1962. But along with bombing part of the Ho Chi Minh Trail, *Barrel Roll* planes also provided close air support for the "neutral" Royal Lao armed forces, as well as CIA mercenaries and special forces from Thailand, as they battled Pathet Lao and North Vietnamese troops in northern Laos.

The air war continued to heat up once we arrived back at Yankee Station and joined up with the aircraft carrier *Ranger*. On February 7, 1965, a FLASH message arrived at Yankee Station: "Execute *Flaming Dart*." Jets from the carriers *Hancock* and *Coral Sea* were catapulted into the air with heavy bomb loads. Meanwhile, several Navy F4B Phantoms rose up from the *Ranger* and passed near the *Higbee* as they rushed to help guard the *Hancock*'s and *Coral Sea*'s fighter-bombers against MiGs.

The *Higbee*'s role in *Flaming Dart I* was simple and very limited: Stay in a four-ship screen; help protect the *Ranger* against possible enemy submarines; and be prepared to rescue any pilots who crashed at sea nearby.

President Johnson himself had picked the targets for *Flaming Dart I*: the North Vietnamese Army's Vit Thu Lu barracks near Dong Hoi. The raid was supposed to be an in-kind reprisal for recent Viet Cong mortar attacks in South Vietnam that had killed eight Americans, wounded 126 and destroyed 10 aircraft.

There was one other supposedly key player in the first *Flaming Dart* attack, Nguyen Cao Ky, a South Vietnamese air force commander who would become one of his faltering nation's final prime ministers.

As Ky later recalled in his autobiography, *Buddha's Son*, "I thought that it was important for both civilian and troop morale in South Vietnam that the VNAF (South Vietnamese Air Force) have a role in this operation, and the Americans agreed." But as Ky led his "Thanh Phong" ("Divine Wind") squadron of 24 propeller-driven A1H Skyraiders toward the VNAF's first strike on North Vietnam, he was greeted by an unexpected sight: "...dozens of U.S. Navy planes bombing and strafing our target."[1]

Ky had not been told that the U.S. Navy pilots had orders to knock out the antiaircraft guns surrounding his target, thus making it "safer" for him and his pilots to bomb. It was just another moment of miscommunications between America and South Vietnam – one of countless that would plague the Vietnam War. Indeed, some of LBJ's advisers had told the president that only "very slight resistance was expected" at Dong Hoi.

Ky quickly chose another target nearby and led his squadron into the first of two single-file attacks (one plane swooping down behind the other). The South Vietnamese pilots soon realized they were diving at 350 miles per hour toward a "headquarters for an antiaircraft division." Tracers and blistering AA fire rose up and hit every plane. But all of Ky's pilots survived, and their new target was damaged. Ky himself escaped death by inches. A 12.7mm slug slammed through his windshield and passed between his arm and chest.

In Washington the next day, during a meeting of the National Security Council, Defense Secretary Robert McNamara apparently told LBJ only that Ky's squadron "had hit a target other than the one they were supposed to hit." Meanwhile, the U.S. Ambassador to South Vietnam, Gen. Maxwell Taylor, told LBJ advisor McGeorge Bundy that such reprisal attacks would "give a clear signal to the North Vietnamese." And Taylor told the U.S. Senate's Foreign Relations Committee that the *Flaming Dart* attack was intended "to change the will of the enemy leadership."

That "clear" signal was *not* received. Or, more likely, it was ignored. No leadership wills visibly changed. Three days later, the Viet Cong bombed a hotel that housed U.S. enlisted personnel in Qui Nhon, a coastal town in central South Vietnam. The attack killed 23 Americans and wounded more than 20 others. In retaliation, President Johnson ordered a second *Flaming Dart* attack. The new targets were North Vietnamese communications and logistics facilities just a few miles north of the Demilitarized Zone.

This time, the *Higbee* played a slightly different role in the new escalation of the Vietnam War. The ship was moved, pawn-like, from the *Ranger*'s screen to the *Coral Sea*'s screen, just before 95 aircraft from the three carriers on Yankee Station bombed and strafed North Vietnamese military barracks at Chanh Hoa.

The *Higbee*'s log recorded a boring litany of *"Steaming as before...Steaming as before...Steaming as before..."* accompanied by routine records of changes to course and speed as the three aircraft carriers swept back and forth across Yankee Station, carefully staying outside the 30-mile no-fly zone claimed by China for its heavily militarized Hainan Island. However, while the carrier jets bombed the new targets in North Vietnam, we kept wary eyes open for any surprise attacks by the Chinese air force or navy, based just minutes away to the northeast.

At one point between *Flaming Dart I* and *Flaming Dart II*, someone high in the Pentagon decided to stage a major show of force in the South China Sea. The exercise apparently was intended to frighten the North Vietnamese into submission and also intimidate the Chinese and Russians. *Operation Candid Camera* massed four aircraft carriers, a guided missile cruiser, a guided missile destroyer, and 12 conventional destroyers, including the *Higbee*, for an aerial photography session.

From the *Higbee*, the armada looked massive – a seemingly invincible gathering of airpower, firepower and naval steel stretching from horizon to horizon. As I stood at the ASROC deck's lifeline and marveled at the sight, I could hear music from Richard Roger's *Victory at Sea* again swelling in my mind. Surely, not even the D-Day invasion fleet had appeared this big or powerful, I thought.

The spy trawler *Gidrofon* had a front-row perch for the unprecedented gathering. Indeed, the Navy was staging the expensive show largely for the *Gidrofon* crew's benefit – for the excited messages the Russian radiomen would send to Moscow, for relay to Hanoi and Peking.

Most of us believed, of course, that Russia's and China's support for North Vietnam was monolithic. It was easy to assume that the three countries were sharing information about everything that happened in the South China Sea and Tonkin Gulf.

However, "[t]he Soviets…were not the loyal socialist allies that they appeared to the rest of the world," Mark Moyar wrote in his book, *Triumph Forsaken: The Vietnam War, 1954-1965*. "At this same time, they were conniving to deny the North Vietnamese a decisive victory, for two reasons. First, the destruction of South Vietnam would substantially enhance China's prestige and power within Asia and the Communist world, undermining the Soviet Union's position. Second, the imminence of a North Vietnamese victory or a victory itself could provoke a sharp U.S. reaction that might harm Soviet relations with the United States or lead to a war between the United States and China in which the Soviets, because of their 1950 treaty with China and their concern about Soviet prestige in the Communist world, would feel obligated to assist the Chinese in some way."[2]

More than once as I watched the bobbing trawler, a dark thought crossed my mind. If a single atomic bomb or missile warhead suddenly exploded in our midst, it would cause much more devastation to American naval power than had been wreaked at Pearl Harbor. We on the destroyers were considered basically expendable. But the loss of four aircraft carriers at once would be catastrophic to America's military capabilities and defenses.

A few days later, copies of the aerial photos were distributed to the participating ships, and the demonstration's big flaw was immediately apparent. To capture the full formation, the Navy's photo reconnaissance plane had been forced to fly at very high altitude. Now, on eight-by-ten glossies, the powerful armada appeared to be simply a bunch of gray toy boats making bright, choreographed wakes on dark water.

The Russians, North Vietnamese and Chinese, if they ever saw the pictures, no doubt were as unimpressed as we were.

Immediately after *Operation Candid Camera*, we returned to carrier screening duties on Yankee Station. But the *Higbee* suddenly experienced a breakdown in one of its two engines just after the second *Flaming Dart* raid. The Captain tried to keep us on station within range of the task group while the problem was investigated. But, our top speed now was 15 knots. We could not serve a useful role, and we would be easy pickings for PT boats or submarines. We were diverted to Subic Bay for emergency repairs.

The crew's rumor mill came alive during the languid, three-day transit.

Rumor #1: *Somebody sabotaged an engine bearing so we can get away from Yankee Station and have some liberty while the ship is repaired.*

This rumor had some believability for a day or so, because we were all weary of steaming inside the big, rectangular box of seawater designated "Yankee Station." Also, word had spread that two or three officers had begun "investigating" the possibility of deliberate damage.

Of course, rumors of about leaving Yankee Station had been a constant, and hopeful, currency among enlisted crewmen since our second trip to the troubled waters. And, often, because of my security clearance and access to ship movement orders, I knew the truth and had to keep it secret. I couldn't even hint. When somebody told me a "I hear we're going to…" rumor, I could only say: "That's interesting." Or, I could engage in a bit of disinformation: "I think I heard somebody say we might go Down Under."

Australia had been one of our rumored "next" destinations for as long as I had been aboard the ship. Almost everyone wanted to stop there. Consequently, I often used Australia as my "go-to" country when some of my shipmates pressed me hard for information about where we might go next.

Within an hour or so after hinting it, I would hear one *Higbee* crewman tell another: "Hey, I've heard we're going to Australia."

The second crewman would ask: "Who told you that?"

And the first crewman would reply with a name, usually a deck ape, a snipe, a gunners' mate, or a mess cook.

"Who told *him*?"

"He said he heard it from the Captain."

"Damn! I bet we *are* going to Australia!"

Rumor #2: *"We'll be at Subic for two weeks. Then we're going to Australia!"*

After we limped into Subic Bay and reached the pier, off-duty sailors started scrambling to get their liberty uniforms ready. They figured liberty call would be sounded soon after we tied up at the pier.

I didn't bother. I already knew. The shipyard had sent us a message during the night saying they had all of the right parts waiting. They would repair the engine in less than 24 hours.

More than 200 faces visibly fell when word was passed over the 1MC that all hands would stay aboard ship and assist with repairs, refueling the ship and restocking food and ammunition.

The next day, when we headed back to sea, our destination was *not* Australia. It was Vietnam again. And we had a new mission: spy ship.

U.S. Navy destroyers periodically were dispatched close to the Paracel Islands to see if the Chinese were expanding their military presence. The Paracels are a string of islands and reefs located about 200 miles east of Da Nang, 175 miles southeast of China's Hainan Island, and a third of the way between South Vietnam and the Philippine Islands.

Yankee Station, the watery home of aircraft carriers now launching strikes against North Vietnam, was almost exactly halfway between Da Nang on the west and the Paracel Islands on the east.

Yankee Station also was almost on top of a Chinese territorial "claim line" in the South China Sea.

The French previously had controlled the islands and considered them part of French Indochina. Then the Japanese seized them in World War II. Next, the Chinese and later the Chinese Communists gained control. Now, as the *Higbee* steamed toward the Paracels, three nations had territorial claims on the islands: South Vietnam, Taiwan and China. And China had possession.

At 0345 Monday, February 22, 1965, the *Higbee*'s radar picked up the first blips from Money Island. The range was 30,000 yards, roughly 15 nautical miles. As dawn's early light increased, we swung by other islands at a range of less than six miles. When full sunlight arrived, the ship slowed to about 12 knots, ran up the biggest American flag on board, and started drifting around our main target, Woody Island, holding a distance of 6,300 yards—just over three nautical miles. We were right outside the limits America recognized but well inside China's territorial-water claims.

With the huge flag waving and popping overhead, we started going through daily shipboard routines, including swabbing the decks and mustering the crew. Soon, a Chinese signalman in a tall watch tower on Woody Island began flashing a light at us.

It was a warning message in Morse code and perfect English: *"Leave our territorial waters immediately."*

We made no effort to leave. We spent the next four hours leisurely completing our first circumnavigation of Woody Island.

Meanwhile, the warning message kept getting repeated every few minutes.

In Radio Central, things initially were calm. Most of the radio gang now was on duty, however, and we took turns going outside on the ASROC deck to watch the Chinese being mad at us.

That afternoon, the *Higbee* moved on and circumnavigated Lincoln Island. There, we saw no warning signals. But things quickly became tense once we moved back to take another run around Woody Island.

The flashing light resumed its unambiguous command.

And the Combat Information Center (CIC) suddenly detected a strong, buzzing radar signal coming from the island.

The signal was patched down to Radio Central, and two officers had me help them try to identify it. It had the rapid buzz of a pulsed radar signal. But it also had periodic bursts of tones that sounded like radio teletype. When we connected the signal to one of our teletype machines, it started printing groups of numbers every few seconds.

We came to the consensus that we were hearing some kind of gun-control or missile-control radar, and Chinese weapons now were tracking us.

Our Woody Island surveillance quickly wrapped up, and we headed out to less-disputed waters.

As the Vietnam War escalated, the *Higbee*'s assignments expanded. We continued to run ASW screens for carriers, and we moved astern into rescue position when planes were launched or recovered. We also began chasing more sonar contacts. Some turned out to be American submarines; others were whales or schools of fish. But a few were "unknowns," likely Russian or Chinese subs playing cat and mouse with us. They fled the area quickly once we pinged them, notified nearby ships and got air support from one of the Navy's sleek new P-3 Orion anti-submarine patrol planes.

We also started challenging and identifying more freighters and other ships in the South China Sea and Tonkin Gulf.

I had bought a new camera in Yokosuka a few weeks earlier and shown off some of my photos. As a result, one of the *Higbee*'s officers quickly had "volunteered" me for a new duty, ship's photographer, on top of my radio duties.

When the *Higbee* encountered a Soviet-bloc freighter, a call would blast out suddenly over the ship's 1MC: "Now the ship's photographer...lay to the bridge!"

It was my call, seasick or not, to run down to my footlocker, pull out my camera, verify that it was loaded with film and rush up to the bridge.

From a small walkway near the port or starboard wing, I would focus a short telephoto lens on the suspect freighter and take as many bow, side and stern photos as I could get as the ship passed by. Once the photo shoot was over, I would carefully rewind my film and give it to one of the officers on the bridge.

No one ever told me where the film went or how it was used. And I never saw how any of the pictures turned out. All of that was beyond my "need to know." The film, which I had purchased myself, likely was developed aboard one of the aircraft carriers or included in the packages flown each day to Subic Bay via "carrier onboard delivery" (COD) flights. Naval Intelligence, I figured, was collecting "mug shots" of Soviet-bloc vessels traveling to or from North Vietnam.

The procedure for challenging a Soviet ship at sea seemed fairly simple. The *Higbee* would speed toward a surface radar contact, and when the contact was within visual range, a signalman on our signal bridge would use a flashing light to send "AA" (for "unknown ship") at the vessel. Once the contact responded, our signalman would flash something like "Where are you bound and what is your cargo?" while we kept speeding closer and moved to parallel them.

The flashing light signals used international Morse code, so I often stood on the ASROC deck and read the replies. Sometimes the cargo was wheat. Several times, however, the Russian freighters responded stating that they were bound for Haiphong, carrying arms and ammunition for the DRV (the Democratic Republic of Vietnam). They knew we could do nothing about it.

During a few encounters, the Russian ships responded with Russian Morse code, which has several extra characters to match the Cyrillic alphabet. Not all U.S. Navy signalmen could copy what the Russians were sending, and not every ship had a crewman or officer who knew enough in Russian to translate what was received. Only one or two signalmen on the *Higbee* could copy Russian Morse, and it required calling out the characters to a "recorder." This was another signalman standing nearby who wrote down the message.

Alec Brewster, a Signalman Second Class aboard one of the *Higbee*'s sister Gearing Class destroyers, recalled how the process worked:

> "In telling a recorder what to write down when we were receiving code, we would call out every letter using phonetic equivalents: Alpha, Bravo, Charlie, and so forth. The problem with the Russian code we were taught was, several of their letters equaled multiple letters (in English). I remember there was 'SH' and 'CH,' and with these we would just say the letters. Another one, though, was 'SHCH,' which, if you stop and think about it, takes a long time to say. So we just shouted 'Shit!' and the recorder knew to write down 'SHCH.'"[3]

After the flashing-light challenges, we sometimes exchanged unenthusiastic waves with Russian crewmen visible on the decks. This struck me as a very strange way to conduct a war.

But things soon would get even stranger. We were about to go on "Cabbage" duty.

The Russian spy trawler *Gidrofon* maneuvers close to a
U.S. Navy ship in the Tonkin Gulf. *(Photo by Steven Henry)*

CHAPTER 16

Dances with Sharks

"Do not move up-stream to meet the enemy. So much for river warfare."

– Sun Tzu, *The Art of War*, circa 500 B.C., translated by Lionel Giles, 1910

In late February, 1964, the *Higbee* received orders to veer away from freighter surveillance and aircraft carrier screening duties. Another destroyer moved up to replace us, and we were sent to relieve the destroyer *USS Lofberg* (DD-759) as the "shadow" for a Russian spy trawler.

The 150-foot-long *Gidrofon* (Russian for "hydrophone") supposedly was a scientific research vessel, making hydrographic surveys in the South China Sea and Tonkin Gulf. But the converted Soviet tuna boat deliberately was doing its surveys amid the Seventh Fleet ships steaming in and around Yankee Station.

The *Gidrofon* may well have performed a few hydrographic studies – most likely to help Russian subs locate underwater hiding places. But it had two other, equally threatening, roles.

Chugging along at a top speed of 13 knots, the trawler periodically attempted to maneuver into the paths of aircraft carriers or other ships and force them to change course while aircraft were being launched or recovered. The *Gidrofon* also bristled with antennas, many more than a vessel its size actually needed. It was a seagoing listening post that had the ability to gather radio and radar intelligence and also warn the North Vietnamese when a new air attack was on the way.

Despite its slow speed and diminutive size, the *Gidrofon* often proved to be a formidable foe.

"Moscow had laid down guidelines for the *Gidrofon*'s conduct on Yankee Station," Zalin Grant noted in his book *Over the Beach: The Air War in Vietnam*. "The skipper was encouraged by his superiors in the Kremlin to harass U.S. warships, so long as he did it while following the international rules that governed sea travel. An excellent shiphandler, he tried always to approach American ships from their starboard side at a perpendicular, thus giving him the right of way and making them yield. Sometimes, when he couldn't manipulate the rules to his advantage, he simply ignored them."[1]

Reporting in 1966 on Russian trawler activity in the Tonkin Gulf, *Time Magazine* noted: "The Russians justify their presence in the gulf by flying the flag of the Soviet hydrographic office, and when they move close to U.S. ships they fly the two red balls and white diamond that identify a vessel engaged in underwater research. International rules of the road give such a ship the right of way, and the Russians use the rules liberally to push into American formations."[2]

The *Higbee*'s new assignment had three components: (1) Watch the "Cabbage" – that was the Navy's unimaginative secret code name for the *Gidrofon*; (2) keep "the skunk" – Navy parlance for an unfriendly vessel – from getting in the way of sea and air operations; and (3) occasionally harass the Russian crew, but don't hurt anyone, damage their ship, or otherwise create an international incident.

That last order was unwritten, of course, but understood.

When the *Gidrofon* was blocked from steering into the path of an aircraft carrier, it often still tried to stay close enough to monitor and report on aircraft launches.

"To launch and recover aircraft, the carriers needed a thirty-five knot wind blowing over their flight decks," Zalin Grant explained in his book.

"They were constantly steaming up and down [within the watery confines of Yankee Station], making frequent course changes in search of the right breeze."

When a carrier steamed into a strong headwind at modest speed, the *Gidrofon* could keep pace.

Otherwise, the trawler could drift along inside Yankee Station, wait for a carrier to approach, then turn into the giant ship's path and force it to change course. When that happened, the carrier often would lose enough headwinds that it would have to temporarily delay catapult launches or aircraft recoveries.

Sudden steering maneuvers also increased the risk that a carrier might collide with a screening destroyer while trying to get out of *Gidrofon*'s way. Thus, staying between the Cabbage and the carriers proved to be a challenging assignment on the *Higbee*'s bridge.

The Officer of the Deck, the Junior Officer of the Deck and the lookouts constantly had to stay on their toes. They had to watch for steering feints as well as real turns by the *Gidrofon*. At the same time, they also had to keep track of the nearest aircraft carrier's position and maneuvers. And they had to maintain safe distances from the other destroyers steaming along in the carrier's antisubmarine screen.

One day, the *Higbee* was given an extra job: Try to jam some of the *Gidrofon*'s radio receivers while a new airstrike was being mounted. I volunteered to help.

Three of us from the radio gang rigged a small UHF antenna on the ship's starboard side, just a few feet above the waterline. It was low enough that the *Higbee*'s hull and superstructure kept most of the jamming signal from being a problem up on the aircraft carrier's flight deck. But the remainder of the signal had a clear, line-of-sight path to the Gidrofon's UHF antennas.

At the appointed time, the carrier slowly turned into a headwind to start launching planes. We hooked the antenna to a low-powered UHF transmitter and locked down the push-to-talk microphone button. The *Gidrofon* tried to turn toward the carrier, but the *Higbee* sped up and slipped smoothly into place between the carrier's starboard side and the trawler. We were now uncomfortably close to the carrier's massive hull, maybe 150 feet away. We had to look straight up to see the flight deck.

At first, we just made random noises into the microphone. None of us knew any Russian. But when planes started being catapulted off the deck, I pulled out a harmonica I had bought weeks ago at the Yokosuka Navy Exchange. I started playing – badly – the few songs I knew, including "Turkey in the Straw," "Moon River" and "Old McDonald Had a Farm."

As I kept playing, the *Gidrofon* tried to maneuver away from our musical jam session. But the *Higbee* stayed with the trawler and gradually forced her to move farther and farther away from the launch operations.

The next day, we had one more irritation for the *Gidrofon* – a truly nasty little surprise.

Whenever the Russians saw something fall overboard from a Seventh Fleet ship, they would race toward the object, hoping to recover something useful to their spy operations. We always had to be careful when moving around on the ship's exterior. A classified message could blow out of someone's hand and sail out onto the water. The same worry applied when burn bags full of old radio messages had to be destroyed in an outdoor cooker on the ship's fantail. Any kind of accident could have provided the Russians with a small treasure trove of sensitive information.

One of the radiomen came up with the surprise, and the rest of us quickly agreed it would make the Soviet crew very unhappy. Even Chief Linn liked the scheme and cleared it with the communications officer.

First, we wadded up some blank teletype paper and stuffed it into a burn bag. Then several of us took turns using the bag to answer calls of nature. Finally, the bag was tightly sealed and carried outside toward the ship's fantail, where other bags were being burned.

The *Gidrofon* was noodling along at low speed, and the *Higbee* was maintaining its shadow. The radioman carrying the burn bag suddenly pretended to trip and fall, and the bag flew overboard. Several of us raced to the fantail rail and watched and pointed in mock horror as the bag hit the blue and bobbed away, riding high on the ship's wake.

The *Higbee* slowed and started to turn. An alert was sounded over the 1MC: "Now set the special recovery detail!"

Several Higbee sailors raced to the ship's motor whaleboat and made preparations to lower it toward the water.

The *Gidrofon* took the bait. It made a sharp turn and raced back to pick up the bag before we could get there. As the *Higbee* pulled up close, a Russian sailor hauled the bag aboard with a long pole and rushed it inside the trawler.

A few minutes later, as several of us watched from the fantail, the same sailor emerged almost on the run. He threw the bag as far as he could away from his ship and made angry gestures at us. We laughed until we cried and our sides hurt. For several days afterward, some of us periodically would pretend to open imaginary bags and growl: *"Look, comrade! Americanski shitski!"*

The surveillance and blocking duties continue for another week and eventually became tedious to almost everyone except the OOD, the JOOD, and the lookouts, who *had* to remain alert to the Russians' every move.

One day, the *Gidrofon* floated in dead-calm water about a mile off our port side, and we floated, too, gently swaying. Amid the boredom, a few *Higbee* crewmen began lobbying for "swim call." Some of the Russians, after all, now were sunbathing on their decks, according to the lookouts.

The rumor that we might get to swim soon grew so strong that a few sailors appeared on deck in swim trunks and shower shoes, ready to jump in. But the notion did not last long. In a matter of minutes, the *Higbee* was surrounded by a sudden swarm of tiger sharks – man-eaters. And more sharks could be seen deeper down in the clear, bluish water, rising toward the ship.

We had no idea what was attracting them, but someone on the bridge rightly decided that the sharks would be an immediate danger if any one of us fell into the sea. Meanwhile, we had to remain on our surveillance station near the *Gidrofon*.

At the weapons officer's command, the ship's small-arms locker was opened, and a few M1 rifles and .45 pistols were handed out. Under strict orders to shoot only toward the open ocean and well away from the *Gidrofon*, armed sailors quickly lined up along the starboard lifelines and opened fire. Sharks now were surfacing just a few yards away from the ship and showing their evil teeth. They made easy targets.

Each time a shark took a slug, it would slowly spiral down into the deep, trailing a dark stream of blood that looked a bit like smoke from a burning World War I biplane. Some of the other sharks would follow the blood trails down and tear into their own wounded. The water remained nearly still and amazingly clear. We could see sharks moving nearly 100 feet beneath us.

The killing continued, at and below the surface, for nearly thirty minutes. When we had used up our training quota of small arms ammunition, a few *Higbee* sailors started putting big pieces of raw meat on grappling hooks with chains attached. Soon, they were hauling man-sized sharks onto the main deck. The beasts flopped around, snapping their deadly jaws. A few sailors pulled out knives, cut open the sharks' bellies and let the beasts' stomachs and other organs spill out onto the steel deck. But the gross orgy ended when two of the ship's mess cooks came running to the scene.

"I said you could have *one* roast, not a whole week's meat rations!" one of them complained bitterly to some of the shark killers.

That night, the crew's mess offered just one main entrée: grilled cheese sandwiches.

The next day, we had beef stew, with more vegetables than usual and almost no meat in any scoop. Dinner was small hamburgers, limit one each. And, true to the mess cook's protest, the rest of the week passed with greatly reduced meat rations.

After a few more days of watching and harassing the *Gidrofon*, we turned the blocking assignment over to another destroyer, the *USS Wiltsie* (DD-716), and moved on to a new assignment.

But as the *Wiltsie* eased into position, we had one final, parting gift for the Soviet spy swabbies. The *Higbee* turned upwind from the trawler a few hundred yards and unleashed a thick, smelly smokescreen.

Black, oily smoke boiled and drifted straight toward the *Gidrofon*. We could see sailors on the trawler's deck pointing, then hurrying inside and slamming shut hatches that normally remained open in calm weather.

The nasty cloud completely engulfed the Russian ship and left it invisible for nearly a minute before gradually drifting away and dispersing.

While I was aboard the *Higbee*, this was the only attack we made on an "enemy" vessel.

The author, a few days from his 21st birthday, near the coastline of South Vietnam, just outside Da Nang harbor, March 8, 1965.
(Photographer unknown)

CHAPTER 17

Seeing Combat (*Seeing* It)

"To combat may be glorious, and success
Perhaps may crown us; but to fly is safe."

– William Cowper, *The Task,* Book II, *The Timepiece*

On March 1, 1965, the Seventh Fleet gained a new "Jehovah." Vice Admiral Paul Blackburn took command of a force that had now swelled to 125 ships, 650 aircraft and 65,000 personnel in Asia and the Pacific. His flagship was the guided missile light cruiser *USS Oklahoma City* (CLG-5).[1]

The *Higbee*'s first assignment from the new Jehovah turned out to be a big one. It would take us inside South Vietnamese territorial waters for the first time and leave us there much longer than we expected.

During the evening of March 4, we joined up with Task Group 76.7 less than 20 miles east of Da Nang. The ships in the task group included the amphibious cargo ship *USS Union* (AKA-106), the attack transport *USS Henrico* (APA-45), and the amphibious transport dock *USS Vancouver* (LPD-2). The task group was ferrying Marines and their combat gear. Two battalions of the 3rd Marine Division's 9th Marine Expeditionary Brigade (MEB) had been waiting off South Vietnam's coast since January.

For the next three days, the task group essentially went nowhere. We steamed a few miles northward, then gradually turned and steamed a few miles to the south. Then we turned around again and repeated the pattern.

As we did this, Washington and Saigon kept hashing over the details of when, where and *if* U.S. Marines would land in South Vietnam.

At 0430 in the morning of March 8, the *Higbee*'s crew was awakened by the sharp squeals of a boatswain's pipe played over the ship's 1MC. An urgent announcement quickly followed: *"Now general quarters! General quarters! All hands man your battle stations! This is* not *a drill! This is* not *a drill!"* Loud electronic *"Blang! Blang! Blang!"* tones quickly followed.

Still under the dim red sleeping lights, we scrambled into dungarees and hurried to our positions. A few minutes later, the Captain made a short speech over the 1MC, telling us that we were now leading a Marine battalion in for a beach landing near Da Nang and that we would be the gunfire support ship if they came under attack.

He warned that we could be in combat in a matter of minutes. Then he wished us godspeed and good luck and urged us all to do our jobs.

My job during general quarters, however, still was to do almost nothing except stay out of Chief Linn's sight. Despite my commendations, my battle station continued to be Radio II, the claustrophobic little transmitter compartment directly across the passageway from Radio Central.

Chief Linn never realized it, but keeping me banished me to Radio II gave me extra freedoms. I had not given up on music completely after I threw my guitar overboard a few months earlier. Indeed, I now had a cheap banjo hidden behind the "Greek," and I often kept a harmonica in my dungarees.

During long drills when I had nothing else to do, I could work on a few chords and songs. And, when the call to General Quarters was real, I could quietly slip out the compartment's door, go through the watertight hatch to the ASROC deck and get a quick glimpse of our situation and our surroundings.

I also could step across the passageway, knock on Radio Central's door, and ask for situation updates. No one in Radio Central took part in the ship's sound-powered phone network. But I did. So I could say "Mount 51 wants to know what's going on," when it wasn't true, and get some of my curiosity satisfied.

Once I had some sense of what we were up against, it was easier for me to hunker down and do my mundane task. Sometimes, I even felt grateful that I was a Navy radioman with access, knowledge and privileges that few other sailors enjoyed. I might not have had this, I realized, if I had become an Army, Air Force, Marine or Coast Guard radio operator.

Indeed, Frank Schley recalls how it felt to be completely in the dark aboard the *Higbee*:

"My remembrance of the morning of March 8, when they landed the Marines at Da Nang, was of walking up the main deck and all of a sudden realizing we were surrounded by more ships than I had ever seen. I remember looking around for 360 degrees and seeing ships as far as the horizon. All I could think was that they had declared war and had not told us. I immediately flashed to the movie 'No Man Is an Island' where a sailor, who is about to be shipped home for discharge, is trapped in the Philippines when the Japanese attack. I suffered an instant attack of depression, assuming my discharge would be delayed 'for the duration.'"

My gratefulness to have information, of course, was tempered always by my frequent bouts with seasickness – and with Chief Linn.

The Chief now was busy in Radio Central, hovering near the 21 MC intercom at the watch supervisor's desk as we led the Marines toward Da Nang. Against regulations, I also had a camera hidden in Radio II, to get to it quicker when I was called to the bridge to be the ship's photographer. So the Chief didn't see me when I slipped out of Radio II with my Pentax and stepped out onto the ASROC deck.

The rising sun was hidden by thick, low clouds. Yet, there was just enough soft, even light to take pictures.

Off the ship's port side, I could see a wall of stubby, steep, tree-covered mountains sliding by less than two miles away. They seemed at first to jut almost straight out of the water. But then I saw a thin stripe of white near their base. Breakers were surging onto a bright, narrow beach that was backed by trees.

One other sailor, someone I barely knew, also sneaked onto the ASROC deck with a camera and started snapping pictures. After a few moments, we traded cameras and took pictures of each other with Vietnam in the background. Then we hurried back to our battle stations.

As lookouts and gun spotters kept close watch on the mountains, the *Higbee* turned and swept into Da Nang harbor, leading the ships carrying the Marines and their support equipment.

When no opposing fire was observed, the *Higbee* turned and patrolled the area with both 5-inch/38 gun mounts manned and ready. Meanwhile, the initial waves of Marines stormed ashore at Red Beach, right at the center of the bowl-shaped harbor. They fully expected combat. Yet, as author Philip Caputo recounted in his book *A Rumor of War*, the Marines "were met, not by machine guns and shells, but by the Mayor of Da Nang and a crowd of schoolgirls."[2] The mayor made a speech; the schoolgirls put flowered wreaths over the Leathernecks' helmets.

The 9th Marine Expeditionary Brigade (9th MEB) represented the first U.S. battalion-sized forces sent to South Vietnam. A second battalion of 9th Marines arrived in Da Nang the same day by air. "Enemy snipers on nearby hills fired numerous rounds at the planes during the landings, but there were no injuries," Edward F. Murphy noted in his book *Semper Fi—Vietnam*."[3]

The Viet Cong were rumored to have at least one old French artillery piece hidden in the mountains near Da Nang harbor. At times, we were within its range, and we were warned to watch out for it. But no one on the *Higbee* reported any artillery or small arms fire during the landings.

As the Leathernecks charged ashore and spread out, their initial assignment was to create a defensive perimeter around the new U.S. airbase near Da Nang. The South Vietnamese port city was situated less than 100 miles south of the Demilitarized Zone that separated South and North Vietnam.

"Though they did not know it at this time," Murphy wrote, "the Marines of the 9th MEB had turned a corner in U.S. involvement in South Vietnam's internal conflict. Their arrival presaged a seven-year war that eventually called into question America's role in world affairs, divided America's citizenry like no other issue since the Civil War, and cost the lives of nearly 55,000 members of the U.S. armed forces."

For the next week, the *Higbee* slowly cruised around in the outer fringes of Da Nang harbor, patrolling back and forth between the Son Tra Peninsula on the north and Canton Rock on the south, in the shadow of Monkey Mountain. Sometimes, the ship briefly veered out into the South China Sea a few miles to take on fuel and supplies from other ships. But we quickly returned to harbor patrol. We had frequent views of Monkey Mountain and the Marble Mountains near Da Nang, as well as numerous green hills and mountains belonging to Annamite Range that runs parallel to the Vietnamese coast. It seemed like a strange and beautiful land, and most of us had little understanding of why we were there.

Initially, as we maneuvered close to the cloud-misted hills and mountains, we worried that Viet Cong snipers might try to take long potshots at us. But as the days dragged on at Readiness Condition Two, we soon just glanced at the haunting landscape and wished we could go ashore—or, better yet, go "home" to the gaudy and pleasurable safety of Yokosuka.

The Marines' arrival may have represented a major escalation of America's involvement in Vietnam's north vs. south civil war. Yet, on the ship, we barely felt it. And to those on beach, we were just a gray, distant shape with big guns.

During the morning on March 12, the *Higbee* finally was released from Da Nang harbor patrol. We were reassigned to chasing carriers with Task Group 77.7. The ship headed east, starting the five-hour journey out to Yankee Statopm. But, early in the afternoon, after taking on fuel, we received an IMMEDIATE message from the Commander of Task Force 77. We were now to go north at 25 knots to a position at 17 degrees north, 107.30 degrees east.

This was a point in the water about 20 miles east of the southern edge of North Vietnam and just 16 miles southeast of the North Vietnamese military facilities on Con Co ("Tiger") Island.

The *Higbee* was instructed to rendezvous there with the *USS Black* (DD-666), a 2,050-ton, Fletcher-class destroyer that had been built a year earlier than the *Higbee* and survived more combat in the Pacific during World War II. The *Black*'s latest WestPac tour, however, had started in late January, 1965, so the she was still considered a "rookie" ship within the current Tonkin Gulf and South China Sea hierarchy. The *Higbee*'s captain was given tactical command of the *Black* and also became Commander of Task Group 71.1 (CTG 71.1).

The two-ship task group met up near sunset and bobbed about 500 yards apart as the *Higbee*'s motor whaleboat transported one officer to the *Black* to brief her captain and officers on the new mission. Afterward, the two ships split up in darkness, turned off all running and navigation lights, and began using their SPS-10 surface-search radars. We were now trying try to catch North Vietnamese trawlers or fishing boats running south past the DMZ.

About three hours later, the *Higbee* turned on its navigation lights again and joined up with two other ships, the guided-missile destroyer *USS Buchanan* (DDG-14) and the Gearing Class destroyer *USS Chevalier* (DD-805). These two ships constituted their own task unit, TU 70.8.7, a designation assigned to search-and-rescue (SAR) training missions in the South China Sea and Tonkin Gulf. The *Buchanan*'s captain was the task unit's commander. However, the Commander of Destroyer Squadron 15 (COMDESRON 15) also was aboard the *Buchanan*, so the *Higbee* "reported for duty" and temporarily became part of yet another organization, Task Group 77.8.

We weren't trapping any gun runners. But we were very efficiently building temporary new bureaucracies at sea.

The four ships did little overnight except patrol along the 17th parallel, each staying within their own small areas, while their powerful radars swept the horizon, looking for southbound vessels that might suddenly turn and head for South Vietnam's coastline.

The next day, March 13, the *Higbee*'s Combat Information Center's air-search radar picked up swarms of aircraft converging on Tiger Island, about 20 miles off the North Vietnamese coast. We didn't know it yet, but this was the second bombing mission of a new operation known as *Rolling Thunder*.

The *Higbee*'s Captain sent an IMMEDIATE message, classified SECRET, to COMSEVENTHFLT, stating that he was moving the *Higbee* closer to Tiger Island to be in position in case pilots needed rescue. The *Higbee* soon reached a point about three miles off the island just as black, propeller-driven A-1H Skyraiders and silvery U.S. Air Force F-100D Super Sabre jets swooped down and attacked radar installations and weapons emplacements. The Air Force jets looked strangely out of place over the ocean.

Aboard the *Higbee*, we were called to battle stations. But some of us were able to watch a few minutes of the action. Bombs were falling, flashing, booming and throwing up mushroom clouds of smoke as plane after plane zoomed across the island. We were now close enough that Tiger Island's shore batteries could have fired at us. But they were too busy trying to survive the big air raid.

None of the attacking planes was shot down, and once they formed up again and flew away, we secured from general quarters and left the area. We had been the only U.S. Navy ship anywhere close to Tiger Island and represented the best rescue hope for any pilot who might have had to bail out. Yet as we steamed south, a new IMMEDIATE message, classified SECRET, arrived from ComSeventhFleet. It did *not* praise the skipper's initiative. Instead, it chewed him out for compromising a TOP SECRET mission with a SECRET message that had revealed the attack to other ships in the fleet.

I carried the message to the Captain and tried to discern the thoughts behind his steely eyes and calm expression as he read it. He just grimaced slightly, initialed it, and handed it off to the Executive Officer and Officer of the Deck.

Their head shakes and expressions as they read it, however, seemed to say: "What the hell kind of war *is* this?"

The Captain sent no reply to ComSeventhFleet except a basic acknowledgement that the ass-chewing had been received. And the *Higbee* returned to its assigned patrol station along the 17th parallel.

The next day, March 15, the *Higbee*'s and *Black*'s joint mission suddenly changed to SAR OPS (search and rescue operations) again. And again we headed north into sensitive waters. A lone A-1H Skyraider from the *Ranger* had crashed into the sea about 60 miles off the southern coast of North Vietnam and about 50 miles from China's militarily sensitive Hainan Island. Apparently, it had been on some kind of patrol, but there was no mention that it might have been shot down.

From the *Higbee*'s deck log: *1923 Stationed recovery detail. 1952. Commenced expanding square search, clockwise rotation, search axis 290°. Search speed 15 kts. Track spacing 1000 yds.* Black *conducting like search independently, axis 335°.*

As the search continued, the flap over the "compromised" attack faded. And a little more information about the Tiger Island raid appeared in the encrypted fleet broadcasts. But it remained very much a hush-hush operation.

Historical accounts released years later offered only a few more details. Some 20 to 24 South Vietnamese Air Force A-1H Skyraiders had made the main assault, attacking barracks and depots on Tiger Island, with Air Marshal Nguyen Cao Ky again reportedly leading his propeller-driven "Divine Wind" squadron. (Curiously, Ky makes no mention of the attack in his autobiography, *Buddha's Child.*) Meanwhile, the U.S. Air Force F-100Ds provided flak suppression and other support with their 20mm cannons and bombs.

Apparently, no one had bothered to plan for the possibility that South Vietnamese or U.S. Air Force pilots might get shot down over the shark-infested waters that surrounded Tiger Island.

The *Higbee* was the only ship close to the scene, and clearly, we were *not* supposed to be there.

On March 17, the search for the lost Skyraider pilot was ended. The ocean had given up not a single clue to his fate.

The *Higbee* and *Black* now were sent south at 25 knots to a new patrol area along the central coast of South Vietnam. Once again, we would be watching for North Vietnamese boats attempting to smuggle guns and ammunition into South Vietnam.

The next morning, the *Higbee* anchored off the South Vietnamese city of Qui Nhon, not far from another Gearing Class destroyer, the *USS Buck* (DD-761). A few minutes later, the Commander of Destroyer Division 72 (COMDESDIV 72) came over by boat from the *Buck* and had new orders for the *Higbee*. We were about to make a bit of military history. We would initiate and lead the new *Operation Market Time* coastal patrols.

We didn't know it yet, but our patrols quickly would demonstrate the limitations of using destroyers to try to block North Vietnam from smuggling supplies and re-enforcements to the Viet Cong.

Small fishing craft and other vessels could evade radar detection and pursuit simply by hugging the shallow waters along the long coastline and blending in with the many other boats. Then they could move inland via South Vietnam's numerous rivers.

These findings soon would help draw the U.S. Coast Guard and its shallow-draft boats into Vietnam and also lead to a major expansion of the U.S. Navy's fledgling riverine forces.

In the meantime, I had other matters on my mind. I was still trying to find any way possible, short of desertion or death, to get off the *Higbee* and away from Chief Linn and seasickness.

Salvation seemed to arrive quite suddenly while we were anchored at Qui Nhon. A small speedboat flying a big U.S. flag zipped up and stopped next to us. It had twin outboard engines and an M60 machine gun mounted on a pole.

It also had vicious shark's teeth painted on its bow, reminiscent of the old P-40 fighter planes that the Flying Tigers had flown in China in World War II.

An officer in combat fatigues disembarked from the boat and came aboard to join the hush-hush meeting with COMDESDIV 72.

The two sailors who remained aboard the speedboat wore a curious mixture of military and civilian clothing and looked very relaxed with their lives. They seemed to be living by their own set of rules.

Indeed, as Admiral Elmo R. Zumwalt would note in later years: "There is no accepted doctrine on the subject...[y]ou have to make up riverine warfare as you go along."[4]

As I stared at the speedboat's crew, thoughts and images flashed through my mind: *Rivers! Lakes! Canals! Flat water!* And: *Radios! They use radios on those boats!*

I rushed into Radio Central, found a special-request form (a "chit"), and filled it out, asking for immediate transfer to the Navy's riverine forces.

I stressed my expertise with radios, the small boats' constant need for efficient communications, and my chronic seasickness.

And, I wouldn't get seasick at all on inland waters, I solemnly promised. Therefore, I could make a much greater contribution to the war effort.

To my surprise, the *Higbee*'s communications officer and operations officer both approved the transfer a few hours later. But the executive officer and the Captain quickly said no.

"Dunn is a good radio operator needed aboard the *Higbee*," the XO's rejection stated.

One stipulation was added, however. I *might* be considered for transfer to the riverine forces *if* I was willing to "ship over" – reenlist for another four years of active duty.

I pulled my short-timer's sheet from my pocket. Fewer than 90 days now remained in my enlistment. I folded up the riverine chit and quietly put it away.

I didn't appreciate it at the time, but being a short-timer likely saved my life.

When the riverine guys got into combat, it often involved Viet Cong guerillas or North Vietnamese troops trying to ambush them from stream banks.

And the intense fire fights frequently played out at very close range.

As John Forbes and Robert Williams noted in their 1987 book *Riverine Force*: "...[T]he US Navy in the mid-1960s was ill-prepared for small-scale small-boat operations in brown waters. But once these operations started, it took just three years—from the spring of 1965 to the fall of 1968—for the Navy to penetrate the furthest reaches of the narrow twisted waterways of South Vietnam."[5]

South Vietnam's inland waters *looked* tranquil and inviting. In reality, however, they were no place at all for a Reservist who had fired weapons at the Pacific Ocean – and never missed.

A fishing junk sails along the South Vietnam coastline near Da Nang, March, 1965. *(Photo by Si Dunn)*

CHAPTER 18

Pirates of the Tonkin Gulf

Operation Market Time had grown out of something that a very alert U.S. Army helicopter pilot spotted while flying a medivac mission near Vung Ro Bay on South Vietnam's north-central coast on March 3, 1965.

Lieutenant James S. Bowers had noticed that a small, tree-covered island seemed to be moving. When he flew lower to investigate, he discovered that the "island" actually was a 130-foot steel-hulled trawler camouflaged with trees in big pots on its decks. Lt. Bowers radioed a U.S. Navy coastal adviser, and the South Vietnamese air force soon attacked the trawler and caused it to roll onto its side near its small, disguised dock.[1]

That night, North Vietnamese engineers secretly were dispatched from somewhere inland. They tried to destroy the damaged trawler with a ton of high explosives. But their big charge merely blew the damaged vessel in two.

The next morning, South Vietnamese troops and U.S. Special Forces soldiers fought and killed some of the surviving crewmen and local guerillas near the beach. Then they investigated the wreckage and found unambiguous proof. North Vietnam was using the sea to smuggle supplies and weapons, including 75mm howitzers and AK-47 semiautomatic rifles, to its units and to Viet Cong guerillas operating in South Vietnam. The supplies were being brought in at night and unloaded at secret docks hidden among a number of small coves and inlets such as Vung Ro.

"The Vung Ro Incident confirmed the sea infiltration of weapons and supplies from North Vietnam," R.L. Shreadley noted in his book, *From the Rivers to the Sea: The U.S. Navy in Vietnam.* Indeed, he pointed out, this had been the destroyed trawler's 23rd trip smuggling war supplies to South Vietnam.[2]

As Lt. Cmdr. Thomas J. Cutler later recounted in his book *Brown Water, Black Berets*: "Á preliminary survey [of the Vung Ro trawler] revealed one million rounds of small-arms ammunition, more than 1,000 stick grenades, 500 pounds of TNT in prepared charges, 2,000 rounds of 82-mm mortar ammunition, 500 antitank grenades, 1,500 rounds of recoilless rifle ammunition, more than 3,600 rifles and submachine guns, and 500 pounds of medical supplies."[3]

The contraband was from several Eastern-bloc countries and China, and the dead crewmen had documents identifying them as members of North Vietnamese army and navy units.

Soon after the trawler's contents were tallied, MACV's Gen. William C. Westmoreland contacted the U.S. Navy's top brass for Pacific operations. He asked them to send officers to Saigon to help plan an operation that could counter North Vietnam's use of the sea as an infiltration and resupply route. The planners met in Saigon for about a week and created a new naval patrol scheme. A number of U.S. vessels would be stationed at the 17th parallel (the 1954 cease-fire line) and southward along the South Vietnam coastline, and they would be supported by long-range patrol planes. The ships and planes would watch for two types of craft: (1) steel-hulled North Vietnamese trawlers staying far out in the South China Sea, then making perpendicular dashes to the South Vietnamese coast; and (2) fishing junks that would hug the coastline and try to blend in with the local fishing craft as they slowly made their way southward from North Vietnam.

Vietnam's coastal waters were alive with fishing boats, especially a type known as *thuyền buồm đánh cá*. This small sailing craft was favored by hundreds of net fishermen on both sides of Vietnam's DMZ. Literally translated, the name means "boat boat hit fish," according to Gary Dale Cearley, a U.S. Navy veteran who became a Thailand-based international logistics and public relations specialist. Cearley, who has worked in Hanoi, Ho Chi Minh City (formerly Saigon) and other parts of Southeast Asia, studied Vietnamese (northern and southern dialects) at the Defense Language Institute.

"*Thuyền* and *buồm* are both words for 'boat,'" he explained. "*Thuyền* generally means 'a paddle boat' and is more generically used as the word 'boat' in southern Vietnam. *Buồm* can be either a round, reed basket boat that is tarred (in the southern language) or, in the northern language, it can mean the same as *thuyền*. Used together, they often mean 'a small sail boat' and *đánh cá* is literally "to hit fish," but generally means 'fishing with a net.'"[4]

To find and investigate suspicious trawlers and *thuyền buồm đánh cá*, the Navy created Task Group 71.1, with the *Higbee* in the lead.

The new patrol plan included one politically sensitive provision that would prove frustrating over the next two months:

"Authorization from the South Vietnamese government was required to allow the U.S. units to 'stop, board, search, and, if necessary, capture and/or destroy any hostile suspicious craft or vessel found within [its] territorial and contiguous zone waters.'"[5]

The problem for the two ships in the new task force was that we had been given no instructions on *how* to obtain this authorization. And we suddenly needed it on the second night of the patrol.

Once again, the *Higbee*'s SPS-10 radar picked up some sea targets that appeared to be converging in the ink-dark night. They were about 15 miles away, a half hour's steaming time if we went to battle stations and flank speed.

This time, the Combat Information Center and the bridge were worried that a North Vietnamese trawler was unloading guns, ammunition and maybe soldiers into several small fishing boats that could smuggle them ashore somewhere south of the Demilitarized Zone.

The phosphorescent radar-screen images were moving just a few miles outside South Vietnam's territorial sea limits. We could not attack in international waters unless we were attacked first. So we needed permission to pursue and engage, especially if any of the targets tried to run toward the coast.

I was the watch section leader on duty in the radio shack. The Captain ordered us to try to communicate with Saigon, just a few hundred miles away.

We decided to call Gen. William Westmoreland's headquarters first. Surely the Military Assistance Command Vietnam (MACV) had radio operators monitoring specific channels, and surely they could communicate with the appropriate South Vietnamese authorities.

J.L. Davis held open a book listing American military radio frequencies used in South Vietnam, and I put the 500-watt AN/URC-32 transceiver into single-sideband voice mode, set a few knobs and dials, and pressed the handset's push-to-talk button.

"MAC-Vee, this is Truck, over." I had no idea what tactical call sign MACV headquarters used. But surely, an Army radio operator would recognize that somebody was trying to reach MACV.

No response. I tried again and again. Each time, I heard only static in the handset.

"What's the secondary frequency?" I asked Davis. He read off some numbers in the 8 MHz range. I set them and worked the handset again.

"MAC-Vee, MAC-Vee, this is Truck, Truck, over."

Nothing.

I tried every voice frequency listed for MACV. No response.

I asked Davis for the frequencies designated for Morse code. I changed the AN/URC-32 over to CW mode and started keying. *"Dah-dah, di-dah, dah-di-dah-dit..."* I sent "MACV DE NHLL K" ("MACV this is *USS Higbee*, please respond.") I had no idea what CW call sign, if any, had been assigned to Gen. Westmoreland's MACV. But I had to use *something*.

Unfortunately, the letters "MACV" also fell within the "MAA-MZZ" call sign groups assigned by international treaty to the United Kingdom and Northern Ireland. My CW transmission could have been interpreted as an attempt to contact a British tramp steamer on frequencies that it might never have monitored.

The 21MC came to life above the watch supervisor's desk. "Radio, bridge. Has Dunn made contact yet?"

Davis ran over to the squawk box and pressed the push-to-talk lever.

"Bridge, radio. Negative, sir. He's still trying."

"Tell him to hurry!"

"Radio, aye!"

I looked at the list of military frequencies and found a few for the South Vietnamese Navy. We were now down to the longest of long shots. I spoke no Vietnamese and no French, and no one else on the ship did, either, as far as I knew. It would have to be Morse code or nothing.

Again, I had no idea what radio call signs the South Vietnamese Navy recognized. So I just took a wild guess. "SVN DE NHLL K." Unfortunately, the letters "SVN" also fell within the "SVA-SZZ" radio call signs assigned by international treaty to Greece. My call to the South Vietnamese Navy also could have been interpreted as a call to a Greek navy shore station. Working as quickly as I could, I tried every primary and secondary frequency on the list.

No go.

At almost any time on a well-disciplined Navy radio net, I could reach halfway around the world, and sometimes farther, with the AN/URC-32. Yet now, I couldn't communicate with any of the U.S. Army and South Vietnamese Navy stations that were within a radius of a few hundred miles. Indeed, some of the stations were coastal and just a few miles away. This didn't give me a good feeling about the future of our strange new war.

The radar contacts soon were lost in the coastal clutter, and the *Higbee* resumed patrol.

Years later, I would find some possible explanations for my frustration, in the book *Riverine Force* by John Forbes and Robert Williams:

"Where coastal operations were concerned the [American-South Vietnamese communications] situation was made even more complex by the fact that the Vietnamese Navy had two different commands involved: the Sea Force and the former junk militia, the Coastal Force. US responsibilities were also split between the Saigon-based Military Assistance Command Vietnam, which concerned itself directly with operational matters; the Naval Advisory Group, which administered the advisory program; and the Pacific Fleet, whose commander in chief was based in Honolulu."[5]

So basically, no one was listening to my calls. Or if anyone heard them, they had no idea what to do with them.

On March 20, 1965, two Navy minesweepers, the *USS Pivot* (MSO 463) and *USS Pluck* (MSO 464), joined the fledgling patrol efforts. These both were Aggressive class, non-magnetic ocean minesweepers built in the 1950s. Their ten-foots drafts enabled them to work closer to coastlines and in harbors and rivers shallower than a destroyer could negotiate. The *Higbee*'s draft was more than 14 feet.

The expanded patrol was designated *Operation Market Time* on March 24, 1965, my 21st birthday. Eventually, it would evolve into a massive effort employing dozens of ships, as well as long-range patrol planes.

We were now operating just a few miles off the coast in an area roughly 100 mile long. It ranged from Vung Ro southward past Nha Trang and Cam Rahn Bay to An Phoc. Saigon was a hundred miles or so south, in an area assigned to other *Market Time* ships.

The air support soon included carrier-based A-1H Skyraiders, twin-engine SP-2H Neptune reconnaissance planes from bases in South Vietnam, and sleek, new four-engine P-3 Orion long-range patrol planes zooming in from the Philippines.

But the necessity to get permission from the South Vietnamese government – and the inability to establish radio communications with MACV – left us unable to do much except steam up and down the coastline, stare at the hundreds of fishing boats and trawlers, and wonder if any of them were North Vietnamese.

As the *Market Time* patrols continued, we quickly discovered the limits of trying to use destroyers as patrol craft on rivers, even rivers deep enough and wide enough to handle seagoing freighters.

One afternoon as we slowly moved up the Cai River near the coastal city of Nha Trang, I helped show a few South Vietnamese naval officers how to use an AN/PRC-10 field radio. This was a relatively light (26-pound) backpack VHF transceiver that I wished I had had during landing party training back on San Clemente Island. The Korean War-era radio had a maximum range of three to 12 miles, depending on terrain. It had only recently been issued to the *Higbee*.

At one point, as I demonstrated how to tune the radio, I happened across a female voice speaking rapidly in Vietnamese. The signal was very strong; clearly, she was close by. I turned up the volume so the students could listen.

The South Vietnamese sailors quickly looked grim, and one of them who spoke a little English pointed at the radio. "VC," he said. "Viet Cong."

"Where?" I asked, ducking down.

He pointed to the nearest river bank, less than 100 yards away. "Maybe there."

A *Higbee* officer observing the training quickly ended the session and led the South Vietnamese officers on a quick walk to the bridge.

I gave the AN/PRC-10 to one of the ship's electronic technicians for storage and went back into Radio Central.

Very soon, the ship slowed, reversed its engines and began backing up. There was not enough room to easily turn around in the river.

Later, as I watched from the ASROC deck, we moved, backwards, into Nha Trang's harbor and sent the South Vietnamese trainees ashore. Then we turned around and steamed back out into the South China Sea, where the ship was much more at home.

During dinner on the mess decks that evening, a couple of *Higbee* crewmen claimed they had heard pops of small-arms fire coming from the shore as the ship was backing up. But, aside from one questionable dent on a metal box on the ASROC deck, nothing and no one had been hit. It was the *Higbee*'s final foray up a river while I was aboard.

We saw few tangible results from the ship's two-week assignment as *Market Time*'s task group commander. At one point, we rendezvoused with another minesweeper, and this one brought us a South Vietnamese naval officer and an enlisted man, both armed.

Now, out in the coastal waters, fishing-boat families stared up at us from their tiny craft while we stared down from the decks of our mighty warship and a *Higbee* crewman stood ready at a .30-caliber machine gun. The South Vietnamese sailors boarded the boats from our motor whaleboat and searched everywhere for guns and ammunition.

Each time, they found nothing but fish.

Then the destroyer sped up to check out new radar targets. But we had to maneuver carefully so we would not swamp any of the dozens of *thuyền buồm đánh cá* or run afoul of their many nets.

"For the most part," Craig L. Symonds wrote in his book, *The Naval Institute Historical Atlas of the U.S. Navy*, "duty on MARKET TIME was boring routine patrol, much of it conducted in oppressive heat."[6]

He added: "This assignment was as difficult and tedious as a full coastal blockade, but even more frustrating, for *this* [his emphasis] blockade was selective, and it was often very difficult to tell friend from foe among the hundreds of wooden junks trading and fishing along the South Vietnamese coast."

Symonds further noted: "By April 1965 the Navy had committed a dozen destroyers, destroyer escorts and ocean minesweepers, which patrolled the Tonkin Gulf near the seventeenth parallel. But the Navy lacked sufficient shallow-draft vessels for the important inshore work."

The Navy turned to the U.S. Coast Guard for help. The Coast Guard had a number of small, steel-hulled cutters equipped so that one man could operate all steering, engine control and communication functions, while other personnel manned machine guns and other weapons.

For all of its inefficiencies, the rapid deployment of Navy ships and aircraft and shallow-draft patrol boats along the South Vietnam coastline did have a dramatic impact north of the DMZ, according to Mark Moyar in his book *Triumph Forsaken: The Vietnam War, 1954-1965*:

"Market Time swiftly brought Hanoi's infiltration operations to ruin as if the stopper had been pulled and all of South Vietnam's coastal waters had gone down the drain. One Vietnamese Communist account explained, 'On many voyages our ships were blocked by enemy warships and forced to turn back. A number of ships managed to penetrate the enemy's outer patrol perimeter, but they ran into enemy naval vessels close to shore.'"[7]

However, Moyar added, "The full effects of Market Time would not be felt on the battlefield until much later, for the North Vietnamese had already stockpiled large quantities of weapons and ammunition in the South by February 1965."

By keeping most of the Seventh Fleet steaming in squares and circles a hundred miles out in the South China Sea and Tonkin Gulf prior to *Market Time*, America essentially had left South Vietnam's coastline unprotected and unpatrolled until it was too late. But we didn't know that yet. We were in the midst of more prosaic aspects of the Vietnam War.

For example, the *Higbee*'s air conditioning could not keep pace with coastal South Vietnam's tropic heat and humidity. The sun bore down relentlessly all day on the gray-painted steel. Then, after nightfall, the stored heat radiated into the sleeping compartments. Officers and crewmen alike slept fitfully, soaked in clammy sweat.

One night, I fell asleep, exhausted after an eve watch, and dreamed that I was slowly baking to death in my rack. I woke up an hour later, hot and drenched.

There was no movement of air, no way to get cool. And the compartment was nearly full of other sailors tossing, turning, groaning in their sleep and cursing the heat when it woke them up. I was desperate for sleep; I would have to be back in the radio room in about five hours.

Finally, after another miserable hour, I made a choice completely against regulations. I slipped out of my rack, rolled my dungarees, shirt and shoes into a bundle and left the Operations compartment in my underwear and shower shoes. Broadway was empty and illuminated with red lights. It was now after 2 a.m.

At mid-ship, both the port and starboard doors had been left open, another violation of regulations and a mostly futile gesture to let in some cooler night air. I carried my bundle outside the starboard door and climbed up the ladder to the ASROC deck.

The ship was moving ahead at fewer than 10 knots, slow enough to dodge fishing boats yet just barely fast enough to generate a discernible breeze. On the ASROC deck, I put my bundle down outside the red warning circle and refashioned my pants and shirts into a pillow. I lay down on the metal and relished the slight movement of air across my sweaty face, chest and legs.

We were just a few miles off the coast. There was no moon, but a few tiny dots of light were scattered across mountains that appeared to rise almost vertically from the beach. As I looked up, I could see a small red running light barely giving visibility to the SPS-10 radar antenna spinning restlessly in the dark. Above the antenna, however, was a rarity: clear sky – and what seemed to be almost every speck of the visible universe. With air moving across my face and the full majesty of the Milky Way sparkling in my eyes, I soon fell asleep. And it seemed that I slept forever, drifting smoothly through space. But suddenly, I felt something nudge my shoulder: a shoe. I opened my eyes.

The stars now were fading back into the sky glow, and the armed guard from the ASROC firing shack was standing over me. "Better get up now," he said. "Reveille in five minutes." I got up, put on my uniform and shoes just a few feet from a nuclear warhead, and went below to shower, shave and get breakfast.

My 21st birthday came and went while we patrolled uneventfully among the fishing boats, then anchored again off Nha Trang. New orders for the ship arrived late that afternoon, and we got underway again, bound at once for our home port. We had not seen Yokosuka since January 31. But just as we headed out of the South China Sea, we had to turn around and join the destroyer screen for the *USS Hancock*. Unhappily, we were back chasing bird farms again and conducting drills at sea. It seemed as if this pattern would never end.

Three days later, our orders were changed once again, and we resumed steaming toward our distant home port. I hoped, once we reached Japan, that we would stay docked long enough for me to reach the end of my enlistment. My focus increasingly was just on getting out of the Navy and going home.

As early as possible each morning, I pulled my short-timer's sheet from my shirt pocket and marked off that day. If I had the mid-watch, I scratched out the coming day as soon as the clock passed midnight. My greatest fear remained that something new and vicious would happen in the Tonkin Gulf or somewhere in Vietnam, and my enlistment suddenly would be extended for many months or even for the duration of a declared war.

When the *Higbee* docked at Yokosuka Naval Station on April 4, 1965, I had about ten weeks left in my active-duty obligation. If my "early cut" for college came through, I could be packing my sea bag in under six weeks.

Each time I had the in-port radio watch, I spent more and more time carefully pouring over all of the incoming radio traffic, even reading routine messages intended for ships far outside the South China Sea and Tonkin Gulf. I listened to news broadcasts from the Voice of America, the BBC and Radio Australia. I kept searching for any kind of news that affected my plans to go home.

There were now persistent rumors that President Johnson might extend all military enlistments, including Reservists. One more big attack by the Viet Cong or some kind of dramatic action by the North Vietnamese might be enough to trigger a formal war declaration, and I would be stuck aboard the *Higbee* for the duration.

"Or," as one of my shipmates, a Navy regular, liked to remind me with a smirk, "until you get killed."

On April 8, 1965, one of the *Higbee*'s radio-teletype machines again sounded the dreaded sound I hadn't heard since the first weeks after the Tonkin Gulf incidents.

Ding! Ding! Ding! Ding!

A FLASH message was coming in. Several U.S. Navy jets and Chinese jets had exchanged fire near Hainan Island. My spirits fell. I figured the Chinese now would openly side with North Vietnam, and a wider war was just beginning.

To my immense relief, however, nothing substantial happened over the next few days. The Chinese issued some stern warnings and increased their construction aid to northern North Vietnam. Chinese air and naval forces were instructed to attack *if* U.S. planes intruded into China's air space or if U.S. ships moved inside the 12-mile limit.

Over the next two weeks, it seemed as if I might get my wish to stay in port until my discharge. But new orders for the *Higbee* arrived on April 19. We were being sent back to Yankee Station by way of Subic Bay. I became deeply depressed as we left port, and I prepared for more days of seasickness. But I was an old hand now – if not exactly an old salt. I knew how to do my duty as a shipboard radio operator.

The trip south once again included gunnery drills, man overboard drills, personnel inspections and busy radio operations. And once again, during the first three days, I repeatedly threw up my guts and begged to die.

On April 23, the *Higbee* was detached from other duties in the South China Sea and sent north into the Tonkin Gulf, this time on "special operations." Within two days, the ship was patrolling about 70 miles off the North Vietnamese coastline, in the vicinity of Ha Tinh and Dong Hoi. We were once again searching for North Vietnamese boats trying to sneak south. But now we were much more vulnerable to MiG attacks.

If MiG pilots decided to go "feet wet" and fly out into the Tonkin Gulf, they would be on us in minutes. Indeed, that was part of the Navy's bigger plan. We were being used as MiG bait – for a Terrier-equipped guided missile cruiser and a guided missile destroyer steaming just over the horizon.

During the next few days, we gradually moved the patrol zone south, closer to the Demilitarized Zone. The end of my enlistment now was growing very close, and I wondered how much longer I could stand the wait and the worry, as well as the apprehension that we might be attacked.

One shot, one MiG, one missile, one torpedo could change everything.

Above: A trawler hugs the South Vietnam coastline near Da Nang, heading north as the *Higbee* keeps watch during Operation Market Time, March, 1965.

Below: Friends or foes? Small fishing boats from North Vietnam rarely had trouble blending in with South Vietnamese fishing vessels as they smuggled supplies and personnel down the coastline.

(Photos by Si Dunn)

CHAPTER 19

Breakaway

By the end of April, 1965, I had a severe case of "tight jaws." Every change or pause in the clacking rhythms of the radio teletype machines seemed ominous and caused me to tense up and clench and grind my teeth until my jaws ached. Also, I remained moody and convinced that some new event or crisis was about to extend my enlistment. It might be something that happened in the Tonkin Gulf, the Formosa Strait, the Middle East, or Moscow. I feared constantly now that *something somewhere* was about to go wrong, and I would be stuck on the *Higbee* forever.

Off duty, I began spending more of my limited free time standing at the portside railing on the ASROC deck, staring at the horizon. Sometimes I watched a carrier launch or recover planes. Or I watched freighters as they glided past us a few thousand yards away.

At times, the universe seemed to be nothing but dome of pale blue sky and a vast, empty disk of endless seawater stretching outward in all directions from where I stood.

When there was nothing else to watch—nothing whatsoever distracting in the water or sky – I studied some of the movements up on the port wing of the bridge. The port lookout kept scanning the horizon – back and back, back and forth—with his binoculars. Occasionally, the officer of the deck, the executive officer or the captain would step out onto the wing next to the lookout and peer at something with their binoculars.

Whenever this happened, I watched them closely, trying to spot any clues that something new was about to happen—something, of course, that might threaten the end of my enlistment.

The "something new," however, almost always turned out to be just another rusty freighter on its way to or from Haiphong, Hong Kong, Macao or some port on the south coast of China. Once the "target" was identified, the officer would move back inside the bridge, and the lookout would continue scanning the portside horizon until the end of his watch.

Ennui was pervasive when nothing was happening at sea. Some sailors found comfort and solace in the boredom. And some seemed to give it no thought at all. I fought it every way I could. Yet there were few ways on a destroyer to make boredom go away. I could not read a book without getting seasick.

I had now sold my banjo to another sailor. I had nothing new to say in letters to my parents. And I couldn't go into Radio Central and play with a shortwave receiver while I was off watch, because there was nothing to hear except broadcasts in Chinese, Vietnamese, Thai and other languages I could not comprehend.

Also, Chief Linn would make me leave his sight, or he would assign me extra POMSEE duty.

Mostly, when I was off duty and not asleep, I roamed around the ship or just leaned against railings and stared at the ever-changing shapes of the waves. I kept trying to imagine what the world would be like once I could again stand on firm ground and not worry about having to leave it again.

Sometimes, I had vague reveries about what might happen once I returned to distant Little Rock, then tiny Conway and the campus of Arkansas State Teachers College. But most of my thoughts stayed focused mainly toward the moment when I could put my uniforms back in my sea bag, sleep normal hours and just be a civilian again. *A once and former sailor.*

One afternoon at the end of April, I felt deeply depressed as I waited to begin my next eve watch. Instead of standing at the railing as I usually did, this time I sat down in the boxy shadow of the ASROC launchers and slumped against the safety lines. Someone, perhaps the guard in the ASROC launching station, or a shipmate up on the signal bridge, noticed my changed demeanor.

Within minutes, I sensed someone suddenly and quietly moving up beside me. I looked slightly to my right and saw brown shoes and khaki trousers. A chief, maybe. Or an officer. I glanced up—and quickly stood up, snapped to attention and saluted the Captain.

He returned the salute. "At ease, Dunn." He leaned slightly against the railing and gestured for me to relax. For a few moments, we quietly shared a view of the bright sky and blue water.

"Dunn," he said finally, almost like a father addressing an unhappy son, "I know you haven't enjoyed being at sea. I know you've had a hard time with sea sickness. But you are a very good radioman, one of the best I've seen. There are shore billets. The Navy needs smart men like you."

I started to speak. The Captain held up a hand and stopped me. "I already know you aren't going to do it," he said, smiling. "But I still hope you will give some serious thought to re-enlisting. I'm not doing my job if I don't at least *try* to get you to stay in."

I stifled a nervous chuckle and thanked the Captain. I told him I was honored to serve in his crew. It was not a lie. But, I added, I had put in many requests for transfer to shore duty, and none of them had made it past the executive officer.

"I know," he replied, trying to look serious but not quite hiding a grin. "You kept showing us you can do a good job, even under the worst circumstances. So, there was no way we could let you go."

"Yes, sir," I answered, trying to indicate that I understood. *The needs of the Navy and the ship came first.*

After a few moments more, he straightened up at the railing. "Well, good luck with college, Dunn." As I straightened up, ready to salute, he stuck out his hand and shook mine, a civility I hadn't experienced in many months.

I came to attention again, and we exchanged salutes. "Thank you, Captain!" I said. He smiled, left the ASROC deck and headed back toward the bridge.

I grinned to myself, greatly relieved. If the Captain knew I was leaving, then I really was about to get out, barring any extension of enlistments or war declarations.

Just as soon as I could talk my way off the ship, I was leaving. Most definitely and most assuredly now, I was ready to exit the Tonkin Gulf and South China Sea and just go *home*. Surely we would head for a port soon, so I could heft my sea bag and stroll down the gangplank one last time.

REPORT OF ENLISTED PERFORMANCE EVALUATION

Period of Report: Nov 64 to 4 May 65

Description of Assigned Tasks

Radio Control Watch Supervisor. Responsible for proper handling of traffic. He has direct supervision of personnel on watch and the equipment in use.

Evaluation of Performance

Dunn requires limited supervision because he tends to be careless at times. Needs experience. His knowledge of radio equipment of radio equipment and usage is excellent. Recommended for reenlistment.

Reason for Reporting

SEPARATION

But the *Higbee* remained at sea on special operations, and, as the first few days of May dragged by, it looked as if I really would *not* get off the ship in time to enroll for the first summer semester at Arkansas State Teachers College. *Couldn't they put me ashore in Da Nang*, I wondered, *and let me catch a military flight?*

I became anxious and depressed again, but kept doing my job as a radioman. And I continued scanning every message, trying to divine any clue that might hasten – or threaten – my impending departure.

I now had my sea bag packed, ready to leave at a moment's notice. But, as one day flowed to the next, the sea bag stood forlornly near my rack. It and I became objects of unmerciful kidding and pranks. For example, I came down from chow one afternoon needing something from the sea bag. It was gone, and several sailors in the compartment pretended they didn't know what had happened to it.

Finally, one of them said: "We thought you had left the ship already, so we threw it over the side."

Actually, they had hidden it on another sailor's rack and covered it with his blankets, but I had to search frantically through the Operations compartment for a long while to find it.

My agonized waiting finally ended on May 7, just as I was finishing a long and tiring mid-watch.

Chief Linn came into Radio Central. "Dunn, get your gear," he told me. "You'll be high-lined off in 15 minutes."

It took me a few moments to realize that he wasn't kidding – or even trying to torment me.

I quickly shook hands with as many radiomen as I could and wished them good luck – even Chief Linn. Then I left Radio Central for the last time and rushed out to the edge of the ASROC deck. When I looked up the port side, I saw that the *Higbee* was maneuvering toward a gray ship, the oiler *USS Taluga,* to take on fuel. The two ships soon would be steaming side by side and positioned for transfers.

I raced down the nearby ladder to the main deck and hurried to the port opening. Then, inside the ship, I hurried down Broadway to the hatch leading to the Operations compartment and opened my footlocker.

After weeks of wearing dungarees, it seemed strange to throw on my dress white uniform while we were still at sea. But dress whites were the Navy's travel uniform in the tropics.

I made one final check of my now-empty footlocker and rack. Then I hoisted my sea bag onto my right shoulder and struggled out of the Operations compartment, staggering under its weight and the ship's movements. At the compartment ladder, I climbed with one hand, pulling my sea bag up behind me. Once I reached Broadway, I grabbed the sea bag's awkward canvas handle and threaded my way forward along the narrow corridor.

When I stepped out onto the main deck, we were already alongside the *Taluga*. I silently prayed that an errant wave would not suddenly rise up and knock me down or wash me overboard. I moved aft with my sea bag and dragged it up the portside ladder to the DASH deck. Everything now was a blur of activity. The king post was up, and two dozen sailors were manning the manila rope that would help control the highline that now was in place between the *Higbee* and the oiler.

A yeoman petty officer was waiting for me, holding my health and service records in a sealed envelope. He had me sign a form and gave me another envelope containing mimeographed copies of my travel orders.

A boatswain's mate put an orange kapok lifejacket on me and kept me safely out of the way as crewmen on both ships finished rigging the lines fore and aft. These lines would help bring aboard thousands of gallons of diesel oil and take me off the *Higbee*.

Suddenly, a "transfer-at-sea chair" was swung into place, and I was put into it. When I tried to hang onto my sea bag, the boatswain's mate pulled it away. "We'll send it over next," he promised.

The boxy metal framework rose from the deck and swayed back and forth. The transfer-at-sea chair started conveying me above the water. On both ships, teams of sailors worked the heavy manila ropes as they guided me across the 120-foot gap between the *Higbee* and the *Taluga*. Several times during my months at sea, I had seen a transfer-at-sea chair suddenly dip into the waves and give a dangerous dunking to its occupant as the side-by-side ships steamed along at 12 to 15 knots. Once, a Navy chaplain who had visited our ship had been roughly and thoroughly "baptized" as he was transported to another ship.

I held tightly to my military records and kept a wary eye on the Tonkin Gulf undulating beneath my feet as I was pulled across. But I also managed a quick, going-away wave to a few Operations shipmates who had stepped outside onto the ASROC deck to watch. And I gave a farewell salute to the Captain as he kept watch on the UNREP operations from port wing of the bridge. When he saw my salute, he promptly and sharply returned it. Then he stepped back onto the bridge.

Within a few minutes, I was standing – dry – on the starboard side of the *Taluga*'s main deck, watching the *Higbee* from an unfamiliar perspective. Now my sea bag made its aerial journey across in the swinging, swaying chair, and it did not fall out.

The oiler's acrid smells quickly turned my stomach and made my nose burn. As I looked around at its gray decks and organized jungle of fueling lines, I was relieved and grateful that I had not spent my entire enlistment in its radio room. No doubt the Seventh Fleet still needed me, needed what I could do, on any of its hundreds of ships and support vessels. But I needed no more, and could stand no more, of the ocean. I now weighed barely 110 pounds, some 25 pounds below my enlistment weight.

I sensed another movement in my peripheral vision. As I looked around toward the *Taluga*'s stern, I saw a massive gray shape moving up on the oiler's port side, getting ready to be the next refueling customer. The aircraft carrier *USS Midway* would be my ride to the Philippines and the Subic Bay Naval Station.

When the oil transfer was finished, the *Higbee* and the *Taluga* cut loose their underway replenishment lines and quickly hauled them aboard. It was time for the *breakaway*, the moment when two side-by-side ships carefully start moving apart again.

On many ships, there was a tradition of having a brief gimmick or performance that would show some pride once an underway replenishment was completed without a serious incident. Some ships had rock bands that played high up on the signal bridge. The aircraft carrier *USS Ranger* loudly played a recording of "the Lone Ranger" theme from the *William Tell Overture*, and someone would shout "Hi-yo, Silver, away!"over its booming 1MC.

One Tonkin Gulf destroyer had a fire truck siren and flashing lights, and crewmen on the signal bridge suddenly would pop into view wearing old-fashioned fire helmets and brandishing fire axes.

The *Higbee*'s breakaway gimmick had long been an old steam train whistle permanently mounted on the port side, close to the main deck and near a high-pressure (150 pounds per square inch) steam line that could be connected quickly. As retired Rear Admiral Tim Jenkins, the *Higbee*'s young operations officer in 1965, later recalled: "The Snipes [engine room personnel] would hate it when we blew the whistle, because it would pull down so much steam that it was difficult for them to keep the boilers at the proper levels."[1]

The *Higbee*'s steam whistle (allegedly stolen years earlier from a train in Sasebo, Japan) sounded very loud aboard the ship. Indeed, its breathy *whooo-ooot* could be made to give off mournful tones reminiscent of a 1940s or '50s freight train rolling through a lonesome, Deep South night.

At sea, however, there was nothing nearby to add any modulating echoes. When the *Higbee* and the *Taluga* began to pull apart, the whistle sounded flat, hoarse – and puny – across the water.

I thought of the E. E. Cummings poem where "the goat-footed balloonMan whistles far and wee."[2] But the ship's breakaway routine included a couple of other finishing flourishes, Adm. Jenkins later reminded. "We would also break (run up) the DESRON 3 Asiatic Squadron flag and, and when we could get away with it, a Navy blue-and-gold 'HIIYA' flag – an acronym for 'Hang it in your ass,'" he said.

One of the *Higbee*'s sister destroyers, the *USS Leonard F. Mason* (DD-852), also flew the HIIYA flag during breakaways, and the ship's captain, Commander Ralph Ellsworth Graham, played "Scotland the Brave" on bagpipes.

For one quick moment as the train whistle sounded, I wondered if I was making a mistake, leaving the ship and the closest friends I had known. I wondered if I could run up to the *Taluga*'s radio shack and signal the *Higbee* to come back and get me. That moment, however, quickly and firmly faded.

I knew well now that the sea was not my home and would never be my home.

I wanted hills, trees and fields far from any body of water larger than a placid lake or gently flowing river. I wanted feel concrete, not steel, beneath my feet and walk on city sidewalks again. And I wanted to hear people speak plain English, not WestPac's pidgin of military acronyms, sailor slang and juked-up Japanese, punctuated always with raw streams of obscenities.

As its steam whistle continued to *whoo-oo-ooo-t*, the destroyer that had been much of my universe for the past year now pulled ahead and made a smooth arc to starboard. Soon, I could no longer see anyone moving on its decks. The *Higbee* gained speed and quickly shrank as it headed away, until it seemed little more than a gray, toy boat sliding across endless blue ocean, beneath endless blue sky.

Now I turned and watched the massive *Midway* surge into view. It was next in line for fuel. And it was my next ride.

Gaunt from frequent seasickness, the author weighed 110 pounds when his duty tour as a radioman ended.
(Photographer unknown)

CHAPTER 20

In Transit

Once the *Midway* was alongside the *Taluga*, I was bundled into another transfer-at-sea chair and highlined across to a loading platform outside the aircraft hanger. The *Midway* was preparing to leave Yankee Station and head to Subic Bay for overdue repairs and R&R for her crew.

On the loading platform, I hefted my sea bag and followed a Marine corporal inside the cavernous carrier.

Saying nothing and looking bored, the Marine handed me off to an equally bored-looking seaman apprentice, who led me through a maze of passageways and compartments to my bunk.

As I put away some of my stuff in my new footlocker, I wondered if I would be assigned to the *Midway*'s radio room. What would it be like to work amid a large group of radiomen, instead of a three-man watch section?

Nothing happened for a while. Finally, a third-class petty officer stopped by and told me I would be given a work assignment shortly. I waited around but finally got bored after two hours. I went to the compartment's front entrance and wrote down its designations. Then I went out into a passageway and found a *Midway* sailor willing to show me how to get up to a small observation platform where I could watch the flight deck.

Even as the *Midway* steamed away from the Vietnam War, it kept recovering old, prop-driven A-1H Skyraiders from missions and launching bomb-laden jets for one final strike.

Over the next three days, no one gave me a work assignment. And I conveniently forgot to request one. After reveille each morning, I stayed in my rack as long as I wanted.

I made all chow calls. And between meals, I wandered through the seemingly endless passageways, marveling at some of the features of carrier life, while staying well clear of the aircraft elevators and areas where bombs and jet fuel were stored.

The *Midway* had a hamburger stand, a movie theater, a big ship's store and rows of vending machines that dispensed candy bars and canned drinks. It was almost like being in a small town, except there were no women and no one speaking any languages except "sailor" and "Marine."

You have to be tough to serve on a destroyer, I thought with a grin, as I stood in a long line to get a *Midway* hamburger.

The *Higbee*'s lone vending machine had served nauseating soft drinks, when it worked at all. You dropped your nickel into a slot, and a little paper cup would drop down – if you were lucky. Then some syrup would spew into the cup – if you were lucky. Finally, whether you were lucky or not, the machine would squirt out a little bit of carbonated water and desalinated seawater. Our Cokes, when we successfully got one, tasted distinctly of fish and brine, as well as soft drink.

A few weeks before I left the *Higbee*, I had found an embarrassing way to get some extra seawater into my Coke. Late one afternoon, just before I was due to go up to Radio Central for the eve watch, I showered, put on fresh dungarees, bought my Coke and carried the paper cup out through the starboard hatch onto the main deck. I just wanted to get a few minutes of fresh air before trudging up to Radio Central to work amid shipmates who smoked endlessly and equipment that reeked of Bakelite, metal and ozone.

Suddenly, the *Higbee* made a quick course correction, a sharp turn to port. The starboard side, where I was standing, heeled closer to the water. A big wave rose up and swept along the deck, knocking me flat and completely covering me with water.

As I struggled back to my feet, cursing and soaked, I heard and saw nearby crewmen laughing and pointing.

"Hey, look!" one of them shouted. "Dunn thought it was swim call!"

"Well, he's a Reserve. What does he know?" another responded, evoking more laughter.

I knew they were just having fun, but now I was angry. I was still holding the paper cup, and it was now filled to the brim with exactly eight fluid ounces of the Tonkin Gulf.

I flung the cup overboard and went below to change uniforms.

When the *Midway* moored at the Subic Bay Naval Base, I took off my dungarees and put on my dress whites. I had a moment of panic when I realized I didn't know how to get off the big ship. But as I looked out into a passageway, I saw another sailor in dress whites lugging his sea bag. Maybe he was getting out of the Navy, too, or just getting transferred to another ship. I didn't care which. He seemed to know where he was going. I grabbed my sea bag and followed him.

Carefully keeping my sea bag on my left shoulder and my service records envelope in my right hand, I made it to the quarterdeck not far behind him. Both of my hands were full, so I couldn't salute the officer of the deck. Instead, I just stopped and faced him.

"Request permission to go ashore, sir!"

The lieutenant (j.g.) responded with a bored and casual salute. "Permission granted."

I nodded my thanks, then glanced toward the stern and nodded once at the American flag as I stepped down the long gangplank.

An old school bus, painted the ubiquitous Navy gray, was parked on the pier. The driver was a beefy third-class with two hash marks on his sleeve, probably someone who had been busted down a rate or two recently. He stood in front of his bus watching the disembarking sailors and Marines.

"Transit barracks!" he called out when he saw me. "Let's go!"

I dragged my sea bag into the bus and had no trouble finding a seat. The bus was empty except for two other riders, sleeping near the back.

The transit barracks was a white, rectangular, one-story building that looked almost exactly like several other nearby buildings. I went inside the front door and stopped at the small check-in desk, manned by a yeoman third class. He examined my records and logged me in on a clipboard.

"Muster is at oh-seven-hundred," he said. He gestured unenthusiastically toward the open doorway near his table. "Find a rack in there."

"There" was a room about half the size of a basketball court, with mostly empty racks—military bunks, this time—stacked two deep. Most were empty.

I picked a rack near the center and stuffed my sea bag into an upright locker, the first one I had gotten to use in nearly two years. It was early afternoon, still three hours or so until liberty call. I knew I was supposed to report to someone and volunteer for some kind of work detail to fill the time. But I was through with volunteering.

I walked out of the transit barrack and strolled around the base, saluting officers when necessary and relishing the solid feel of land beneath my feet. Very quickly, however, I began to feel weighted down by the windless heat and very high humidity. After less than an hour, I was thoroughly drenched with sweat. I went back to the transit barracks to gulp cold water from the "scuttlebutt" – the water fountain – and take a shower. When I emerged from the shower, the petty officer on barracks fire watch had news for me.

"Your new orders have arrived." He handed me a small batch of papers.

They were not what I expected. I had figured the Navy would shuffle me aboard another ship for the long trip to Treasure Island, California. Then I would be released from active duty at the last possible moment, too late to enroll for the first summer semester. But the Navy had a different – and seemingly better – idea. It was putting me on a Military Air Transport System (MATS) cargo plane that could also carry a few passengers.

My flight was supposed to take off at 0800 the next morning, a good 15 hours away. It was now late afternoon, and I had liberty. So I decided to make one more visit to Olongapo, the infamous town long known as "Shit City" among Seventh Fleet sailors. The crude sobriquet stemmed from the stagnant, sewage-laden stream that barely moved beneath the bridge separating the navy base's front gate and the town.

Much of Olongapo was off-limits to Subic Bay's sailors and Marines. Virtually the only area on-limits was the city's dusty, unpaved main street, which was lined with bars, garish night clubs and small hotels that offered rent-by-the-hour rooms. In Olongapo, you could drink, dance to jukeboxes or live Filipino rock bands, and take a bargirl to a hotel next door or across the street. Otherwise, there was little else to do except fight with a shipmate or duke it out with someone from another ship. As long as you didn't fight and obeyed the midnight curfew for getting back to base, the Shore Patrol would leave you alone. If you did get into a fight, the bar owner or hotel staff quickly called the SPs. And it was bad to still be there when they arrived.

During one of the *Higbee*'s first stops at Subic several months earlier, J.L. Davis and I had gone into a big nightclub that featured a Big Band-style orchestra, a Forties-style floor show – and strippers.

As one stripper shimmied after removing absolutely everything, a drunken sailor in dress whites suddenly staggered into the spotlight and tried to dance with her. She burst into tears and fled, her artistic routine ruined.

Quickly, two of the sailors' shipmates tried to grab him and pull him back to their table. But he decked one of them with a roundhouse punch.

Other sailors rushed in to try to quell the disturbance. One of them went down as a punch broke his glasses. Some of that sailor's shipmates immediately joined the melee. In moments, the inside of the nightclub was in danger of being destroyed. Dozens of sailors now were wrestling, kicking, swinging at each other, knocking over chairs and tables and sending the band, singers and strippers all fleeing for safety.

One punch had dissolved into exactly the kind of nightclub fight scene that often showed up in movies about American soldiers, sailors, pilots or Marines on the verge of going off to World War II.

Davis and I were not able maintain our Hemingway-esque, neutral-observer poses for long. Somebody shoved a young seaman apprentice against our table, tipping it over and spilling our drinks. "Let's get out of here!" we said, almost in unison.

We made our way around one edge of the growing fray and shoved our way toward the night club's the front entrance. Over the shouts and noise of breaking glass and tumbling furniture, we could hear the sounds of Shore Patrol jeeps arriving outside. We knew anyone inside the club likely would be arrested.

We burst out the front door just as SPs charged toward us blowing their whistles and pulling their truncheons.

In a burst of desperate genius, Davis and I each grabbed an ornate door and held it open for the SPs as they rushed in.

We could hear police whistles, clubs hitting heads and other noises of order being restored as we let go of the doors and hurried toward the bridge over the fetid river.

Frequently, it proved better to avoid Olongapo and remain within the relative, if boring, safety of Subic Bay Naval Station.

Just as I expected when I crossed the bridge, a crowd of shoeshine boys and beggars immediately swarmed around me, babbling in Tagalog and broken English.

Two shoeshine boys tried to start polishing my shoes while I walked. I pushed them away and continued toward the long, dusty street that was lined with neon lights and signs for San Miguel Beer, Lem-o-Lime and Coca-Cola.

Once I entered the "commercial" district, the beggars and shoeshine boys fell back and left me alone. Their territory, in the hierarchy of Olongapo commerce, was the short block between the bridge and the first bars.

Colorful – sometimes garishly colorful – "jeepneys" sped up and down the wide dirt street. These were war-surplus jeeps and old cars that had been reworked so they could carry up to six passengers or more in the back. Sailors sat on two facing benches beneath a canvas canopy, typically tan or olive drab. The canopy shaded riders from the painful heat and the frequent rain showers. Sometimes, a jeepney ride was the only way to feel any kind of breeze at all in the steamy air. A quarter would buy a ride of several blocks up the main street or back to the main gate.

A jeepney ride was good on the trip away from the main gate, just after liberty call in late afternoon. But taking a ride back to the main gate near midnight, in a jeepney full of inebriated sailors and Marines, was guaranteed trouble. Either someone would throw up and pass out or try to jump out of the jeepney to get one more drink – and throw up on those who tried to restrain him.

Olongapo gave us few tales we could tell our parents, spouses or offspring.

As I walked through Olongapo for what I now knew would be the last time, a cacophony of Beatles songs and other rock tunes was pouring out the open front doors of the bars. Some of the bands were live, with Filipino guitarists, drummers and singers doing good jobs of imitating the sounds of some of America's newest hit songs.

About halfway down the first block of bars and hotels, I realized Olongapo no longer held any appeal at all.

I just wanted to get the hell out of Asia and go home.

I turned back toward the main gate.

The shoeshine boys and the beggars moved toward me again and once again badgered me for shoeshines and money.

I pulled out all of my Filipino money, perhaps $30 worth in small bills and coins, and stared at my tormentors. They stared at me, not sure what I was doing.

Suddenly, I threw all of the money up into the air. It made a small cloud of coins and pesos between us.

My first thought was: *I don't need this anymore. I don't need any of this shit.*

My second thought was a shameful realization. With one impulsive gesture, I had created another *Ugly American* moment. The shoeshine kids and the beggars immediately dove for the cash and started fighting each other for it, even before it all hit the ground.

As they battled and struggled to take it away from each other, I hurried across the bridge and did not look back as I flashed my ID card at the main gate. A Marine guard grimaced at me but said nothing as he waved me forward and I walked back into the comfort, security and cultural isolation of the naval base.

That was my last sight of Olongapo: a dirty, bloody street brawl I had started.

Early the next morning, I climbed aboard another old Navy-gray school bus for the 60-mile ride to Clark Air Base outside Manila. To my surprise, it would be a strange and dangerous trip.

Philippine presidential elections were in progress. Campaign posters were everywhere along the winding roads and in the villages. Some villages seemed to be solidly for the challenger, Ferdinand Marcos, while others clearly were for the incumbent, Diosdado Macapagal.

A few of the signs evoked the memory of Ramon Magsaysay, the popular Philippine leader who had been killed eight years earlier in a plane crash. But I could not tell which candidate was claiming his posthumous endorsement.

About halfway into the trip, as the bus passed through a small village and back into the countryside, the driver suddenly speeded up. Now we were going much faster than seemed safe.

Two petty officers sitting across from each other in the front seats suddenly pulled their sidearms – gleaming .45s – and jammed clips into the handles. They set their safeties and started peering out the windows intently while they held on to their seat frames with one hand.

I didn't understand what was happening, but there was no time to try to figure it out. The swaying bus had no seat belts. We passengers had to grab onto whatever we could and just hang on. We bounced up from our seats as we hit bumps and potholes, and some sailors were thrown into the aisle as the bus whipped around a sharp curve and came to a long straightaway.

On the outskirts of the next village, Philippine Boy Scouts in full uniform were lining both sides of the road for some reason. They saluted the Navy bus as it sped past and enveloped them in a cloud of dust. But the need for the speed soon became apparent once we reached the other side of the village. The driver suddenly pushed his accelerator to the floor and the two armed petty officers tensed and held their pistols ready.

Up ahead, more people were grouped along the road, and this time, they weren't Boy Scouts.

A shower of rocks and bricks flew toward the bus. Most of them missed, but the bus took several hits. The windshield and several side windows, including mine, were cracked.

As the bus raced away from the village and moved into more open countryside, the driver lifted the accelerator a bit, and the petty officers put away their guns. A few miles later, the battered bus rolled into the relative safety of Clark Air Base.

The Air Police gate guard gave the bus driver a sympathetic nod and a wan smile as he waved us through.

When I got off the bus, the late-spring heat and oppressive humidity almost baked me into immobility. There was no breeze at all, just the hot pressure of tropical sunlight bearing down with no trees or jungle canopy to provide any cooling. It had been hot at sea, particularly inside the metal ship where the air conditioning could not quite keep up. But even on calm days, we could find a cooling wind out on the decks as the ship surged forward.

It was too hot at Clark to do anything except drink. And, unfortunately, Navy enlisted men could go to an enlisted airmen's club that had afternoon specials on mixed drinks.

I ordered a hurricane, not really knowing what one was, and paid for it with a dime, the special price. Thirty cents later, a sailor and a Marine (I think) helped carry me out the door and back to the transit barracks. The next morning, I woke up with a massive hangover and a ticket to ride a Military Air Transport System (MATS) Boeing 707 – not to Honolulu as I had expected but to Yakota Air Force Base in Japan.

If I had known what next awaited me, I might have spent a few more dimes, perhaps even a dollar, in the airmen's club.

The MATS 707 four-engine jet transport plane was partially filled with cargo but also had a small number of backward-facing passenger seats. These were filled with officers and enlisted men from several service branches, as well as a few military wives and children. There were no windows to look out. Once the 707 started its takeoff roll down the long runway, I tried to settle back and relax for the flight. But just as we neared takeoff speed, the engines suddenly roared much louder, and the MATS transport started shaking violently and vibrating all over. As we slowed, we terrified passengers realized that the pilot had aborted the takeoff. Immediately, we were grateful that the runway had been built for the long takeoff runs of heavy bombers.

The MATS plane taxied over to a hanger filled with other planes, and one of the crewmen informed us that the 707's hydraulic system had failed during takeoff. We had been lucky to still be on the ground when it happened, he admitted. We got off the plane, gathered up our gear and rode a bus back to the transit barracks. The repairs would take at least until tomorrow, we were told.

The next morning, we boarded the same plane and started down the same runway. This time, the pilot throttled back the engines well before we reached takeoff speed. The hydraulic system had failed again. Once again we taxied to the repair area and rode buses back to the transit barracks.

Later that day, we were taken again to the same plane. Either our luck would run out or the third time would be the charm, some of us joked grimly. We took off without crashing, cheered as the wheels went up, and made it to Yakota, Japan, several hours later.

Almost immediately after landing, I was put on another MATS flight, this time going to Honolulu. I worried that the flight might have to stop at Clark Air Force Base on the way, taking me straight back to where I had started. But the flight went from Yakota to Honolulu nonstop with a full load of military men, women and dependents—and no incidents. I tried to sleep, but I was too keyed up about getting closer and closer to home.

Foolishly, I had brought nothing to read and no writing materials. So I just sat and stared at the back of the seat in front of me and tried to let the Tonkin Gulf and South China Sea slowly drain from my mind.

A long climb. Steps near the Clinton Presidential Library,
Little Rock, Arkansas, November, 2007. *(Photo by Si Dunn)*

CHAPTER 21

The Long Way Home

Getting from the Vietnam War to Little Rock took 10 days and involved several modes of transportation. But I did not really arrive "home" from my experiences and disillusionments until years afterward, long after the terms "Vietnam syndrome" and "post-traumatic stress disorder" had been coined.

I felt a sense of culture shock soon after I arrived at Hickam Air Force Base. I took a taxi into Honolulu for liberty and heard civilians speaking normal English for the first time in almost a year. It seemed almost like an incomprehensible foreign language. Aboard the *Higbee*, I had lapsed into speaking and understanding a strange pidgin that consisted of Seventh Fleet Navy lingo mixed with distorted Japanese, Chinese and Tagalog, plus bits of California surfer slang, all punctuated with copious quantities of raw profanity.

The second half of my trip home, from Hawaii to Arkansas, gave me a little extra time to decompress and find my civilian bearings again.

My first stop in the continental United States was the transit barracks at the Treasure Island Receiving Station. I had loved walking around San Francisco while stationed at Hunters Point Naval Shipyard in 1963. Strolling again through the fog-shrouded city, I briefly toyed with the idea of staying in California, going to film school and becoming a cinematographer. But once my travel orders to Little Rock were in hand, I went straight out the front gate carrying my sea bag and almost immediately started talking to another sailor, a 22-year-old boatswains mate named Snider, who was leaving the Navy, too.

"I've got a car. I need another driver to split the gas," Snider told me. He said he had bought a used sedan while on liberty recently and intended to drive it across the U.S. to rural Maryland.

I hadn't touched a steering wheel in nearly two years, but after almost a year at sea, I was eager to see some land – as much land as possible.

"I can go as far as Kansas City," I told him. "I can take a bus from there."

Clearly eager to get moving, Snider quickly agreed. We hailed a cab, tossed our sea bags in, and rode through downtown San Francisco. The cab finally dropped us off at a shabby parking lot, and Snider introduced me to his "new" ride, a beat-up black 1955 Mercury Montclair with almost-bald tires.

"I got it from another sailor for fifty bucks," Snider told me. "It needs a little work, but it'll get us there."

He took the wheel, and we headed east across the Oakland Bay bridge, lapsing into the small talk of sailors. We had almost nothing in common. He had spent his entire four-year enlistment working aboard tugboats and other auxiliary craft in West Coast harbors.

As we rode along, I realized his car was worth just about what he had paid for it. The engine ran, but the shocks were gone, and the brakes made grinding and squealing noises.

Also, Snider periodically kept making strange, back-and-forth movements with the steering wheel as he drove.

A few hours later, I figured out why he was doing that. I got behind the wheel for the first time and took us back onto Interstate 80. Sometimes, the car would drift toward the shoulder or move from one lane to another no matter how I adjusted the wheel. Then, suddenly, the steering would reengage and yank us back into our lane.

Fortunately, the tricks for avoiding a head-on crash or plunging off the roadway were simple: (1) remain alert to oncoming traffic and the conditions of the shoulders; and (2) start moving the steering wheel at least five seconds before it needed to be moved.

We drove that way, like two drunken sailors, from California into Nevada, constantly gambling with our lives.

We decided to *not* stop in Reno, so we could conserve our meager travel cash. Snider and I figured we had just enough money between us for gas and food. And I had some cash tucked back for a bus ticket once we got to Kansas. But we didn't have enough resources to make any repairs to Snider's junkyard Mercury. So we just pressed our luck and kept surging – and weaving – ahead.

Halfway between Fernley and Winnemucca, Nevada, however, we both realized we needed a rest stop, and we finally succumbed to the late-night "CASINO" neon signs glowing along highway. The Mercury rattled and ground to a stop outside a small club in tiny Lovelock, and we went inside.

Snider quickly lost $10 at a slot machine and visibly got distressed as he pushed in more coins and kept yanking handle without success. I was soon down by almost the same amount and grew equally concerned that we were throwing way our travel money.

At the Enlisted Men's Club in Yokosuka, it had been no big deal to go broke on the slots. You simply walked out the door and strode a few hundred yards to your ship. There, you always had food, a place to sleep and plenty of buddies willing to make you a five-for-seven or five-for-ten payday loan. If you were really smart, you probably even kept a few bucks hidden inside your footlocker.

I didn't relish the notion that we might gamble away everything in Lovelock and strand ourselves in the Nevada desert. I still had my bus money to fall back on. But it wouldn't be enough to get me to Little Rock from here. And Snider would be left on his own.

Even if we had nothing in common, he was still a shipmate and a buddy while we were under travel orders and had on our blues.

Suddenly, I won $20 in dimes. Snider stared enviously as my machine pumped them out with satisfying rattles. "Here," I said, quickly scooping up the coins. I gave Snider a fistful and stuffed the rest in my pocket. "Let's call this a wash and get the hell out of here!"

Snider agreed. "Was this my stupid idea – or yours?"

We got back on the road and kept the Mercury moving past Battle Mountain, Elko and, finally, West Wendover. Soon, the sun rose in front of us, and we rolled out of Nevada's deserts and mountains and crossed into Utah. We emerged onto a flat, ruler-straight stretch of Interstate 80 that arrowed toward the southern end of the Great Salt Lake.

In Salt Lake City, we split a sandwich at a restaurant and stared for a few minutes at the nearby six-spire Salt Lake Temple and the domed Mormon Tabernacle. Then we jumped back in the car and continued east until we found U.S. Highway 40. There, we turned southeast and made the winding run into Colorado, taking turns at the loosey-goosey steering wheel every four hours like sailors standing watch on a ship.

The real challenge came when we reached the Rocky Mountains and realized that driving over them with bad steering and bad brakes was an insane idea.

Naturally, it was my turn at the wheel. And, on more than one mountain, as gravity pulled us downhill, I wasn't always sure we would have enough steering and brakes left to negotiate the onrushing next turn. But after surviving four typhoons, never-ending seasickness, multiple run-ins with Chief Linn, *and* sleep-deprivation in the Tonkin Gulf, I was *not* ready to take a 5,000-foot plunge off a mountainside in a runaway Mercury Montclair. While Snider dozed, I steered for dear life and tried to use the motor and the slipping automatic transmission to hold our speed down a little. I also kept my right foot ready to grind the brakes down to their last molecules of bare metal, if necessary.

By the time we crossed into Kansas, I had had enough. Keeping the Mercury on the road and out of the oncoming lane was wearing me out. And now, I couldn't sleep out of worry that Snider might make a wrong move and lose control. Furthermore, we were growing weary of each other's sea stories. He couldn't really relate to my Seventh Fleet experiences, and I had no interest left in hearing more about the process of moving boats and ships around San Francisco harbor and getting drunk on Market Street.

Kansas City now was less than 200 miles away. Yet, on the flat, dull Kansas prairie, it seemed as if it might take forever to get there.

Western Kansas had no big towns along Interstate 70. Colby and Hayes looked too small to have bus stations, and they were not names I recognized, even from my numerous ham radio contacts with Kansas operators. The flatness seemed to stretch to infinity. I was ready to get out *now* and hitchhike with my sea bag, just to get a change and feel the world steady again beneath my feet.

Suddenly, a mileage sign swept past. Salina, Kansas, was 30 miles ahead. *It'll do*, I decided. *It will do absolutely*. Salina was a *city*, albeit small, and surely it had a bus station. Even if the bus had to take me all the way to Topeka or Kansas City before finally turning south, it would do.

Snider drove me into the heart of Salina, and I bought him $2 worth of gas before I got out at the bus station.

"Good luck with the drive, Snider," I said. I hoisted my sea bag and tossed it up on my shoulder.

"Yeah, good luck, Dunn," he replied. He pushed the accelerator, and the Mercury Montclair waddled away. It turned a corner somehow and disappeared.

The Navy had always called us by our last names, and that was how enlisted sailors generally knew each other. During our two-day drive, I had never learned Snider's first name. And he had never asked to know mine. I hoped he would make it to Maryland alive. But very quickly, I pushed him and his fifty-dollar Mercury Montclair out of my mind.

My dress blues now were wrinkled and dirty as I carried my sea bag into Salina's Continental Trailways bus station. I bought a one-way ticket to Little Rock and plopped wearily into a lobby seat for the two-hour wait.

A couple of men who might have been military veterans strolled around the waiting room looking bored. They glanced at the rating patch on my left sleeve and at the *USS Higbee* patch at the edge of my right shoulder. The ship's name obviously rang no bells, so they left me alone and moved on.

At Wichita, I dozed in the lobby until dawn. Then I took a bus to Joplin, Missouri. At Joplin, I changed buses again, this time for Little Rock. The bus from Joplin rolled out and headed down through Neosho and across the Arkansas border, stopping in Rogers, Springdale, Fayetteville and Fort Smith. Then it turned southeast on Interstate 40. I awoke each time the bus driver called out a new name and stopped the coach to let off or pick up more passengers: *Clarksville, Russellville, Morrilton, Conway*—all names I knew and could visualize; towns of my childhood. The Tonkin Gulf and South China Sea already were starting to seem like a distant, bad dream.

I reached Little Rock early in mid-afternoon and shoved my sea bag into the back seat of a taxi cab. In my weariness, I mistakenly gave the cabbie the address for the house that had been my home when I left for active duty. He gave me a funny look but said nothing and drove along a new road I did not recognize. Eighth Street now was a freeway.

The cabbie exited at Pine Street, headed north through a neighborhood that I still recalled, then circled around to go south on Cedar Street. Part of the old neighborhood was the same. But most of my block and the house where I had grown up were gone, replaced by a brand-new freeway entrance ramp. I felt a moment of shock. It was not unlike the shock I had felt the first time I saw the naked hull and main deck of the *Higbee* sitting up on blocks in dry dock at the Hunter's Point Naval Shipyard in 1963, waiting to be rebuilt.

"Now where?" the cabbie asked, eyeing me in the rear-view mirror. I pulled open my sea bag and found a letter from my parents. I gave him an address on Louise Street. "Where's that?" he asked. I had no idea. I was lost in my own hometown. He got on his radio and called his dispatcher. Louise Street turned out to be a very short street just a couple of miles away.

Home is the sailor, home from the sea...[1]

In the time-honored tradition of not telling parents when their sons were coming home from the service, I had not told my mother or father anything except that I was safely back in San Francisco and would be home sometime in the near future.

I looked at my watch. My father would still be at work, editing stories and writing headlines for late editions of the *Arkansas Democrat*. My mother's health was not good and had gotten worse while I was at sea. So I knew she would be at home, perhaps watching soap operas, doing light housework and starting to plan dinner.

My arrival was not nearly as big of a surprise as I had hoped. My mother had spotted me almost as soon as the taxicab stopped in front of the house. Later, she would tell me she had sensed that I was back in town, nearly an hour before I arrived.

As I climbed out and paid the cabbie, she was standing on the front porch in her bathrobe, smiling as only she could smile, and crying only as she could cry.

By the time I was halfway up the sidewalk with my sea bag on my shoulder, trying to look like a war-toughened swabbie, I was crying, too.

#

At the Vietnam Wall, Washington, DC, July 3, 2009.
(Photo by Si Dunn)

Epilogue I

I was among the first to return from the Vietnam War. Thus, for many months, I did not encounter anyone else who had been there or knew anything about what it was like.

As a sailor, I had seen only a tiny handful of the real horrors of war. But I had been a witness to some of war's randomness and to some of the absurdities that occur at the spear-point of policies created half a world away by people who are both ill-informed and driven by political agendas.

Once I returned home to Little Rock, I did not stay there long. The dark dreams of being at sea, trying to copy undecipherable messages, faded quickly. So did the disturbing memories of being called to battle stations in the blackness of night. But I had trouble finding a focus for my life, and I soon started a restless pattern of changing jobs every few months and changing colleges almost as often.

I had managed to save $800 from my Navy pay by sending home occasional money orders. With part of the funds, I paid for a semester of summer-school tuition and housing at Arkansas State Teachers College in Conway. With the rest, I bought a low-powered motorcycle that was just one step above a motor scooter.

Less than a month after I had left the Tonkin Gulf, I signed up for a tennis class and a class in basic journalism, virtually the only courses that still had some enrollment spaces. Then I went in search of part-time jobs to help me stay in school.

I knew now that I wanted to be a journalist, and Conway had a newspaper. But I didn't apply there. Neither did I try to be a Conway correspondent for either of Little Rock's two daily newspapers, even though my father might have been able to help me. I didn't feel ready, so soon after leaving active duty.

Instead, between classes, I became something of a land-based "deck ape." I worked as a general laborer in the campus maintenance department. I helped move mattresses into and out of dorm rooms. I rode on the back of the campus garbage truck and dumped trash cans into its hopper. I mowed swaths of campus grass with big, red Yazoo mowers.

Cutting the grass was the easiest detail. No one watched over the Yazoo crew. So sometimes, we mowers could just start our machines and let them run while we took short naps behind some of the bushes.

The naps were important, because I also had found a night job as a sheet-metal worker in a Conway school bus factory. I would ride my motorcycle the mile or so from the campus to the factory just before 6 p.m., punch a time clock and take my position at a "fade-out" machine. This was a huge metal-stamping mechanism that pushed down on flat, foot-square pieces of steel using 60 tons of pressure and molded them into "fade-outs."

Fade-outs were metal ovals about six inches wide, with multiple ridges. Each time I stamped one, I tossed it into a nearby bin almost full with other fade-outs.

Another worker standing at another machine pulled fade-outs from the bin as fast as he could and loudly sawed the metal ovals in half.

Each fade-out eventually became two end pieces for the raised black stripes that ran down the sides of yellow school buses.

Over the next few weeks, I made many dozens of fade-outs each shift, standing at the big machine until 2 a.m. I slid a piece of metal into place and pushed the stamping button. Then a drop of machine oil fell from somewhere overhead and landed on my head. It felt like a greasy form of Chinese water torture.

I tried wearing one of my old Navy work caps and letting it soak up the falling oil. Soon, the cap was nasty and grimy, and it quickly mirrored my growing dissatisfaction with sheet-metal work.

I had not understood how "deck apes" could keep reenlisting in the Navy so they could spend their lives chipping paint, swabbing decks and waiting for the next chow call. But now, the school bus factory made them seem almost like wise philosophers; for the sea constantly changed and the ship frequently traveled somewhere new. The bus factory did not.

Some of my bus factory co-workers had been working at the same place all of their adult lives, and a few of them had lost at least one finger, or more, to the machines they served. The plant was dingy, smelly, noisy and often unsafe. And my boss, while no Chief Linn, was easily angered when people were producing parts at rates below the night's assigned quotas.

"Step it up! Step it up! Let's go! Let's go!" he would grouse at me when he walked over to the fade-out machine and looked into the box of new pieces I had produced.

Break time came at 10 p.m., and we had 30 minutes to eat dinner. Usually, I had a ham sandwich and a small container of milk purchased from the factory's small commissary. Then I would sit outside and watch the sky.

I seldom ever talked to any of my co-workers, because they seldom talked to each other, and none of them seemed to have anything interesting to say.

We all just sat a little ways apart from each other, ate our late dinners, stared at the sky and waited for the buzzer to sound and send us back to our machines.

After I got off at 2 a.m., I rode my motorcycle back to my dorm room and try to unwind by quietly playing a guitar for a few minutes.

Often, I discovered – painfully – that I had small bits of metal embedded in my fingers. Sometimes my fingers bled small drops on the frets and strings.

I hated the work, but I needed the money to stay in school. There was not yet a GI Bill for Vietnam veterans.

Still, I had a breaking point.

After a few weeks, I realized I was now spending a lot of my break times just staring at my motorcycle in the parking lot and fantasizing about riding off to new places. One night, I forgot my oil-soaked destroyer cap and had to endure warm oil falling into my hair every time I punched a new fade-out. By break time, my hair and scalp were soaked, oil was getting onto my clothes, and my fingers had several small cuts that stung when I tried to wipe the oil off my head.

'Step it up!" my boss complained as he checked my production. "Punch 'em out, Dunn! You're *way* behind!"

When break time finally arrived, I wiped as much oil as I could out of my hair. Then I bought my dinner, went outside and sat on an old folding chair while I ate.

A full moon was high in the sky, and my motorcycle now seemed to have an extra glow. The more I looked at it, the more I knew my brief career as a metal worker was reaching its ignoble end.

When the buzzer sounded to end our break, everyone headed for their machines. Everyone except me. This time, I kept staring at my motorcycle.

The boss saw me looking at it and seemed to realize what I was thinking.

"Get in here!" he ordered.

He sounded nothing at all like Chief Linn. Yet the effect was the same.

I got up and walked straight toward the parking lot.

The boss hurried out of the factory, chasing after me. He knew what I was about to do. But he was middle-aged and overweight.

I ran to my motorcycle, hopped on it and started it with one firm kick.

"Get back here and finish your shift!" the boss yelled. "Fill your quota!"

He was almost on me when I slammed the motorcycle into gear and steered away from him. I felt like Steve McQueen in the 1963 hit movie *The Great Escape*. I wanted to do a wheelie and a grand leap as I sped out of the factory parking lot. But I figured I would just crash and break my neck. So I settled for opening the throttle wide and doing a little two-wheel hop as I crossed a big bump in the road.

"Finish your shift!" I heard him shout one last time.

That night, after I got back to my dorm room, I decided that perhaps the aptitude tests I had taken in junior high school and high school had been right all along. I did have some aptitude for technical things, but my strongest test scores always had pointed straight toward working with words: being a writer or an English teacher.

I rolled some paper into the old Underwood typewriter that my parents had given me for my second try at college. I picked the little shards of school-bus metal out of my fingers. Then I let the words flow, whatever came to mind, and I didn't worry that I was literally leaving little drops of blood on the keys.

Within a month, I had made my first meager sales as a freelance writer, and I started replacing the lost income from the school-bus factory job by selling short articles to newspapers and little-known industrial magazines, such as *Southern Pulp & Paper Manufacturer*.

Initially, my biggest worry in civilian life was that I would be called back to active duty. The Navy was still short of radio operators, and I had three years remaining in my Navy Reserve commitment. But in 1965, President Johnson chose to increase the nation's draft quotas rather than call up reservists.

Luckily, I did not descend into the drug and alcohol problems that befell many Vietnam veterans. Still, for many years afterward, I experienced repeated difficulties with anger and alienation, and I was unable to stay focused on jobs for longer than a year to 18 months.

Restlessly, I moved – from Little Rock to Denton, Texas, to Austin, to Houston, back to Denton, then to Arlington, Dallas, Denton, Dallas, and Denton again. During this time, I became a photojournalist and earned a bachelor of arts degree from North Texas State University (now the University of North Texas).

In 1968, while still a journalism undergraduate student, I tried to return to Vietnam as a war correspondent and photojournalist. I gathered several letters of endorsement (but no financial support) from several publications. By then, however, inflation was running wild in Saigon, and famed Associated Press photographer Horst Faas urged me to "bring lots of money" if I went there. But I hated the idea of having to raise money, so I soon gave up the idea.

Over the next decade and a half, I worked at the *Dallas Morning News* four different times, sometimes staying on the job two or three years and other times lasting just 18 months or less before getting angry about something and quitting to go freelance. Then I would stay self-employed for a year or so, working seven days and nights a week as a freelance writer and editor, until the *News* or *Denton Record-Chronicle* had an opening and let me come back.

I did not go near an ocean again for nearly six years after I left the active-duty Navy. And when I did, my first act was to stand at the water's edge for a long time and watch the Gulf of Mexico wash up toward, but not quite to, my feet.

Soon afterward, newspaper reporting and photography assignments in Houston and Dallas began to require that I go back out onto the water.

First, there was a shrimp boat in Galveston Bay. The fisherman had no crew and needed someone to steer his boat and dodge ferries while he worked his nets and pulled in his catch. The water was calm, so I made it through the day without getting ill or running us aground. A few months later, I ventured a little farther out, aboard a boat taking sports fishermen out to catch red snapper. I got queasy once the boat stopped and started rocking in the swells not far from offshore drilling rigs.

Finally, I took a one-week cruise aboard the *MV Odessa*, a Ukrainian-Russian semi-luxury cruiser that sailed from New Orleans to Cozumel and Playa del Carmen, Mexico, plus a small port in Honduras, then back to New Orleans. I got seasick twice, but fought it each time by standing at a safety rail, watching the horizon and letting the wind blow in my face, just as I had done aboard the *Higbee*.

I did not find any real roots in my post-Vietnam life until I married at age 35, some 14 years after leaving the Tonkin Gulf, and then bought a house and had a family.

The lingering regret from my long-ago ten months in Japan and Southeast Asia is that I went there knowing nothing about their cultures and geographies and came home not much better informed.

What I *did* learn was how it feels to fear imminent death and how easy it is to let imagination fill in the blanks when nature and technology collide in the dark.

Many factors of history and circumstance led America to plunge into the disastrous Vietnam conflict. And an event other than the Tonkin Gulf Crisis might have thrust us into it at some later time. But I and many others knew almost from August 4, 1964, that false radar echoes had led us to attack North Vietnam and send ground, air and naval forces into South Vietnam.

As a disillusioned radioman petty officer aboard a lowly destroyer, I could do absolutely nothing about it.

Nothing except keep sending and receiving the dark signals of war.

The *USS Higbee* soon after completion and commissioning, 1945.
(U.S. Navy, photographer unknown)

Epilogue II

A week after I left the *Higbee* in May, 1965, a new captain came aboard. The ship continued its special patrols in the Tonkin Gulf and South China Sea. It also performed screening duties for aircraft carriers that launched new bombing missions over North Vietnam.

In early June, the ship served as part of the recovery fleet for the Gemini IV space mission. (Less than a year later, a sister destroyer, the *USS Leonard F. Mason*, would make headlines when it rescued the capsule and crew of Gemini VIII after astronauts Neil Armstrong and David Randolph Scott were forced to make an emergency splashdown well off target.)

On September 1, 1965, during Tropical Storm Polly, the *Higbee* helped rescue 30 sailors from the French tanker *Arsinoe* after it ran aground on a coral reef at Scarborough Shoal, about 130 miles west of Subic Bay. Navy and Coast Guard seaplanes, a Navy helicopter, and an oiler, the *USS Neches* (AO-47), also participated in the dangerous operation, which took place in 20-foot swells.[1] Along with France's official thanks, the French Embassy in Manila sent numerous cases of champagne to Subic Bay for the air crews and the crewmen of the *Higbee* and *Neches*.[2]

A week later, off the coast of South Vietnam, the *Higbee* fired its first shots in anger since the Korean War and hit some suspected Viet Cong targets.

Over the next few months, the *Higbee* took part in more firing and screening missions, and then returned to Yokosuka for repairs.

Later, it made a brief goodwill visit to Taiwan and once again shadowed the Soviet spy trawler *Gidrofon*, as well as a Russian submarine tender that serviced the trawler periodically.

The destroyer steamed back to the South Vietnamese coastline in late January, 1966, and fired at more Viet Cong targets. The firing missions continued well into 1966, and the ship expended thousands of 5-inch/38 shells.[3]

The next time the ship appeared prominently in naval history summaries was 1968.

The *Higbee* was sent to patrol the Korean peninsula after the North Koreans captured the *USS Pueblo* (AGER-2) and towed it to their port city of Wonson. The *Pueblo*, a Banner-class auxiliary general environmental research ship, had been gathering electronic intelligence both from North Korea and from Soviet naval activity in the waters nearby, and its capture meant that the North Koreans and the Russians got their hands on KW-7 and KW-37R encrypted radio teletype systems, plus a treasure-trove of other secret equipment.

The *Higbee* almost played a much bigger role as that tense international incident unfolded, according to Major Daniel P. Bolger in his book *Scenes from an Unfinished War: Low-Intensity Conflict in Korea, 1966-1969*. According to Bolger, the Commander in Chief of the U.S. Pacific Command, Admiral Ulysses S. Grant Sharp, proposed that the *Higbee* could steam directly into Wonson's harbor, covered by U.S. Navy fighter jets. "The *Higbee* would demand release of the *Pueblo* and its crew, promising air strikes on Wonson if unheeded." But the plan received no support from the Johnson Administration, Bolger noted.[4]

In April 1972, during Operation Freedom Train, the *Higbee* was among the first U.S. Navy ships to shell targets in North Vietnam. The ship also sank a North Vietnamese patrol boat. But North Vietnam soon retaliated. On April 19, two MiG-17 jets suddenly went "feet wet" and roared out over the Tonkin Gulf at very low altitude. One of them dropped two 250-kilogram bombs toward the *Higbee*. One bomb hit the water near the fantail; the second bomb scored a direct hit on the ship's aft 5-inch/38 gun turret.

Luckily, the gun mount's 12-man crew had just been evacuated after a shell jammed, and only a few sailors received injuries, none serious. A Terrier missile fired by the *USS Sterett* blew the MiG out of the sky.[5]

The second MiG dropped its bombs near the *USS Oklahoma City*, with little damage and no injuries. Later, it was alleged that the two MiG pilots had been trained in sea-attack methods by a Cuban advisor.

With no rudder control, the *Higbee* limped into Da Nang harbor for temporary repairs. Later, following extensive work at Subic Bay, the *Higbee* returned to duty and remained active in the Seventh Fleet until the war finally ended on Jan. 27, 1973.

The *Higbee* returned to Long Beach, California, and was assigned to training and support duties in Destroyer Squadron 27. Less than two years later, the ship moved north to Seattle's Todd Shipyard. There, it underwent another major overhaul and modernization and was reassigned to Destroyer Squadron 37, with Seattle as its home port.

By 1979, however, the *Higbee*'s active-duty career was over. Despite holding the best overall gunnery scores in the U.S. Navy at the time, the "Top Gun" ship was taken out of service. An article in the July 1995 issue of "The Tin Can Sailor," written by former *Higbee* crewman A.C. Edmunds, describes the destroyer's slow demise:

"HIGBEE was decommissioned at the Inactive Ship Facility, Bremerton, Washington, 15 July 1979. In 1980, her hull was prepared for target ship duties and, in July 1980, she was transferred to the Pacific Missile Test Range where she served for the next six years, receiving impacts from the dummy warheads of 25 cruise missiles. The old ship succumbed to a live warhead test 26 April 1986. Her final resting place is in 1,000 fathoms of water approximately 35-40 miles SSW of San Nicholas Island, California."[6]

More precisely, the ship went down at 32° 28' 0.4" North, 119° 58' 0.7" West.[7]

Several Gearing-class destroyers were transferred to the navies of Greece, Turkey, Taiwan and other nations in the 1970s and 1980s and eventually retired and scrapped. Only a few Gearing-class destroyers were still above water in 2012. The most visible of these were museum ships, including the *USS Joseph P. Kennedy Jr.* DD-850 Destroyer Museum in Massachusetts and the *USS Orleck* Naval Museum in Louisiana.

The Mexican Navy still had one Gearing-class destroyer in active service in 2012, the ARM *Netzahualcoyotl* (D-102). Nicknamed "Netza," the ship originally was the *USS Steinaker* (DD-863).

The *Netza* was believed to be the last of the class, the lone survivor.

"A grateful nation remembers those who fought in Indochina."

Above: A plaque in Paris, France, photographed in 2010, commemorates troops who fought in the French Indochina War, which began in 1945 and ended in 1954. It was fought mainly in North Vietnam.

Below: Other than briefly going up a river, this was the closest the author got to Vietnam. *(Photos by Si Dunn)*

NOTES

Chapter 1: "War!"

1. Eric Burdon Official Website, **http://www.ericburdon.com**

2. *Dictionary of American Navy Fighting Ships*, Department of the Navy, Naval Historical Center, **http://www.history.navy.mil/danfs/h6/higbee.htm**

3. Commander, U.S. Seventh Fleet web site, **http://www.c7f.navy.mil/about.htm**

4. *Higbee Log 64-66*, edited by Lt. (jg) R. B. Ely; Daito Art Printing Co., Ltd., Tokyo, Japan, *circa* 1967

5. "Welcome Aboard USS Higbee DD-806," pamphlet, circa 1973, **http://www.navsource.org/archives/05/806.htm**

6. "USS Higbee (DD-806)," article by A.C. Edmunds, **http://www.destroyers.org/histories/h-dd-806.htm**.

7. On Sept. 6, 1997, the U.S. Navy commissioned the Arleigh Burke Class guided missile destroyer *USS Hopper* (DDG-70), named for Rear Admiral Dr. Grace Hopper, who developed the first computer compiler and the first computer programming language. **http://www.hopper.navy.mil**.

8. Email message from Raymond Heflin, Oct. 13, 1999

Chapter 2: The Radio Kid

1. *Popular Electronics*, **http://www.swtpc.com/mholley/PopularElectronics/Popular_Electronics.htm**

2. Heathkit, **http://en.wikipedia.org/wiki/Heathkit**

3. Hallicrafters, **http://en.wikipedia.org/wiki/Hallicrafters**

Chapter 3: Reservist

1. *Wesley K. Clark: A Biography* by Antonia Felix (New York: Newmarket Press, 2004): 1-4

Chapter 4: Sailor

1. *Skate*:
http://en.wiktionary.org/wiki/Appendix:Glossary_of_U.S._Navy_slang, "Sailor who avoids work in general while not being detected; for example the ability to 'skate' out of work undetected while being assigned to a 14 man working party."

Chapter 5: Radioman

1. *Radioman 3 and 2*, Bureau of Naval Personnel (Washington, D.C.: Government Printing Office, 1964): p. 77

2. *Time Magazine*, May 17, 1963, **http://www.time.com/time/magazine/article/0,9171,830348-2,00.html**

3. *Area Handbook for North Vietnam* by Harvey H. Smith and Donald W. Bernier, Frederica M. Bunge, Frances Chadwick Rintz, Rinn-Sup Shinn, and Suzanne Teleki (Washington, D.C., U.S. Government Printing Office, 1966): 401

4. *JFK and Vietnam: Deception, Intrigue, and the Struggle for Power* by John M. Newman (New York: Warner Books, 1992): 18-19

5. *In Retrospect: The Tragedy and Lessons of Vietnam* by Robert S. McNamara with Brian VanDeMark (New York: Random House, 1995): 32)

Chapter 7: Underway

1. DASH system: *Quicksilver: A Greyhound at Sea* by Jack L. Wells (West Conshohocken, PA: Infinity Publishing, 2007): 72

Chapter 8: Attack

1. *Tonkin Gulf* by Eugene G. Windchy (Garden City, N.Y.: Doubleday & Co., Inc., 1971): 224

2. *Truth Is the First Casualty: The Gulf of Tonkin Affair— Illusion and Reality* by Joseph C. Goulden (New York: Rand McNally & Co., 1969): 152

3. *In Love and War*, James Bond Stockdale. and Sybil B. Stockdale, (New York: Harper & Row Publishers, Inc., 1984): 24

4. Ibid., 25

5. Stockdale, 25

6. *Chained Eagle* by Everett Alvarez (New York: David I. Fine, 1989): 13

7. *Ibid.*, 5

8. *Point of No Return: Tonkin Gulf and the Vietnam War* by Earle Rice Jr. (Morgan Reynolds Publishing, Greensboro, NC: 2004): 54

9. Lt. (jg) Everett Alvarez's ejection from Skyhawk: Message photocopy provided to author by National Archives and Records Administration, Washington, D.C.

Chapter 9: Landing Party

1. *U.S. Asiatic Fleet Regulations, 1931* (Navy Department Library, Naval Historical Center.):41

2. *Landing-Force Manual*, 1920 (Washington, D.C.,: U.S. Navy, Government Printing Office): 24

3. "Electrical Experimenter," September 1918, p. 316, as displayed on the "United States Early Radio History" website, **http://earlyradiohistory.us/1918sc.htm**

4. "Sailors as Infantry in the U.S. Navy," by Capt. Patrick H. Roth (October 2005, Department of the Navy, Navy Historical Center) **http://www.history.navy.mil/library//online/naval_infantr y.htm#prac**

5. *The Channel Islands of California: A Book for the Angler, Sportsman, and Tourist* by Charles Frederick Holder, (Charleston, S.C.: BiblioLife, 2009): 168

Chapter 10: Dark Signals

1. *The President's War* by Anthony Austin (New York: J.B. Lippincott, 1971): 299

2. Ibid., 299

3. Op. cit., Windchy, p. 248

Chapter 11: Rough Rider

1. Undated commendation letter from Commodore V.P. Healey, Commander Destroyer Squadron Three

Chapter 12: Sea Ghosts

1. *Tonkin Gulf and the Escalation of the Vietnam War* by Edwin E. Moïse (Chapel Hill, N.C.: The University of North Carolina Press, 1996): 107-108

2. "On this Day: 1960-75 > Vietnam Era,"
   http://www.navyhistory.org.au/category/navy-day-by-day/1960-1975/page/6/

3. "Tonkin Gulf, sanctuary of 4,500 biological species," article published Sept. 16, 2008 on "Organ of the Military Central Commission and Vietnamese Ministry of National Defense" website, **http://army.qdnd.vn/vietnam.economy.Outstanding-activities.18704.qdnd**

4. Moïse, op. cit., 108

5. *Truth Is the First Casualty: The Gulf of Tonkin Affair—Illusion and Reality* by Joseph C. Goulden (New York: Rand McNally & Co., 1969): 159

6. Ibid., 159

7. Goulden, 159

8. "Chronology of Events of 18-20 September 1964 in the Gulf of Tonkin," dated Jan. 15, 1965. Declassified and released to public February 13, 2006, by the National Security Administration "pursuant to E.O. 12958, as amended."

Chapter 13: Wearing Out

1. "Enter the Water King" by Richard H King,
   http://www.gyrodynehelicopters.com/the_water_king.htm
)

2. Desegregation of America's armed forces: Executive Order 9981, July 26, 1948

Chapter 14: First Casualties

1. Email from Jim Checkett, April 6, 2007

2. *Choosing War: The Lost Chance for Peace and the Escalation of War in Vietnam* by Fredrik Logevall (Berkeley, Calif.: University of California Press, 2001): xxii

Chapter 15: R & R

1. *Radioman 3 & 2*, (Fourth Edition, 1964): 40

Chapter 16: Back on the Line

1. *Buddha's Child: My Fight to Save Vietnam* by Nguyen Cao Ky, with Marvin J. Wolf (New York: St. Martin's Press): 122-124.

2. *Triumph Forsaken: The Vietnam War, 1954-1965* by Mark Moyar (New York: Cambridge University Press, 2006): 358

3. Email message from Alec Brewster, Sept. 17, 2008

Chapter 17: Dances with Sharks

1. *Over the Beach: The Air War in Vietnam* by Zalin Grant (New York: Cambridge University Press, 2006): p. 360

2. *Time Magazine*, Oct. 14, 1966

Chapter 18: Seeing Combat

1. Vice Adm. Paul Blackburn obituary, *New York Times*, July 27, 1992

2. *A Rumor of War* by Philip J. Caputo (New York: Holt, Rineheart and Winston, 1996): 53

3. *Semper Fi – Vietnam* by Edward F. Murphy (New York, Ballantine Books, 2000): 8

4. *Black Water, Brown Berets: Coastal and Riverine Warfare in Vietnam* by Thomas J. Cutler (Annapolis, MD: Naval Institute Press, 1988): 286

5. *Riverine Force* by John Forbes and Robert Williams (Annapolis, MD: Naval Institute Press, 1992): 27

Chapter 19: Pirates of the Tonkin Gulf

1. *From the Rivers to the Sea: The U.S. Navy in Vietnam* by R.L. Shreadley (Annapolis, MD: Naval Institute Press, 1992): 78-82

2. *Black Water, Brown Berets: Coastal and Riverine Warfare in Vietnam* by Thomas J. Cutler (Annapolis, MD: Naval Institute Press, 1988): 76-77

3. Gary Dale Cearley, email, August 26, 2008

4. Op. cit., Cutler, 79

5. Op. cit., *Riverine Force*, Forbes and Williams, 31-32

6. *The Naval Institute Historical Atlas of the U.S. Navy* by Craig L. Symonds (Annapolis, MD: Naval Institute Press, 2001): 210

7. *Triumph Forsaken: The Vietnam War, 1954-1965* by Mark Moyar (New York: Cambridge University Press, 2006): 357-359

Chapter 20: Breakaway

1. Rear Admiral Tim Jenkins, email message, 6/02/08 3:15 p.m.

2. "Chansons Innocentes: I" by E. E. Cummings, *Complete Poems, 1913-1962* (New York: Harcourt Brace Jovanovich, Inc., 1972): 24

EPILOGUE II

1. *Subic Bay News*, "Rescue at Sea" (Sept. 10, 1965): 9.

2. *Subic Bay News*, date and page number of clipping unknown

3. *Higbee Log 64-66*, (Tokyo, Japan: Daito Art Printing Co., Ltd., 1966)

4. (Fort Leavenworth, KS. Combat Studies Institute, 1991): 67-69.

5. "Battle of Dong Hoi," author unknown, **http://en.wikipedia.org/wiki/Battle_of_%C4%90%E1%BB%93ng_H%E1%BB%9Bi**

6. Website, **http://www.destroyers.org/Histories/h-DD-806.htm**

7. "NavSource Naval History – Photographic History of the U.S. Navy," **http://www.navsource.org/archives/05/806.htm**

Made in the USA
Middletown, DE
26 August 2015